P9-BZD-661

Essays on Life Writing

From Genre to Critical Practice

Life writing is the most flexible and open term available for autobiographical fragments and other kinds of autobiographical-seeming texts. It includes the conventional genres of autobiography, journals, memoirs, letters, testimonies, and metafiction, and in earlier definitions it included biography. It is a way of seeing literary and other texts that neither objectifies nor subjectifies the nature of a particular cultural truth.

Marlene Kadar has brought together an interdisciplinary and comparative collection of critical and theoretical essays by diverse Canadian scholars, most of whom are women engaged in larger projects in life writing or in archival research. In the more practical pieces the author has discerned a pattern in the autobiographical text, or subtext, that has come to revolutionize the life, the critic's approach, or the discipline itself. In the theoretical pieces, authors make cogent proposals to view a body of literature in a new way, often in order to incorporate feminist visions or humanistic interpretations.

The contributors represent a broad range of scholars from disciplines within the humanities and beyond. Collectively they provide an impressive overview of a growing field of scholarship.

MARLENE KADAR is Canada Research Fellow and Assistant Professor in the Humanities Division and at the Robarts Centre for Canadian Studies, York University.

THEORY / CULTURE

General editors:
Linda Hutcheon and Paul Perron

Essays on Life Writing:
From Genre to Critical Practice

Edited by Marlene Kadar

UNIVERSITY OF TORONTO PRESS
Toronto Buffalo London

© University of Toronto Press 1992
Toronto Buffalo London
Printed in Canada

ISBN 0-8020-2741-5 (cloth)
ISBN 0-8020-6783-2 (paper)

(∞)

Printed on acid-free paper

Theory / Culture 11

Canadian Cataloguing in Publication Data

Main entry under title:

Essays on life writing

(Theory/culture ; 11)
Includes bibliographical references.
ISBN 0-8020-2741-5 (bound) ISBN 0-8020-6783-2 (pbk.)

1. Autobiography – Women authors.   2. Autobiographical
fiction – History and criticism.   3. Women –
Biography – History and criticism.   4. Literature,
Modern – History and criticism.   5. Self in
literature. . I. Kadar, Marlene, 1950–   .
II. Series.

PN471.E77 1992   809'.93592   C92-093476-5

This book has been published with assistance from
the Canada Council and the Ontario Arts Council
under their block grant programs.

Contents

Y = yawn

y + ? = yawn, why leave ?

OK

153 SH²⁰ +

Acknowledgments

For their efforts and influence I want to thank Linda Hutcheon, Sean Kane, Earle Birney, Jean van Heijenoort, Ella Wolfe, Ellen Anderson, Sally Cole, and especially Gary Penner.

For their contribution to the critical practice of life writing I want to thank my exacting Humanities (4000M) students and my uncommon colleagues, the Canada Research Fellows.

For its assistance under the Canada Research Fellowships program, I want to thank the Social Sciences and Humanities Research Council of Canada.

For their help with this book, I want to thank Gerry Hallowell, Laura Macleod, John St James, and Cecilia Abrusci.

To Emma and Jacob

Essays on Life Writing

When writers want to be read they have to be more flexible and take more chances than the standard scholarly style allows: often, they have to be more direct and more personal. In a very real way (although my writing includes precious few autobiographical revelations), I could not think of myself as a writer until I risked exposing myself in my writing.

I am not talking here, necessarily, about full-scale autobiographical writing – though I am not ruling it out either. But I am saying that writerly writing is personal writing, whether or not it is autobiographical. Even if it offers no facts from the writer's life, or offers just a hint of them here and there, it makes the reader know some things about the writer – a fundamental condition, it seems to me, of any real act of communication.

Marianna Torgovnick, 'Experimental Critical Writing'

❧ ❧
Coming to Terms:
Life Writing – from Genre
to Critical Practice

There are at least three ways to view life writing, each of which
includes an attempt to define or redefine what exactly life writing
is. Let me go over the two that have been and still are used in the
scholarship to date, and then let me tell you about the one 'She'
made me do. This 'she' is a reading presence which reminds me
that life writing is not a fixed term, and that it is in flux as it
moves from considerations of genre to considerations of critical
practice. 'She' also ensures that the text does not become fully the
distant and mastered 'object' of my discourse (Torgovnick 26; Gallop 19–21). After all, I am a particular kind of white reading woman
(Behar 228) in the 'West,' interpreting the texts, or self-construc-
tions, of others. Issues of representation enter into the configuration of what does or may constitute life writing. What follows
is a progressive three-part presentation and exploration of the term
life writing alongside a suggestion that it may represent both a
genre and a critical practice. There is also the suggestion that
changes in how we perceive life writing evolve as political and
literary movements evolve.

Life Writing: The Original Genre

Life writing may be viewed strictly as a limited and limiting genre,
as it was in the eighteenth century. At that time it was equivalent
to 'biography,' and biography used to be considered more generally
to *include* autobiography, and *perhaps* other kinds of autobiographical writing. First mention of the word 'biography' is recorded in the *Oxford English Dictionary* as John Dryden, 1683;

the root is the Greek *bios*, meaning 'quick, vital.' The biographical, then, treats a subject that is vital to the subject, but the self of the author does not necessarily intrude into that subject. In this kind of life writing, it has often been considered preferable if the author remains 'objective.' An autobiography then, as M.H. Abrams's definition reveals, can be thought of in relation to biography: it is a biography written by the subject about himself or herself (15), with a certain degree of 'objectivity.'

The term autobiography derives from the Greek *autos*, meaning 'of or by oneself, independently,' and the first mention is recorded, again in the *Oxford English Dictionary*, as Robert Southey in 1809. Autobiography is a genre that obeys the laws which have governed the writing of one's self. Although the author is not 'distant' or even 'objective,' the text exhibits certain formal conventions, and adheres to certain protocols that are different from those of biography.

What is not always revealed in the scholarship about autobiographical writing, however, is that for a part of the eighteenth century, before the Greek and Latin rooted words 'biography' and 'autobiography' fell into current usage, the Anglo-Saxon rooted phrase 'life-writing' was popular. Life writing has always been a more inclusive term, and as such may be considered to have certain critical advantages over 'biography' and 'autobiography.' Thus life writing, put simply, is a less exclusive genre of personal kinds of writing that includes *both* biography and autobiography, but also the less 'objective,' or more 'personal,' genres such as letters and diaries. A particular branch of textual criticism has adopted this version of the term life writing – such as one might find in the journal *Biography* – and has also broadened it. A contemporary source for this use of the term may be found in Donald J. Winslow's *Life-Writing: A Glossary of Terms in Biography, Autobiography, and Related Forms*, and amplified in Linda S. Coleman's dissertation 'Public Self, Private Self: Women's Life-Writing in England, 1570–1720.'

In general, however, the usefulness of this version of life writing is limited, for the following reasons. First of all, it has a history of being androcentric, and may therefore (re)generate androcentric interpretive strategies, thus underlining the marginalization of what may be called gynocentric ones (Schweickart 129). Moreover, this version of life writing privileges objective truth and narrative regularity, leaving less room for non-linear narratives and fragments, and unpublished documents. I will consider a second view of life writing as genre which, therefore, improves on these two limitations.

Life Writing: Still a Genre but ...

The most broadened version of the term 'life writing' as a specific genre is the one often celebrated by feminist literary critics concerned with the proliferation, authorization, and recuperation of autobiographical writing, especially in recent decades. Here life writing is the subject of 'gynocritics,' a literature that has been identified according to its subject matter – women's texts, personal narratives, Patrocinio Schweickart's 'female texts' – and the critic's job is focused on content. It is a kind of writing about the 'self' or the 'individual' that favours autobiography, but includes letters, diaries, journals, and (even) biography. This kind of life writing may be written by literary men and women, or it may be written by 'ordinary' men and women. When it is the latter, it is often referred to as 'nontraditional literature,' and may include personal narratives, oral narratives and life testimonies, and anthropological life histories (Behar 223–8).

Although this version of life writing takes into account women's writing and the suppression of women's writing, it is still potentially problematic because it tends to privilege an idea about what constitutes 'the personal,' or the ('unary') 'subject' (P. Smith 103–8), and it also may forget about the complex configuration of the reader (see Jacobus 22–4). This kind of life writing is understood by new critics, for example, as primarily 'non-fictional,' a term with which Quebec feminist fiction theory, deconstruction, and postmodernism have some difficulty. Nicole Brossard wrote: 'In reality, there is no fiction' (Lovhers 15). (As Cixous and Clément underline, as far as women are concerned, there is the added problem that there is too little fiction available in which 'her' reality is embedded by 'her' [96–7].) As Linda Hutcheon has said in her discussion of Coming through Slaughter – a book she calls 'a fictionalized biography of the real Buddy Bolden' – 'to write of anyone's history is to order, to give form to disparate facts; in short, to fictionalize' (The Canadian Postmodern 82).

Apart from disputing an epistemology that separates fiction and non-fiction, the postmodern vision also enjoys contesting the boundaries between fiction and autobiography. Postmodernist

critics, respectful of Jacques Derrida's inquiry into the utterance
'Genres are not to be mixed' ('The Law of Genre' 202–3), are uncomfortable with the inscribing of genre with laws and law-mak-
ing, suspicious that this inscription will serve to censor the
'different,' and valorize the 'same.' Thus, 'she' made me explore
this unfixed term, life writing, further, starting with the consequences of dualistic thinking: non-fiction (that is, autobiography)
vs. fiction; and literary non-fiction vs. non-literary non-fiction.
This latter dualism is usually framed this way: high culture vs.
low culture. In order to avoid jeopardizing the contesting of categories of culture that life writing enacts, we might prefer the
terms high culture and non-high culture.

Personal Narrative and Non-high Culture

Both ordinary people (mainly men) and great people (mainly men)
have written in the autobiographical voice 'in the past,' a past that
undeniably also includes women's 'natural,' or 'ordinary,' autobiographical voices. These voices are often represented in what
Leonore Hoffman and Margo Culley have called 'women's personal narratives' (10–13). Hoffman makes the point that women's
personal narratives have been wrongly labelled 'nontraditional'
literature, because they are only nontraditional 'in the sense of
their exclusion from the literary canon' (1). We are unable to say
exactly how long ago women's past reaches because, as Virginia
Woolf wrote in 1929, 'all these infinitely obscure lives remain to
be recorded,' and consequently 'all the novels, without meaning
to, inevitably lie' (*Room* 85). As Hoffman and Culley illustrate,
what is recorded in 'lower culture' has had a difficult time competing with the higher, especially in the curriculum of literary
studies. This is confirmed by Harriett Hawkins's serious but humorous study of 'high' art and popular modern genres, especially
as she compares film heroes with 'deep' tragic heroes to show both
the differences and the revealing similarities (3–37).

Letters

When I think of non-high culture, I think also of, for example,
archival materials by women or men who never became celebrities,
or diaries and letters to loved ones and friends, some notable examples of which have been uncovered in recent years. The sev-

enteenth-century philosopher-nun Sor Juana Inés de la Cruz, for example, recorded her own life in what has been called 'an epistolary self-defense' and an 'intellectual autobiography,' titled the 'Response to Sor Filotea.' The main segment of the letter – only brought to light late in this century – is autobiographical and contemplative; it includes a self-criticism, and is propelled by sophisticated ironies. Electa Arenal and Stacey Schlau go so far as to say that Sor Juana, like many Hispanic nuns, used Catholicism 'to structure a feminist ideology' (341), and used the opportunity to write to a colleague in order to voice her ideas. We will remember that even Virginia Woolf wrote *Three Guineas* in *response* to a 'political' letter requesting donations for an educational fund that overtly excluded women.

Sor Juana's and Woolf's letters are both examples of women's life writing, and they are both concerned with the condition of women, and especially the condition of women in relation to (epistolary) writing (Goldsmith 46–59) and education. Their apparently non-fictional letters comprise life writing; and their expectation is that their readers will read the letters as such. Although epistolary literature is a legitimate and necessary function of – or even a step in our progressive consideration of – life writing, I prefer to include as well the fictional frame in which we might find an autobiographical voice. This is especially relevant in our consideration of experimental women's writing, such as *Heroine* and other English-Canadian postmodern texts, or Elena Poniatowska's epistolary novel *Dear Diego*.

Feminism and Postmodernism

Even though life writing claims to represent women, 'feminist' conclusions are not always the appropriate conclusions in our consideration of women's life writing. As Gail Scott sees it, feminism is not prescriptive. Instead, it creates the conditions in which 'she' may be *'herself-defined'* (*Spaces* 88–9).

The difficulty with a strictly feminist (in both form and theme) view of life writing is that it may institutionalize a defensive posture for women, or for the unofficial writer of either gender. Though she is often female, 'she' may also be male (think of black slave narrators such as Frederick Douglass). That is, gender has determined genre in the past; in the future, we want to avoid any further 'gendrification.' If, for example, we accept the stated antagonism between high and non-high culture, we are unable to read, compare, interpret, or know those who have been antagonized – or even those who have done the antagonizing – without having our vision of them coloured by the critical posture of having-been-antagonized. As Harriett Hawkins has illustrated in an indirect fashion, this often means we patronize when what we want to do is include. Moreover, we find here too that content is considered most significant in the assignment and evaluation of meaning; we want to avoid the unary feminist self-portrait. Not doing so may lead to unnecessary rivalries – rivalries not based on substantive difference, but rather on confused semi-political comparisons (that is, this text is more feminist than that). One might say here that May Sarton's *Journal of a Solitude* (1973) is not as feminist as Audrey Lorde's *A Burst of Light* (1987) – for political reasons that may be legitimate, but that may compare authors' personal habits and origins more than the more mysterious habits and origins of texts, many of them extremely political in another metaphorical sense. The conversation between the reader and the critic must not stop at context, nor must it be reduced to text alone. Otherwise it can go nowhere else and thus risks becoming tautological.[1] Once one critic decides this text is more feminist than the other, it is difficult for the other critic to say something other than 'it is not so.' At this point, it is difficult to *resist* continuing dualistic arguments that separate us out into the authorities (of 'gender coherence') and the not-authorities. As Judith Butler says,

> The fixity of gender identification, its presumed cultural invariance, its status as an interior and hidden cause may well serve the goals of the feminist project to establish a transhistorical commonality between us, but the 'us' who gets joined through such a narration is a construction built upon the denial of a decidedly more complex cultural identity – or non-identity, as the case may be ... It seems crucial to resist the myth of interior origins, understood either as naturalized or culturally fixed. Only then, gender coherence might be understood as the regulatory fiction it is – rather than the common point of our liberation. (339)

If gender coherence is a regulatory fiction, it will make itself known in what we have referred to as the habits and origins of texts. The habits and origins of texts have something to do with what the tradition calls 'style.' It is said that this 'style' is knowable because of what is read. But were we to progress in our discussion of life writing on its way from being only a genre to being also a critical practice, we can discern style also because of the nature of reading or the assumptions of readers (Rimmon-Kenan 37). 'She,' a kind of feminized reading consciousness, understands that style belongs, in the first instance, to the text; but 'she' also resists this knowledge. Style also belongs to the author and the reader, and finally to the interpretation and criticism that come out on the page. We have been taught that what comes out on the page is meant to be proof of our authority; it is meant to enter into the 'theatre' of debate and critique, the theatre of sorties (Cixous and Clément 63–132) and war. But in a magnanimous, progressive consideration of life writing, this page-proof is also not proof at all that the 'critic' has read the text the most, the best, the latest, the clearest, but has only read it in the best way 'she' knows how. 'She,' it seems, must be self-consciously created as the reader goes along, and as she collects other readings, other theories, other orbits of a thing she might recognize as self-consciousness herself (or, 'herself-definition'). 'She' must be vulnerable (Gallop 19); she must try not to be fully decided (Johnson 14–15). Postmodernism and deconstruction argue for this critical area somewhere in between a feminism with clarity and a feminism that suffers its own ignoble glitches and moves on.

At the same time, however, there is good reason for 'feminisms' to suspect postmodernism, even when they try to incorporate it. As Hutcheon writes, 'their political agendas would be endangered, or at least obscured by the double coding of that complicitous critique' ('Incredulity toward Metanarrative' 41). Anthropologists Frances E. Mascia-Lees, Patricia Sharpe, and Colleen Ballerino Cohen go further in their condemnation of postmodernism. They are irritated by 'postmodern trends in epistemology and literary criticism' because they see these trends as unaware of their own politics (7–8). My own sense is, however, that perhaps a politically conscious postmodernism is able to appreciate the canon, revise it where it sees fit, and forget it where it also sees fit. As Arun Mukherjee has illustrated, the canon cannot be used to fill up all the holes. It is, for example, in trying to determine why women's writing has been undervalued, simplistic to say only that it has been forgotten (see Sherry 20–30), ostensibly because the canon has been dominated by patriarchal modes of thinking and the values that valorize those modes. The canon *has* been dominated by patriarchal modes of thinking, and this has affected all of us interminably. But it is the forgetting itself, that must be 'read' (and recorded) and again, not as if the 'feminine' were simply the antithesis of the 'masculine' (Giuseppina Moneta 106). Reading the 'forgetting' incorporates feminism into its decisions about the text, but it also uses deconstruction to understand the effects of the forgetting in the text and in the reader. This way, moreover, 'feminine' is not understood only as (heterogeneous) opposite, or, worse still, simply as victim – pointblank. Nor is it read only as white American feminist.

Life Writing: A Critical Practice

At the most extreme end of the spectrum, life writing is a way of looking at more or less autobiographical literature as long as we understand that 'autobiographical' is a loaded word, the 'real' accuracy of which cannot be proved and does not equate with either 'objective' or 'subjective' truth. Instead, it is best viewed as a continuum that spreads unevenly and in combined forms from the so-called least fictive narration to the most fictive. Even so, masks are either explicitly minimized or minimized implicitly through complex narratological 'levels' or strategies (as in metafiction). Under pressure from the reading presence I refer to as 'She,' my own working definition of life writing is as follows:

> Life writing comprises texts that are written by an author who does not continuously write about someone else, and who also does not pretend to be absent from the [black, brown, or white] text himself/herself. Life writing is a way of seeing, to use John Berger's famous phrase; it anticipates the reader's determination on the text, the reader's colour, class, and gender, and pleasure in an imperfect and always evolving hermeneutic – classical, traditional, or postmodern.

Reading a kind of metafictional life writing, one that overtly resists a proof-positive reading, leads us to ask questions about our critical practice, questions about 'standard academic style'

(Torgovnick 27). However, having thought about both the conflicts in actually reading to the best of my (self-)knowledge and the important considerations of a term developing from a genre to a critical practice, we are able to reconsider the possible functions of life writing now, functions that would allow us to include metafiction and, even, narrative poetry; that would enable us to include both 'high' and 'non-high' forms of writing; that would let us reread the canon while inserting the prejudices of women, and women's 'styles'; and that would concede to unfinished or imperfect styles, both those that have been designed into the text and those that have been designs or accidents of history. As Susan Winnett has recently cautioned, 'we have been taught to read in drag and must begin to question seriously the determinants that govern the mechanics of our narratives, the notion of history as a sense-making operation, and the enormous investment the patriarchy has in maintaining them' (516). At the same time, we mustn't ignore the investment we have in overthrowing these determinants, and the influence which that desire to overthrow will have on our critical practice.

For now consider that this way of seeing literature is really a way of knowing that does not necessarily judge the text according to how 'realistic' the autobiographical truth may be, and therefore how good or bad the life disclosed. If anything, it acknowledges that the involved reader takes great pleasure in inventing a persona for himself or herself as he or she reads. In this sense a feminist model of life writing is necessary to correct former misreadings of women's writings. As Dr Johnson said, no man was better qualified to write his life than himself. The same holds true for women. The problem is that in the eighteenth century (and before) few women dared; few women were able; few women were qualified; few women had a life to write.[2] But to say this and then carry out the 'feminist' analysis that one would then expect seems too linear and rational to encompass the complexity of women's life writing, or the act of reading itself. Moreover, the feminist reader may want to fulfil a commitment as she (or he?) stands between conventional aesthetics and new critical practices. Finally, she stands between the influence of feminist practice – a position on gender inequality – and feminist revolution, a desire to celebrate what is already there in the name of women, *herself-defined*. Celebrating what is already there while acknowledging inequities in the social contracts that have defined gendered relationships assumes the

inherent quality of the words and the self who arranges them.[3]
That self defines a new text or life-in-the-text when she or he is
not in a defensive position. The remaining problem then is: Does
she or he have the strength to persist in light of the tremendous
pressure to conform to what her colonizers have defined as intellectual excellence? As Elizabeth Fox-Genovese has explained, in
literary studies depersonalization and abstraction have often been
associated with superior intellectual pursuits (162–5). As unfixed
as the term life writing may be, it defies this equation and therefore
does its part to resist and reverse the literary and political consequences we would have to expect were we to carry through with
'depersonalization' and unrelenting 'abstraction.'

Conclusion

Life writing as a critical practice, then, encourages (a) the reader
to develop and foster his/her own self-consciousness in order to
(b) humanize and make less abstract (which is not to say less mysterious) the self-in-the-writing. Thus, there are many forms, or
genres, in which a reader may glean this written self, but we usually think immediately of autobiography, letters, diaries, and anthropological life narratives, genres in which the conventional
expectation is that the author does not want to pretend he/she is
absent from the text. Add to these original life-writing genres the
fictionalized equivalents, including self-reflexive metafiction, and
life writing becomes both the 'original genre' and a critical comment on it, and therefore the self-in-the-writing. At its most radical, the critical practice of life writing enhances reading as a means
of emancipating an overdetermined 'subject,' or various subject-
locations. It is, to use Marianna Torgovnick's phrase, 'writerly
writing,' even if it is not what we understand as strictly autobiographical. In the end, life writing problematizes the notion of Literature. Without wanting to deny Literature, life writing allows
us to see it, too, as only one possible category of special writing.

NOTES

1 Teresa de Lauretis has summed up the possible impasse in feminist
   critical studies this way: it may reveal itself in 'the even more insid-
   ious opposition between theoreticism and empiricism, where accu-

sations of jargon, bad writing, or elitism from one camp are met with counteraccusations of essentialism and unsophisticated thinking by the other.' See her article 'Feminist Studies / Critical Studies: Issues, Terms, and Contexts,' 7. Domna Stanton addresses the specific impasse between North American and French feminists in her article 'Language and Revolution.' Paul Smith also refers to the impasse in *Discerning the Subject*.

2 For an ironic look at 'patterns in the suppression of women's writing' see Joanna Russ, *How to Suppress Women's Writing* (Austin: U of Texas P 1983), especially the pensive chapter 'Aesthetics,' 110–21. Russ writes: 'The techniques for mystifying women's lives and belittling women's writing that I have described work by suppressing context: writing is separated from experience, women writers are separated from their tradition and each other, public is separated from private, political from personal – all to enforce a supposed set of absolute standards. What is frightening about black art or women's art or Chicano art – and so on – is that it calls into question the very idea of objectivity and absolute standards' (118). Elizabeth Fox-Genovese argues that the situation is even more militant in the case of Afro-American women's autobiographies because 'the white male cultural elite has not, in fact, abandoned the podium. It has merely insisted that the podium cannot be claimed in the name of any particular personal experience. And it has been busily trying to convince the world that intellectual excellence requires depersonalization and abstraction. The virtuosity, born of centuries of privilege, with which these ghosts of authors make their case, demands that others, who have something else to say, meet the ghosts' standards of pyrotechnics' (163).

3 These questions of value are pursued in *Autobiograpical Voices* by Françoise Lionnet, who reads Augustine and Nietzsche for their contribution to a feminist anti-racist notion of 'métissage' (braiding or blending, pp. 1–29). For a specific analysis of how systemic literary 'visibility' is, see also Mukherjee's 'South Asian Poetry in Canada,' in *Towards an Aesthetic of Opposition*, 52–68. For a treatment of the issue of value as it intersects with women's pleasure in the text, see Susan Winnett's 'Coming Unstrung.' For a presentation of the 'values' deconstruction uses in reading texts of all sorts, see Barbara Johnson's 'Nothing Fails Like Success' and Judith Butler's 'Gender Trouble.' For comments about why a reader may not want to master the narrative, see Jane Gallop's *Reading Lacan*, especially pp. 13–30, which begins with a personal inquiry into the grammar of 'Women's Studies.'

For specific essays on feminism and autobiography, see *The Private Self*, ed. Shari Benstock, and Felicity Nussbaum, *The Autobio-*

graphical Subject; The Female Autograph, ed. Domna C. Stanton;
Life/Lines, ed. Bella Brodzki and Celeste Schenck; and Sidonie
Smith, *A Poetics of Women's Autobiography*. See also Shirley Neuman, 'Autobiography: From Different Poetics to a Poetics of Differences' (pp. 213–30 of this book), for a full discussion of the
difficulties inherent in categorization and reading.

WORKS CITED

Abrams, M.H. *A Glossary of Literary Terms*. 5th ed. Fort Worth: Holt,
Rinehart and Winston 1988
Arenal, Electa, and Stacey Schlau. *Untold Sisters: Hispanic Nuns in
Their Own Works*. Trans. Amanda Powell. Albuquerque: U of New
Mexico P 1989
Behar, Ruth. 'Rage and Redemption: Reading the Life Story of a Mexi-
can Marketing Woman.' *Feminist Studies* 16 (Summer 1990): 223–58
Benstock, Shari. 'Authorizing the Autobiographical.' In *The Private
Self: Theory and Practice of Women's Autobiographical Writings*. Ed.
Shari Benstock. Chapel Hill: U of North Carolina P 1988
Brodzki, Bella, and Celeste Schenck, eds. *Life/Lines: Theorizing Wom-
en's Autobiography*. Ithaca: Cornell UP 1988
Brossard, Nicole. *La lettre aérienne*. Montreal: Remue-ménage 1985
– *Lovhers*. 1980. Trans. Barbara Godard. Montreal: Guernica 1986
Butler, Judith. 'Gender Trouble, Feminist Theory, and Psychoanalytic
Discourse.' In *Feminism/Postmodernism*, 324–40. Ed. Linda J.
Nicholson. New York: Routledge 1990
Cixous, Hélène, and Catherine Clément. *The Newly Born Woman*.
Trans. Betsy Wing. Theory and History of Literature 24. Minneapo-
lis: U of Minnesota P 1986
Coleman, Linda S. 'Public Self, Private Self: Women's Life-Writing in
England, 1570–1720.' Ph.D. diss. U of Wisconsin, Milwaukee, 1986
DATA and ACTA: Aspects of Life Writing. Ed. Evelyn J. Hinz. Winni-
peg: U of Manitoba *Mosaic* 1987
de Lauretis, Teresa. 'Feminist Studies / Critical Studies: Issues, Terms,
and Contexts.' In *Feminist Studies / Critical Studies, Theories of
Contemporary Culture* 8: 1–19
Derrida, Jacques. 'La Loi du genre / The Law of Genre.' In *Glyph*,
176–232. Baltimore: Johns Hopkins UP 1980
Fox-Genovese, Elizabeth. 'To Write My Self: The Autobiographies of
Afro-American Women.' In *Feminist Issues in Literature Scholar-
ship*, 161–80. Ed. Shari Benstock. Bloomington and Indianapolis:
Indiana UP 1987
Gallop, Jane. *Reading Lacan*. Ithaca: Cornell UP, 1985. Esp. 'Prefatory

Material' (13–30), 'Reading the Phallus' (133–56), 'The Dream of the Dead Author' (157–85)

Goldsmith, Elizabeth C., ed. *Writing the Female Voice: Essays on Epistolary Literature*. Boston: Northeastern UP 1989

Hawkins, Harriett. *Classics and Trash: Traditions and Taboos in High Literature and Popular Modern Genres*. Toronto: U of Toronto P 1990

Hoffman, Leonore, and Margo Culley. *Women's Personal Narratives: Essays in Criticism and Pedagogy*. New York: MLA 1985

Hutcheon, Linda. *The Canadian Postmodern*. Toronto: Oxford 1988

– 'Incredulity towards Metanarrative: Negotiating Postmodernism and Feminisms.' *Tessera* 7 (Fall 1989): 39–44

Johnson, Barbara. 'Nothing Fails Like Success.' In *SCE Reports* #8, 7–16. Seattle: Society for Critical Exchange 1980

Kadar, Marlene, ed. *Essays in Life-Writing*. Robarts Centre for Canadian Studies Working Paper 89-WO3. North York, Ont.: York U 1989

Lionnet, Françoise. *Autobiographical Voices: Race, Gender, Self-Portraiture*. Ithaca: Cornell UP 1989

Mascia-Lees, Frances E., Patricia Sharpe, and Colleen Ballerino Cohen. 'The Postmodernist Turn in Anthropology: Cautions from a Feminist Perspective,' *Signs, Journal of Women in Culture and Society*, 15.1 (1989): 7–33

Moneta, Giuseppina. 'La pensée comme écoute de la parole.' In *L'émergence d'une culture au féminin*, 101–6. Ed. Marisa Zavalloni. Montreal: Les Editions Saint-Martin 1987

Mukherjee, Arun. *Towards an Aesthetic of Opposition*. Stratford, Ont.: Williams-Wallace 1988

Nussbaum, Felicity A. *The Autobiographical Subject: Gender and Ideology in Eighteenth-Century England*. Baltimore: Johns Hopkins UP 1989

Poniatowska, Elena. *Dear Diego*. 1978. Trans. Katherine Silver. New York: Pantheon 1986

Rimmon-Kenan, Shlomith. *Narrative Fiction: Contemporary Poetics*. New Accents. London and New York: Methuen 1983

Schweickart, Patrocinio. 'Reading Ourselves: Toward a Feminist Theory of Reading.' In *Contemporary Literary Criticism: Literary and Cultural Studies*. 2nd ed., 118–41. Ed. Robert Con Davis and Ronald Schleifer. New York: Longman 1989

Scott, Gail. *Spaces like Stairs*. Toronto: Women's Press 1989

Sherry, Ruth. *Studying Women's Writing: An Introduction*. London: Edward Arnold 1988

Smith, Paul. *Discerning the Subject*. Theory and History of Literature 55. Minneapolis: U of Minnesota P 1988

Smith, Sidonie. *A Poetics of Women's Autobiography: Marginality and* the *Fictions of Self-Representation*. Bloomington: Indiana UP 1987

Stanton, Domna, ed. *The Female Autograph: Theory and Practice of Autobiography from the Tenth to the Twentieth Century*. Chicago: U of Chicago P 1987

- 'Language and Revolution: The Franco-American Dis-Connection.' In *The Future of Difference*. Ed. Hester Eisenstein and Alice Jardine. New Brunswick, NJ: Barnard College Women's Center 1980

Torgovnick, Marianna. 'Experimental Critical Writing.' *Profession* 90 (1990): 25–7

Winnett, Susan. 'Coming Unstrung: Women, Men, Narrative, and Principles of Pleasure.' *PMLA* 105 (May 1990): 505–18

Winslow, Donald J. *Life-Writing: A Glossary of Terms in Biography, Autobiography, and Related Forms*. Honolulu: U of Hawaii P 1980

Woolf, Virginia. *A Room of One's Own*. 1929. London: Grafton 1977

- *Three Guineas*. 1938. Harmondsworth: Penguin 1977

PART ONE

LITERARY WOMEN WHO WRITE THE SELF

Autobiographical Documents by Literary Women as Primary Texts

In PART ONE the contributors focus on primary texts by literary women whose reputations have been made on the basis of published fiction and non-fiction works, that is, texts other than the life-writing documents considered here. Elizabeth Smart's early journals, for example, were published in 1986, but Smart is known for her novel, *By Grand Central Station I Sat Down and Wept*, 1941. Similarly, Marian Engel's *cahiers* and notebooks, part of the Marian Engel Archive at McMaster University, complement Engel's published fiction, including *Sarah Bastard's Notebook* (1968); *Bear* (1976); *The Glassy Sea* (1978); and *Lunatic Villas* (1981). These life-writing documents have become the subject of literary critics who are trying to better understand the thought and life of the author. They do not necessarily simplify the questions we ask about the authors, nor do they present us with any one kind of life-writing document. If anything, they illustrate how complicated the genre of life writing can be as the subject of literary analysis.

In this section scholars experiment with new words with which to name the documents they study, and within the rubric they have set they attempt to locate the subject within. This is particularly evident in the piece on Anna Jameson, where the major 'Canadian' work is called an 'epistolary dijournal'; and in the essay on Mary Wollstonecraft, where *Letters Written During a Short Residence in Sweden, Norway, and Denmark* (1796), often identified as a travel book, is also described as an epistolary novel.

For reasons of genre and gender, the distinctions and ambiguities in naming the specific types of life writing here are explored and played with. For in each case a legitimately autobiographical document – that is, a document written in the first person from the point of view of a self-disclosing narrator who assumes he/she is writing non-fiction – begs the question of the relation of 'simple' autobiographical truth to the construction of self and/in a 'personal' narrative. It is assumed that the primary texts in part one represent life writing in its 'simplest' or least self-conscious form. But there are also ironies and paradoxes in this assumption, ironies that are further exploited in part three, where life writing appears to use fiction in order to deliver a 'truer' picture of the self in a particular subject location.

Here, in part one, life writing is considered in its original eighteenth-century application as an alternative to autobiography and biography, terms that often come to stand for a specific genre in its own tradition, and a genus for autologous writings that are structured in diverse ways (Linda S. Coleman, 'Public Self, Private Self' 1–2; see p. 14, above). To use the term 'autobiography' to represent two distinct but related categories of literature in this way can lead to confusion. But this usage also avoids detailing structural specificities and the critical norms that come into play as a consequence of this avoiding. Using autobiography as an umbrella term leads, for example, to the uncritical privileging of autobiography over the less 'structured,' less unified, less retrospective genres treated here: such as diaries, letters, and notebooks. Life writing then is used in this section primarily as signifier of a generic category; and specifically as an alternative umbrella term (to autobiography and biography) to include all kinds of autologous texts – diaries, journals, notebooks, letters, travel books, epistolary narratives, and, also, autobiography. Apart from generic concerns, however, life writing also allows more critical scope for genderic concerns. The literary history of autobiography has also been a womanless history, whereas life writing offers a feminist canon, among others.

❧ 1 ❧
'Life out of Art':
Elizabeth Smart's
Early Journals

ALICE VAN WART

Elizabeth Smart was an avid journal keeper. As a child she used her journals to compose poems, short stories, and plays, and throughout her life she continued keeping journals, recording in them her daily activities and reflections, as well as drafts of her writing. Her early journals, now published as *Necessary Secrets*, provide an early record of a life that was both single-minded and unconventional, and a repository of all her writing, up to that time.

During her life, Smart was never without a notebook. Essentially she thought of her journals as her writing apprenticeship and they were: out of them came her classic work *By Grand Central Station I Sat Down and Wept* (1941), *The Assumption of the Rogues and Rascals* (1978), published poems, and the unpublished work collected in *In the Meantime* (1984).

Smart's journals reveal a curious process. Whereas most writers generally translate the experience of their lives into art, Smart created a romantic ethos by which to live and out of which she wrote, an ethos that ironically shaped the course of her life. For Smart, life and art were inextricably intertwined.

Editing Smart's journals revealed to me the intricate connection between the events of Smart's life and her writing and, viewed in conjunction with other women's journals and diaries (I use the words interchangeably), suggested to me the importance of women's journals as a form of narrative. The proliferation of the publication of women's letters and diaries (since 1970) has only recently created a necessary critical inquiry and theoretical response to them, a response concerned with the broader implications of the publication of journals, or diaries, as life writing (and here I am using the word as the term is beginning to be defined, as a genre of documents written out of a life that consists of life-narratives, or narratives that tell a story in their own right, even though they may not be fiction). Consequently, I found myself considering the importance of the publication of Smart's journals in more theoretical terms, particularly in the terms of what Nicole Brossard calls l'écriture féminine (a term that loosely translates as writing in the feminine and carries with it implications of style).

Historically, women were drawn to diaries because in them they were able to express themselves in times when they were not encouraged to practise other forms of expression. For this reason alone, the tradition of women's diaries is important because the diaries contribute to our growing knowledge of the history of women (herstory) in Western and other cultures, and the social history of people in general is given more detail than it might otherwise be because of women's attention to details and the texture of everyday life in their diaries.

In general, flexibility is a distinguishing feature of the diary form. In the hands of women it points to a potent form of rhetoric different from the conventional modes of rhetoric based on inductive or deductive thinking and organization. Unlike the framed, contained, and closed thinking revealed in this conventional (or male mode), the writing in women's diaries generally proceeds by indirection and reveals female thinking to be eidetic (presented through detailed and accurate visual image reproducing a past impression), open-ended, and generative. The diary's form is capable of an endless flexibility, a quality well suited to encompassing the multifarious nature of women's lives.

Poet and critic Adrienne Rich has said that writing is renaming. Writing out one's thoughts, feelings, or ideas enables a person to understand, to question, to challenge, to conceive of alternatives. For character to take shape, for understanding to occur, a certain freedom of mind and thought is needed, a freedom to press on, to enter the currents of one's own thoughts and feelings. In their diaries, women begin to analyse the very process of the development of their thoughts and feelings, and in turn often re-create the process of their thinking and their writing style as they do.

Smart's journals, which are both a private revelation of the self and an apprenticeship into writing, provide a powerful narrative in which the genesis of an ethos for living and art create a language and writing style that is perfectly suited to the dictates of her heart, as well as her art.

Smart had a profound need to express herself and there is in her journals a cumulative sense of emotional and artistic development as the narrative unfolds. Certainly Smart's life makes good drama. The myths behind her life are romantic ones perpetuated by herself, and largely bound to the story of *By Grand Central Station I Sat Down and Wept*. The events of this story are based on her love affair with the British poet George Barker, a married man with whom Smart fell in love in 1939 after reading a book of his poetry, and for whom she later disregarded social convention by having an affair with him. Although they never married and only sporadically lived together, over the course of the next ten years she had four children by him, whom she raised more or less single-handedly and often in poverty.

Ironically, as Smart's journals make clear, she had been brought up for a life much different from the one she lived after she had met Barker and became a single mother and a working woman. She was born into an upper-class Ottawa family in 1913 and grew up socializing with people of political and social importance. At the age of seventeen she was taken to London to study the piano with a concert pianist. In London, she socialized with the bright young men of external affairs and dated a lord. She was 'brought out' in Ottawa in 1935, and in 1936 she travelled around the world.

By all standards Smart was brought up to live a privileged life. However, she had decided by the time she was seventeen that she wanted to be a writer, not a pianist. In 1937 Smart decided to live a life that would prepare her for her chosen vocation; that is, she began to live the life she believed would give her something to write about.

Between 1937 and 1940, Smart went to France with a group of artists to begin what she intended to be a new and independent life as a writer; she worked for a short time on a newspaper in Ottawa; she lived briefly in New York, Mexico, and Los Angeles, during which time she lived with the sculptor Jean Varda; she had an intimate relationship with a French poet, Alice Paalan; and she fell in love with George Barker. At the age of twenty-eight she was living in a small schoolhouse in Pender Harbour, pregnant with her first child and writing the first full draft of *By Grand Central Station I Sat Down and Wept*. Smart's journals show that

her eventual abandonment of her background was not so much
rebellion against social convention as it was the imperative of a
highly romantic sensibility searching for the vital moments in life
that she believed could be found only in love, art, and the natural
world.

Although *By Grand Central Station I Sat Down and Wept* is
loosely based on the events that preceeded Smart's pregnancy, it
is not strictly autobiographical. Contrary to the general belief that
this is a confessional novel written in a moment of passion, Smart's
journals reveal this is not the case. By the time she had met the
British poet George Barker, Smart had already defined the myth
of love and passion that would shape her life and her art; furthermore, parts of the novel were written previous to her relationship with Barker.

In an interview with Bruce Meyer and Brian O'Riordan published in *In Their Words: Interviews with Fourteen Canadian
Writers*, Smart makes a careful distinction between what she calls
'facts' and what she calls 'emotional truths': 'The two things are
quite different. Something might be factually untrue but might be
emotionally true. Therefore, it is fiction and it is made with what
one hopes is art. If you have an emotion and you have no craft,
then you will not have art. You have to have the craft first' (191).
Smart's journals validate her point. Most of what she wrote before
By Grand Central Station I Sat Down and Wept was a preparation
for that work. Before she had met Barker, and by the time she had
written her novella 'Let Us Dig a Grave and Bury Our Mother' (a
fictional work loosely based on her relationship with Alice Paalan
published in *In The Meantime*), she knew what she wanted to
write about. In a journal entry 26 November 1939, a few months
before she met George Barker, she wrote, while on a boat on her
way to Mexico to visit the Paalans:

> These grey days all sky and sea are wild with innuendo
> and submerged life ... the whitecaps' foam, the gull's
> flight – the strong warm wet air – like the spring message
> wind it goes through everything, through every pore, the
> brain, the sex, the mouth, the hair; it ravishes, exhilarates,
> possesses, cannot weary – O leap only into the sea – to be
> sea – to be sky – to be air ... The sea's rhythm is love en-
> veloping, surrounding, adoring and expanding. The sky's
> melting meeting.

You knew love – you thought of it as warm. Now you know these are its origins ...
Before love I knew this. But thought its premonition told of love to come– specific love.
Now love has come. But by it I only take this world more slowly, more specifically. Love loosened each several part to love this whole more willingly ... I want my book to be about love. But love is so large and formless. (But so full of new worlds.) (*Necessary Secrets* 198)

In a later entry in December she writes:

> Drapery. What of drapery? I mean the oblique camou-flaged form of putting the truth in a work of art. A poem, a note, a diary. These are the raw moments, the raw thoughts. I do not want, I am irritated with the devious method and hidden indirectness of the novel, for instance, or even the short story, or play. Poems, notes, diaries, letters, or a prose such as in 'The House of Incest,' in *The Black Book*, only meet my need.
> Yet would I not be happy to make a book like *Green Mansions* or *Wuthering Heights, The Waves*, or *Tess of the D'Urbervilles*? Well, yes. But when I think of the things I want to say, I cannot think *that* way of saying them. The fierce impart things, drawn over this hugh irrelevant skeleton. But what form? ... (But) I need a new form ... each word must rip virgin ground. No past effort must ease the new birth. Rather than that, the haphazard note, the unborn child, the bottled embryo.
> (*Necessary Secrets* 201–2)

Smart wanted to capture these raw moments in her writing, what she thought of as emotional truths. In *By Grand Central Station I Sat Down and Wept*, Smart was writing about 'emotional truths'; in that work the narrator proclaims, 'there is no reality but love ... in all states of being, in all worlds, this is all there is' (72).
Curiously, before Smart had met Barker, she was already attempting to write about emotional truths in her novella 'Dig A Grave and Let Us Bury Our Mother,' the precursor in style, voice, and form of *By Grand Central Station I Sat Down and Wept*. The subject of this novella was also love and the genesis of *By Grand*

Central Station I Sat Down and Wept can easily be traced to it. In this earlier work, her writing style went through radical transformations reflected in the diary entries that become the basis of the novella.

In the drafts of various early incomplete stories found in Smart's early journals and in her personal entries, there is an external focus and an interest in character and event, apparent in her 'Juvenilia,' in the early accounts of her life in London and Ottawa, in the records of her various trips, and in her first full-length fictional work, 'My Lover John.' However, the external focus gradually shifts to an internal one, with the consequent movement away from incident and character in her fiction. The changes in voice and style correspond to the growing complexities in Smart's life and to a growing need, on her part, as reflected in her journal's entries, to find a language that would re-create as it articulates emotional truths.

Smart's language changes in her journals as she begins to experiment with voice and style. By the time she had finished her novella in 1939, she had found both her voice and style. To express the abstract emotions of love, Smart had created 'a language of love,' a language of feeling that is at once subjective and universal, passionate and extravagant; it is the language that characterizes and distinguishes *By Grand Central Station I Sat Down and Wept*.

By the time Smart met Barker, she had already written parts of *By Grand Central Station I Sat Down and Wept*. Her affair with Barker provided her with the skeleton on which to hang the flesh of the emotional truths she had already begun to explore in her writing. Ironically, the romantic ethos that shaped her art worked now to shape her life.

In Smart's journals, there is a gradual shift in her writing from closure, a style characterized by being framed, contained, and closed to indirection; it becomes generative, eidetic, and open-ended, the general characteristics that determine the writing in *By Grand Central Station I Sat Down and Wept*. Here a language of openness and expansiveness reconciles the differences or the polarities of good and evil, glory and ruin, ecstasy and agony, faith and betrayal that structure the novel. Both the language and style emphasize the simultaneous existence of the mundane and the magnificent, the squalid and the marvellous; love itself is sacred and profane, spiritual and earthbound, specific and universal. It is a language that obfuscates the boundary between the self and the author and the subject of the discourse.

In all of Smart's writing there is the exploration of the self in relation to an external world. In 'Dig a Grave and Let Us Bury Our Mother,' the narrator says: 'I am the only thing I know. And even that I only see through a glass darkly from time to time, as a great way off' (*In the Meantime* 73). In her journals and in her published work, Smart mythifies the exploration of the self; yet it is not a mythification that sets the exploration apart, but a relentlessly honest search that transcends the impulse to document or to confess by extraordinary perceptions and the power and the beauty of her language. For Smart life and art were one and the same thing. All her writing was life writing; her journals are the documents of this process.

WORKS CITED

Meyer, Bruce, and Brian O'Riordan. 'Elizabeth Smart: Fact and Emotional Truth.' In *In Their Words: Interviews with Fourteen Canadian Writers*. Toronto: Anansi 1984

Rich, Adrienne. 'When We Dead Awaken: Writing as Revision.' In *On Lies, Secrets, and Silence: Selected Prose 1966–1978*. New York: Norton 1979

Smart, Elizabeth. *By Grand Central Station I Sat Down and Wept*. Toronto: Popular Library 1966

– *In the Meantime: A Collection of Unpublished Poetry and Prose* by Elizabeth Smart. Ed. Alice Van Wart. Toronto: Deneau 1984

– *Necessary Secrets: The Early Journals of Elizabeth Smart*. Ed. Alice Van Wart. Toronto: Deneau 1986

2

Between the Lines:
Marian Engel's
Cahiers and Notebooks

CHRISTL VERDUYN

> First thought: I am hooked on orthodoxy. Kosherdom classicism. Have to learn to accept that a lot of the good things are like me, somewhat between the lines.
>
> I am autobiographical ... I am told my novels are ... But my own history is the history of hundreds of people I know.
>
> Marian Engel[1]

An important accomplishment of recent literary criticism has been its revision of what can be considered a literary text. Modern critical movements such as feminism and postmodernism have been instrumental in legitimizing forms of literary expression that fall outside familiar genre categories such as the novel or poetry. Analysis of the relation between genre and gender in particular has resulted in an expansion of the literary canon to include forms of writing that frequently, though not exclusively, have been practised by women. Such revision has had particularly interesting results in the field of Canadian literature. Canonical revision has established the importance of work by numerous women writers who chose alternative literary practices. For example, at the end of the nineteenth century, Quebec writer Laure Conan problematized the dominant literary mode of the historical novel with her book *Angéline de Montbrun*. Incorporating letters, journal, and narrative, Conan's novel has become known as Canada's first psychological novel and its complexities continue to be revealed by modern criticism.[2] Another Quebec woman writer, Jovette-Alice Bernier, took the exploration of the psychological novel a step further with her controversial *La Chair décevante*, published in 1931. Unlike the then dominant 'roman du terroir,' Bernier's novel recounted in journal form the story of unwed mother Didi Lantange's struggle with societal pressures. Expanding the canon has also reinstated the work of English-Canadian women writers such as Anna Jameson, Laura Goodman Salverson, Lily Dougall, and Marjorie Pickthall, among others.3 The new literary terrain now includes travel writing, letters, diaries and other private papers, oral history and narrative, fiction-theory (represented by the work of Nicole Brossard),4 and the more recently identified category of 'life writing.' This last category is especially intriguing, as exemplified in the notebooks and *cahiers* of writers such as Marian Engel.

In an essay entitled 'Whose Life Is It Anyway? Some Preliminary Remarks on Life-Writing,' Marlene Kadar describes life writing as a 'genre of documents or fragments of documents written out of a life, or unabashedly out of a personal experience of the writer' (*Essays in Life-Writing* 5). Life writing comprises many kinds of texts, both fictional and non-fictional. All are linked by a common thematic concern with a life, or the self. While life writing may include some of the elements of the more familiar genre of autobiography, it steps beyond genre boundaries and disciplines, particularly with regard to narrative unity, 'objective' thinking, and author/ity. As Kadar explains, life writing performs two serious intellectual and cultural tasks: 'First, it allows the canonical, or marginally canonical, to be considered alongside the legitimately marginal ... The second important cultural task that Life-writing performs is related to gender. [Life-writing] is concerned with the documentation and reconstruction of women's lives ... Women have found it easier to write *in* their lives, for one, and for another, they have not always written, or spoken, in a language or style which suited the judges of good taste.' (13–14). Kadar identifies the culmination of life writing in 'its combination of feminism and narrative, fictional or non-fictional, in what has come to be known as *Ecriture féminine*, often translated ... as writing-in-the-feminine' (16). A key concept in recent feminist literary criticism, 'l'écriture au féminin' is linked to the equally important concept of 'jouissance.' Simultaneously sexual, political, and economic in its overtones, as Kadar explains, 'jouissance' implies 'total access, total participation, as well as total ecstasy' (16). It is the result of writing that, in the words of French theoreticians Hélène

Cixous and Catherine Clément, 'undermines notions of representation and truth which hold that there is some original presence,
some source of truth that can be restored to the text.'[5]

There have been a number of empirical demonstrations of the
concept of life writing:[6] the court testimonies of non-élite young
women in early seventeenth-century Rome describing their loss
of virginity; the work of Sor Juana Ines de la Cruz, who wrote at
the end of the seventeenth century; and the journals of Elizabeth
Smart, which span the decades of the mid-twentieth century. There
are additional writings that illustrate the notion of life writing, as
the present volume reveals. Among these are the notebooks Marian Engel kept throughout her life.

Marian Engel (1933–85) belonged to the generation of women
writers in Canada who came to prominence during the 1970s.
Mother of twins, first president of the Canadian Writers' Union,
Engel published seven novels, two collections of short stories, two
children's books, and numerous other short stories, essays, and
articles.[7] Her novel *Bear* won the 1976 Governor General's Award
for best English-language fiction. But Engel's *oeuvre* is arguably
more than her published novels and short stories. It comprises as
well a variety of writings contained in the author's papers, including the notebooks or *cahiers* (the terms are interchangeable
for her) that she wrote throughout her life. The Marian Engel
Archive, the collection of the author's papers located at McMaster
University Mills Memorial Library, comprises nearly thirty of her
cahiers.

In the brochure describing Engel's McMaster papers, archivist
Dr K.E. Garay notes:

> Marian Engel ha[d] a Gallic Passion for the *cahier*, and
> early in her career acquired the habit of recording ideas,
> notes on books read, drafts of letters never sent, plot out-
> lines and many other things in her notebooks. While
> some notebooks relate entirely to a particular novel (e.g.
> the *Monodromos cahiers*) others seem to have no relation
> to any novel or relate to several. Few of the notebooks
> contain dates and ... to complicate matters somewhat,
> early notebooks containing blank pages were sometimes
> 'rediscovered' and include much later entries by the au-
> thor. (*MEA* 34)

Engel's notebooks should be considered seriously in the first instance for their obvious link to her published work. The complete genesis and evolution of the novel *Monodromos*, for example, can be traced through the author's notebooks and papers.[8] The same can be said of *Bear*. In some instances, texts undergo considerable subsequent revision; in others, passages remain virtually unaltered. In all cases, fiction writing coincides with other writings, ranging from personal introspection through financial accounts to recipes. The effect is to break down the traditional separation of fiction from other forms of writing. Engel's notebooks thus complete the tasks of life writing Kadar identifies in her essay. First, they unite the canonical and the marginal by interspersing passages of subsequently published novels or short stories with fragments of other writings produced by the author during her lifetime. And second, they document Engel's life as a woman and as a writer.

As Marlene Kadar explains, life writing is a genre practised most often, though not exclusively, in this century by women writers who 'are caring for women's *bios* ['life, course or way of living'], women's *aute* [authority and originality], women's *graphia* [signs], women's hermeneutics' (18). The highest goal of this newly identified 'genre,' Kadar proposes, is 'self-knowing,' which is linked to a notion of self-care' (17). Engel's *cahiers* reflect this goal of life writing while exhibiting its generic traits. A notebook embargoed until after the author's death stands as witness to the difficult acknowledgment of self turning 'human ... becoming a person ... *taking care of myself*' (*MEA* 6:28).[9] Engel's *cahiers* fill in 'between the lines' of Engel's published work. They provide a unique expression of the concerns and themes that shaped her life and informed her writing. Foremost among the ideas recurring in the notebooks is the experience of the writer as woman, and woman as writer or, more generally, artist. Other recurrent ideas include the obstacles presented to the woman writer, among them familial and societal stereotypes about women; literary theory and criticism; literary innovation; and the relation of reality and imagination, fact, and fiction. These recurring ideas will be explored briefly in the remainder of this essay.

One of the most clearly articulated themes in Engel's notebooks is her desire and determination to be a writer. 'I decided to be a writer when I was 10. I bought a notebook and said, "I'm going to be a writer, Mother." And she said, "That's very hard." I said, "I don't care"' ('Beginnings'). This recollection of the early decision to become a writer identifies some significant elements that lend shape to Engel's experiences as a writer: the presence, from the outset, of the notebook; the role of the mother, and by extension, the family; and the hardships to be faced by the writer. Engel's determination to be a writer was matched by her awareness of the difficulties involved in being a writer, more specifically, being a woman writer in Canada in the 1960s. In one entry, she equated the notebook with 'the knowing that you will not be understood because you are not big enough to say what you want' (MEA 6:3).

Feeling 'small' derived from a combination of factors.[10] Most important were the fact of being female, the way in which this was understood by family and society, and how this understanding was realized through social values and upbringing. Engel reflected regularly on the subject of upbringing in her notebooks and all her major fictional characters grapple with the question of how they were raised. 'The years from five to ten are influential ones,' Engel observed in an essay recalling her childhood in Galt, Ontario ('The Girl from Glat'). As she explored her upbringing, Engel interrogated the values it was intended to instill as well as the role played by family figures – particularly the mother.

The mother figure is important in Engel's novels and short stories and a key presence in her notebooks and letters. This feature of her writing is particularly interesting in light of recent feminist critique that has undertaken to measure the extent to which the mother-daughter relationship shapes women's lives and work. In literature, relationships between father and son, or between lovers, have often eclipsed the relationship between mother and daughter. Engel consciously chose to write about the relations between mothers and daughters, and between women in general, thereby situating herself among the increasing number of women writers who privilege these previously neglected relationships.

The notebooks explore the closely related role of the family, and exhibit an ambivalent attitude. On the one hand, family is presented as providing a sense of belonging, a feeling important to the author and her characters alike. 'I am not naturally a rebel,' Engel recorded; 'I want desperately to belong when there is something around to belong to' (MEA 6:3). On the other hand, family was seen by Engel as potentially stifling female self-expression, particularly when its values are steeped in stereotypical attitudes towards women. 'What are the values?' Engel queried in notes to an early unpublished play 'The Deception of the Thrush.' In answer she wrote: 'Family solidarity, feminine modesty, feminine chastity, feminine obedience' (*MEA* 6:3). Engel's notebooks disclose a keen awareness of what she identified as southern Ontario, middle-class puritanism. She equated the state of 'middle-classness' with decorum, conventionality, and doing as one should:

> Should? Isn't that the great Canadian word, though? It's hassled me all through my life, through school and Sunday School and a Baptist university, which I thought was about books and turned out to be about people hanging in your doorway saying Marian, you shouldn't hang about with those people who read so much, you should curl your hair.
> Should, should, should, until you think you're going to die of it. ('Housework Gives Me the Crazies')

In her notebooks, as elsewhere, Engel pursued the matter of 'should' and its various agents – notably family and formal education – and the generally negative impact it exerted on different areas of her growth from girlhood to womanhood. With regard to human sexuality, for instance, Engel observed: 'I was brought up to be a nice, refined, Ontario girl ... I was Miss Square, and, having been handed 'Sex, Marriage and Birth Control' at a tender age, I decided it was just as well. Besides, I wanted to be a writer' (*MEA* 26:13). Becoming a writer did not ensure that questions of sex, marriage, and motherhood would not present themselves. On the contrary, and they are taken up at length in Engel's notebooks.

'Relying on sex only drives one into frantic self-disgust,' Engel wrote in an earlier *cahier*. 'Denial, on the other hand, eventually distorts one's whole life' (*MEA* 6:3). Sex is first in a list of 'embarrassments' that Engel identified in a 1963 notebook, a list that includes writing, religion, adoption (*MEA* 6:7). If matters such as sex, writing, and religion were awkward, it was at least in part because Engel's upbringing located them in the realm of instinct as opposed to the terrain of logic and control.

Engel explored the ostensible antithesis of logic and instinct, particularly as it related to writing, where feelings were perceived to play a critical role. 'Never mind what the story says,' Engel jotted in one *cahier*; 'it proves that the instincts are right' (*MEA* 6:1). But when instinct was linked to 'femaleness,' Engel as writer and woman experienced insecurity on both accounts. A 1963 notebook entry recorded this, and its unhappy consequences:

I am on the defensive about being a woman.
I am on the defensive about my own illogical (i.e. emotional) attitudes.
...
1) I drink more and more
2) I am less and less logical
3) I am less and less sure of which level things come from: hysteria. (*MEA* 6:3)

As she was setting out on a career as a writer, Engel's notebooks reveal that she experienced the sort of distress that feminist investigation suggests is characteristic of the lives of women artists.[11] When emotion/instinct assert importance within a context of logic/control, hysteria is the verdict assigned by both the individual and society. Engel highly valued instinct and emotion in writing. She considered novelists synthesists rather than analysts: 'The operation of the creative mind is one of synthesis, and the operation of the critical mind is analytic. The synthesizing process happens first: the novelist writes his first draft. Then the critical sense takes over. I trust my unconscious more and more' (Matyas, 'Interview with Marian Engel'). When writing was going well, the overwhelming sense was one of 'disobeying orders – living instinctively instead of logically ... riding high' (*MEA* 6:10). But the belief in approaching reality through synthesis, instinct, and emotion was subject to constant challenge. 'What was it taught me not to trust my own instinct & rationality?' Engel queried in one *cahier* and in partial response, wrote: 'pain, self-sacrifice, & instruction [of] the female virtues ... led to their logical conclusion – destruction of the self and of other women's selves' (*MEA* 6:28).

The traditional options for women, the ones that *should* be chosen, were consistently restrictive. It was always the case for Engel that 'respectable was ... the key word, rather than intellectual. That was beaten into me' (*MEA* 26:12). As one notebook entry stated, 'Gentility became the aim, "no thing stronger than tea" a whole philosophy' (*MEA* 6:10). But the world of emotion and imagination, of writing and intellectual pursuit emerged against this background of respectability, gentility, and logic.

The notebooks confirm that Engel read widely and critically. Literary theory was an important lifelong interest. 'I want to work out an aesthetic [of writing],' she noted on 25 August 1972 (*MEA* 6:22). It was also an expertise shaped by her studies at McMaster and McGill. The *cahiers* contain notes taken in class and lists of books read during her university years. After Engel left university, she remained interested in the intellectual questions of the day. For example, she took copious notes on the theory and practice of the *nouveau roman*. An entry dated 30 January 1970 urges: 'The Nouveau Roman, the Old Roman & the New Roman. Straighten out your ideas before you continue' (*MEA* 6:18). Engel tracked the development of the idea of art becoming its own subject and the role of language in this new self-conscious representation. Reading Maurice Blanchot's *Le Livre à venir*, she noted that a 'special lit.[erary] language [is] now being created in America' (*MEA* 6:24). She was taken with Borges's concept of fabulation: 'He says a great deal to me,' she recorded. 'His parables deal w[ith] what one can refer to as 'artistic creation' – or creation or discovery. His labyrinths are tunnels for *seekers* – and writers are *par excellence* seekers (if I can't find it, I'll invent it)' (*MEA* 6:18). She argued on paper with Robbe-Grillet about the 'myth of depth' and the need to see things as they are: 'He may be right but what I need is to place the rare joys of reality against those few elements of reality that seep through to me' (*MEA* 6:18). She devoted considerable attention to the demise of literary realism, recording under a notebook title 'Butor – Repertoire II,' that 'realism is hostile to morality & the intellectual. It is made of mediocrity, hate, flat sufficiency' (*MEA* 6:22).

As she rehearsed and reflected on literary process and criticism, Engel remained intently interested in innovation. However, the options available to her were conjuncturally limited. A writer intent on publishing at the time Engel was beginning her career could not be innovative in the ways subsequently facilitated by feminist literary practice or embraced by the concept of life writing. Although she tried (and even published) poetry, Engel was soon aware that this would not be her literary métier. 'I wrote poetry when I was in my early twenties ... then I had a run-in with Louis Dudek at McGill, who didn't like my work. I stopped writing poetry and realized that if I *could* stop, I was no poet' (Matyas, 'Interview with Marian Engel').

Plays presented another option. Engel's unpublished work features a number of plays that Hugh MacLennan thought were good. McLennan was Engel's mentor at McGill, where he directed her *MA* thesis on the Canadian novel.[12] MacLennan remarked that an early Engel piece entitled 'Beat Up the Rain' was 'true, vivid, vital

and excellently constructed ... the work ... of a very observant
writer who has produced some real if naive characters, thrown
them together and made them live.'[13] But Engel did not pursue
playwriting past the period after her return from Europe in the
mid 1960s, when she wrote radio and television plays and scripts.
Instead, she turned to the novel, which offered her the possibilities
for innovation and the room for 'looseness' that she required for
literary expression. 'I want to cut the novel up,' a notebook entry
recorded, 'cut loose from conventional plod [sic]' (MEA 6:24).

The notebooks provided an excellent outlet for this impulse.
'Writing in so many notebooks,' Engel noted on 4 June 1965 (MEA
6:10), 'as ever, disorganized.' This admission is not a self-criticism.
Engel's writing shows respect for attitudes and modes of being
subsequently legitimized by the contemporary cultural critiques
of feminism and postmodernism. Reading Maurois's life of Balzac
in 1966, she noted her admiration for 'the multiplicity of the man.
The love of the chaos hugger-mugger. Junkshop or splendid museum of a mind? Versailles and Highgate Cemetery. Means of
knowing people – profilic intimacy. How many people's stories
do I know this way?' (MEA 6:11). Engel perceived simultaneousness
and multiplicity as ways to realize intimacy with others and self
alike. Apparent chaos can generate self-knowledge. 'Fragmented
is the word for my mind,' Engel recorded on 30 August 1968 (MEA
6:13). Similar perceptions and reflections appear throughout the
notebooks, as well as via the female protagonists of Engel's novels
and short stories. Reading Harold Nicolson on 10 October 1968,
Engel noted: 'I must keep a diary, keep it regularly as an act of
self-discipline and labour and sanity.' But, she added knowingly,
'my pen will run out. Always I fight against the grain of my upbringing' (MEA 6:13).

At the time Engel was beginning to publish, literary unconven-
tionality was a difficult project to pursue. Feminist and postmodern critiques had not yet facilitated rebel perspectives in the realms
of social values and human expression. The cahiers offered a solution, but publishing a notebook was an idea whose time had not
yet come.[14] In the interim, the notion was subsumed in Engel's
first published book, a novel called, not coincidentally, Sarah Bastard's Notebook.[15]

The idea of the 'novel as notebook' may not originate with
Engel's Sarah Bastard's Notebook, but the latter was a 'novel' publication. This first book brought its author public attention in

Canada, albeit not for the notebook aspect. This analytical lacuna reflected the absence of critical literary applications sensitive to alternative (female) approaches to representing experience. As a fuller critical context has emerged, *Sarah Bastard's Notebook*, like the *cahiers* that preceeded and followed it, can be considered to anticipate modern experimentation with literary form and representation. Engel's notebooks certainly provided her a vehicle of expression for concerns and practices of writing that modern and feminist criticism have subsequently validated. Among these are the departure from linear narrative and the clear separation of genres. The *cahiers* display little concern for chronology and sequence and present a blend of writing practices: fiction, theory, introspection, autobiography, and so forth. The overall effect is to blur the margins of 'reality' and fiction.

In her notebooks, Engel returned several times to the 'dilemma' of 'where fiction begins and reality leaves off and the synthesizing of these two' ('Canadian Writing Today'). She expressed the view that writers cannot live on the theorizing plane alone: 'We write out of another piece of ourselves which we hope to make universal, out of reality. And that is not to say that fiction is not reality, but it is not to say that fiction is reality either' ('Canadian Writing Today'). Engel's reflections on the relationship between reality and fiction can be juxtaposed fruitfully with those of Quebec feminist writer and theoretician Nicole Brossard. In her 1985 collection of essays *La lettre aérienne* Brossard asserts: 'For most women "reality" has been a fiction, that is to say the product of an imagination that is not theirs and to which they cannot really adapt. Let's name some fictions: the military, the rise in the price of gold, the news, pornography ... At the same time, one can also say that women's reality has been perceived as fiction. Let's name some realities here: maternity, rape, prostitution, chronic fatigue, violence (verbal, physical and mental' (75). Brossard probes the ostensible realities and fictions generated by the dominant understanding of the world. She undermines the authority of those named within a male-oriented order, and privileges those identified within a more female-focused order. Her work punctures the structures and fictions of male-shaped reality to allow a new female reality to emerge and be expressed. Engel was engaged in a similar project. She also doubted the existence of one, unified Truth and challenged the distinction between fiction and 'reality' in her notebooks. 'The truth *lies*,' Engel jotted in a 1968 cahier; 'the truth lies somewhere

between' (*MEA* 6:7). Engel did not suggest that truth is to be found
in fiction. Of *Monodromos* she noted: 'Without wanting to say
"what is truth?" I want in Monodromos to *depict* but differently
... But also to admit failure in the end' (*MEA* 6:22). For Engel, the
'necessities of fiction' left no room for 'literal truth,' in which she
was not interested ('Do You Use Real People in Fiction?'). Rather,
Engel was concerned with that which lies 'between the lines.'

Engel's notebooks trace her life as a woman and a writer, detailing the points of tension between the poles of daily reality and
imaginary life and writing. This tension characterizes her life and
her *oeuvre* alike. Pages of notes on literary theory and reflections
on intellectual life are offset by vignettes recording everyday 'real
life.' Dozens of undated entries, both fictional and philosophical,
sit beside equally numerous entries carefully noting time and place
and conscientiously outlining the contours of 'reality.'[16] To read
Engel's notebooks is to shift constantly with the author from a
commitment to a life of the imagination and writing to a commitment to the here and now – reality as presented in a given time
and place. Even as she was attracted to the world of the imagination, Engel was aware of the practical consequences of that attraction – at least for the woman writer. For example, there was
the tendency to lose track of time and to forget about such domestic tasks as housekeeping: 'Like Virginia Woolf, I have a won-
derful gift for not seeing dust' ('Housework Gives Me the Crazies').
In addition, there was the appearance of inactivity and passivity,
at odds with any work ethic. 'For me thinking = action,' Engel
noted; 'No wonder I'm static. Imagination stronger in effect than
action ... confronted with action, I fade into dreams' (*MEA* 6:7).
'Urgency kills me' (*MEA* 6:11).

If she maintained the value of dream and imagination, writing
and fiction, Engel always remained grounded in 'reality' – a reality
that in turn was grounded in female experience. This is what the
notebooks record. In them, fiction writing converges with writing
that conveys life as Engel – a woman and a writer – experienced
it. In this way, the notebooks constitute the writings of a life –
Marian Engel's life writing.

NOTES

1 The first citation is found in papers described as 'jottings, ideas, in-

trospection, 1960's to 1980's, transcript, 5 pp. holograph 8pp.' and located in Box 26 File 45 in the Marian Engel Archive. The second citation is taken from a carbon typescript entitled 'The Greening of Toronto: A Footnote to Mordecai Richler (13p),' located in *Archive* Box 26 File 12. Compiled by Dr K.E. Garay, with the assistance of Norma Smith, the *Marian Engel Archive* is an issue of the *Library Research News*, a publication of the Division of Archives and Research Collections, McMaster University. With her permission, this essay uses the brief descriptions Dr Garay provides to identify Engel's papers, otherwise organized under Box and File numbers. Most citations are from files in Box 6, which contains the author's notebooks and *cahiers*. Following are the descriptions of files cited in this essay:

Box 6 File 1 (*MEA* 6:1): [1962–3] 'I,' Cyprus and Toronto: mostly notes for a planned novel [Sarah Bastard?] and a reading list.

Box 6 File 3 (*MEA* 6:3): [1962–3] 'Tome IV,' Cyprus: ideas, outlines, introspection, lists of books.

Box 6 File 7 (*MEA* 6:7): [1963] 'II.' Monodromos.' This *cahier* appears to have been kept as a journal in Cyprus and later used as one source of *Monodromos*.

Box 6 File 10 (*MEA* 6:10): [1965?] This notebook begins more like a journal, April – June [1965?], mentions the finishing of *Death Comes for the Yaya*, then includes notes on books read, ideas for *Sarah Bastard*, and a 'bibliography of the 20's' on last page. It includes also three visiting cards from Cyprus.

Box 6 File 11 (*MEA* 6:11): 1966–8 'Passmores and Minn.' Notebook begins with notes on a Passmore ancestor but most of the *cahier* is taken up with notes on Minn [for *The Honeyman Festival*]. There are also journal entries, an account of the launching of *No Clouds of Glory* [1968], lists of names and notes on books read. Includes newspaper cutting.

Box 6 File 13 (*MEA* 6:13): 1967 'Minn.' Almost entirely notes and draft passages for *The Honeyman Festival* with some journal entries and lists.

Box 6 File 18 (*MEA* 6:18): 1970 'Monodromos 1st': outlines, lists, ideas, draft paragraphs and 'notes from letters' – all for *Monodromos*. Also notes on books read and ideas on women's liberation.

Box 6 File 22 (*MEA* 6:22): 'Aug. 25/72: Holstein Book.' Ideas and lists for *Monodromos*, notes on books read and 'the poetry of the novel.' Only 6 pp. of the *cahier* are written on.

Box 6 File 24 (*MEA* 6:24): 1972–3 Notes for *Monodromos*, lists of names of places, people, flowers, etc., notes on books read, ideas and paragraphs for Ziggy short story.

Box 6 File 28 (*MEA* 6:28): 1974 This notebook, containing notes relating to the Marshallene character, to *Monodromos*, and to *Bear* as well as journal entries, [was] embargoed for five years [i.e., until Spring 1988].

Box 26 File 12 (*MEA* 26:12): 'The Greening of Toronto: A Footnote to Mordecai Richler,' carbon typescript, 13 pp.

Box 26 File 13 (*MEA* 26:13): 'Growing Up at Forty: Or the Real Joanne' – incomplete annotated typescript, 24 pp. total.

2 See, for instance, Patricia Smart's analysis of *Angéline de Montbrun* in *Ecrire dans la maison du père* 41–86.

3 See essays in Shirley Neuman and Smaro Kamboureli, eds, *A Mazing Space*

4 Others may be cited, but Brossard has been at the forefront of this new mode of writing that overrides traditional genre distinction by merging fiction, essay, theory, autobiography, and so on.

5 Kadar, 16–17, quoting Hélène Cixous and Catherine Clément, *The Newly Born Woman*, trans. Betsy Wing, intro. Sandra M. Gilbert, in *Theory and History of Literature* 24 (Minneapolis: U of Minnesota P 1986) 165–6.

6 See *Essays in Life-Writing*.

7 Engel's published books of fiction include *Sarah Bastard's Notebook (No Clouds of Glory)* (1968), *The Honeyman Festival* (1970), *Monodromos* (1973), *Inside the Easter Egg* (1975), *Joanne* (1975), *Bear* (1976), *The Glassy Sea* (1978), *Lunatic Villas* (1981), *The Tatooed Woman* (1985). In addition, there are two children's books: *Adventure at Moon Bay Towers* (1974) and *My Name is Not Odessa Yarker* (1977); and a book entitled *The Islands of Canada* (1981, with J.A. Kraulis).

8 *Monodromos* exists in numerous drafts and multiple variations in the *MEA*. Garay notes that this novel appears to have been the most difficult one to write and certainly presented the most complex problems of archival arrangement (*MEA* x).

9 The underlined words in the quotation are Engel's emphasis.

10 The embargoed notebook (*MEA* 6:28) is especially revealing in this regard. In it, Engel records insights into her personality and her relationships with her husband, her mother, her children, her analyst, and her writing, achieved during a course of therapy in the mid-seventies.

11 See, for instance, Sandra M. Gilbert and Susan Gubar, *The Madwoman in the Attic*.

12 Engel's *MA* thesis, 'A study of the English-Canadian Novel Since 1939' (144 pp., 1957), was one of the first critical examinations in the field of Canadian literary criticism.

13 Letter from McLennan to Engel dated 14 December 1959

14 Now we do find 'published notebooks' among Canadian publishing-

house selections. A recent example would be Antonio d'Alfonso's *The Other Shore* (Montreal: Guernica 1988).

15 *Sarah Bastard's Notebook* (Don Mills: Paperjacks 1974) was published earlier under the title *No Clouds of Glory* (Don Mills: Longmans 1968). The comment appears more than once in the author's papers that the book ought to have been issued only under the first title, that preferred by the author, and that which most effectively captures the book.

16 This is even more true of the many letters Marian Engel wrote, especially during her sojourn in Europe, and especially to her parents.

WORKS CITED

Bernier, Jovette-Alice. *La Chair décevante*. Montreal: Editions Albert Lévesque 1931

Brossard, Nicole. *La lettre aérienne*. Montreal: Remue-ménage 1985; *The Aerial Letter*. Trans. Marlene Wildeman. Toronto: Women's Press 1988

Conan, Laure. *Angéline de Montbrun*. Quebec: Léger Brousseau 1884

Engel, Marian. 'Housework Gives Me the Crazies.' *Chatelaine* (October 1973) 34:83–6

– 'Canadian Writing Today.' *Creative Literature in Canada Symposium*, 2–9. Toronto: Ministry of Colleges and Universities 1974

– 'The Girl from Glat.' *Weekend Magazine* 25.30 (26 July 1975): 6–7

– 'Do You Use Real People in Fiction?' *Saturday Night* (November 1975): 6–7

Garay, K.E. *The Marian Engel Archive*. McMaster University, Archives and Research Collections 8, no. 2 (Fall 1984)

Gilbert, Sandra M., and Susan Gubar. *The Madwoman in the Attic*. New Haven: Yale UP 1979

Kadar, Marlene, ed. *Essays in Life-Writing*. Robarts Centre for Canadian Studies Working Paper 89-WO3. North York, Ont.: York U 1989

Matyas, Cathy, and Jennifer Joiner. 'Interpretation, Inspiration and the Irrevelant Question: Interview with Marian Engel.' *University of Toronto Review* 5 (Spring 1981): 4–8

Neuman, Shirley, and Smaro Kamboureli, eds. *A Mazing Space: Writing Canadian Women Writing*. Edmonton: Longspoon-NeWest 1986

Smart, Patricia. *Ecrire dans la maison du père: l'émergence du féminin dans la tradition littéraire du Québec*. Montreal: Editions Québec/Amérique 1988. Translated by author: *Writing in the Father's House*. Toronto: U of Toronto P 1991

3

Anna Jameson's *Winter Studies and Summer Rambles in Canada* as Epistolary Dijournal

HELEN M. BUSS

'I am no longer Anna – I am metamorphosed – I am translated.'

In naming twelve features of 'life writing,' Marlene Kadar offers us rubrics that she hopes will facilitate the consideration of the 'canonical, or marginally canonical ... alongside the legitimately marginal' (13). This activity will allow us to 'theorize a new genre' to 'name what is now' (6–7). This naming will facilitate the serious consideration of varieties of writing, including many women's writings, that have been especially marginalized because of its 'unabashedly' autobiographical nature and its ambiguous generic placement. I would like to urge that it is equally important, if we wish to have a sense of the wholeness of our literary tradition, one that includes works most typical of women in the past, to name not only what is 'now' but what was *then*.

As one concerned with early Canadian literature, a literature still in the process of being 'named,' I find the text that most needs naming is Anna Jameson's *Winter Studies and Summer Rambles in Canada*, the English writer's account of her Canadian visit in 1837–8, which included a winter in Toronto and a summer spent touring the Great Lakes. It occupies a marginal but continuing place in Canadian literature, reappearing in scholarly commentary under various generic guises, ones that never quite suit it, and which too often suggest that it is Jameson's text and not the method of classification which is flawed.[1] I would like to consider *Studies and Rambles* in a gendered generic context and in doing so 'name' it as a specific variety of life writing. In *A Poetics of Women's Autobiography*, Sidonie Smith draws our attention to three important considerations in the critical examination of women's accounts of selfhood. These are '(1) the ways in which the autobiographer's position as women inflects the autobiographical project and the four marks of fictiveness that characterize it – the fictions of memory, of the 'I,' of the imagined reader, of the story; (2) the ways in which the autobiographer establishes the discursive authority to interpret herself publicly in a patriarchal culture and androcentric genre that have written stories of woman for her, thereby fictionalizing and effectively silencing her; and (3) the relationship of that literary authority to her sexuality and its presence or absence as subject of her story' (45).

Traditional autobiography assumes the facticity of memory, that what St Augustine or Benjamin Franklin or John Stuart Mill 'remember' is in some way the actuality of their lives. Belief in the facticity of memory has created the specific form and the great problem of retrospective autobiogrpahy: that it creates a consistent self, one that subsumes its experience in the world into a meaningful, directed and stable portrait of self. But memories are as much acts of imagination as they are acts of recall; they are a 'play of seeking, choosing, discarding words and stories that suggest, approximate but never recapture the past' (Smith 45–6). Women autobiographers, seeking a less unitary 'I' than the male autobiographer of the past, have often played a different game with the 're-membering' process, one that acknowledges the tentative and conditioned nature of memory.

Anna Jameson's format in *Studies and Rambles* reflects this alternative 'game' in that she admits the personal idiosyncratic nature of her thinking process: 'I know no better way of coming at the truth, than by observing and recording faithfully the impressions made by objects and characters on my own mind – or, rather, the impress they *receive* from my own mind' (16). She acknowledges that new experience is conditioned by predispositions, biases, and cultural assumptions brought to the experience. At the same time, Jameson attempts to establish her 'discursive authority' on autobiographical grounds through the repetition of the phrase 'my own mind.' Although, she apologizes in her 'Preface' for the 'impertinent leaven of egotism which necessarily mixed itself up with the journal form of writing' (10), her apology masks her typical strategy vis-à-vis the fiction of memory, that it is the undisguised subjectivity of that act, the 'flimsy thread of sentiment,' that 'sustain[s] the facts and observations' (10). Her admission that the text

as 'journal' is a conscious formal choice, rather than an accidental
or convenient occurrence, deconstructs the authority of retro-
spectivity and establishes revisionism as the primary act of memory.

Such a stated stylistic position predicts the way in which Jameson intends to structure the 'I' in her account of her experience
while visiting Canada. I have noted in my article 'Canadian Wom-
en's Autobiography' that the use of a writing style that is 'part
practical journal, part diary, part letter' (155) is a useful one for
women coming to Canada and intent on showing the growth of
self involved in their Canadian experience, because it offers the
combination of the sense of a journey through selfhood (paralleling
the actual journey in the new land), an intimate diary style, and
the address to a beloved 'other' that meets several psychic needs
at once while conveniently disguising itself as practical information to family or friends in the old country.

Smith points out that the woman autobiographer may create
'competing ... versions of herself' (47) to make up for her inability
(or unwillingness) to create a unitary 'I.' Jameson overcomes the
problems presented by 'competing versions' of the self by writing
in a mode that I would name the 'epistolary dijournal,' which uses
the actual journey of the subject along with her first experiences
in new communities, recorded in an intimate diary form and addressed to a beloved 'other' to perform an autobiographical act.[2]
This formal blend allows for multiple subject positions to be presented as coexisting rather than 'competing' and therefore eliminates the need for resolution into unitary selfhood that the term
'competing' implies.[3] The term 'epistolary dijournal' is meant to
imply the values of correspondence and alterity that the epistolary
form suggest, as well as those values of intimate self-disclosure
and self-construction suggested by our contemporary concept of
'diary,' along with the facticity and externalization present in the
travel 'journal.' But as well, I wish to gesture towards the biblical
meaning of 'epistle' as we would use it in the Pauline sense, of a
letter that is also instruction to the faithful (in Jameson's case the
feminist readers of her text), and to suggest something of the 'dialogic' possibilities of 'dijournal' as it might exist in a Bakhtinian
sense of the 'dialogic imagination,' that way of thinking which
sees identity as something the autobiographer can only constitute
as a variety of discourses created from the interaction of person
and culture (Smith 48).

What are the various 'fictions,' or more accurately in a dialogic sense, the various linguistic constructions, of the 'I,' posed by *Studies and Rambles*? Obviously, the title of the work itself indicates at least two, the studious, literary, and cultural critic (her very European public self) that Jameson poses in her early chapters and the rambling, adventurous, and independent voyageur (her imagined Canadian self) posed by the later chapters. But such an obvious dichotomy suggests the frame of binary opposites, the fiction of the 'divided self,' which informs traditional male autobiography that seeks either conversion from one subject position to another or a resolution of opposites. Anna Jameson slides through various constructions of the 'I' as her journey unfolds. I say 'slides' because we must look sharply to see which Anna is speaking.

The first Anna that discloses herself is the disappointed, neglected, insulted, helpless, unoccupied, unhappy, and frustrated Anna: in short, Anna the wife. Although the text does not mention her position as one of the 'wives of the officials' of the colonial government until page 93, any aware contemporary reader would have had easy access to the fact that Jameson went to Canada as wife of Robert Jameson, the attorney general of Upper Canada (Thomas 98–108). But it is not whose wife she is, but her subject position as wife that interests us in much of *Studies*. The questioning sadness in the German epigraph that begins the text sets the tone for the revelation of this 'I': *Sind denn die Bäume auch so trostlos, so verzweiflungsvoll in ihrem Winter, wie das Herz in seiner Verlassenheit?* ('Are then the trees also so desolate, so despairing in their winter, as the heart in her loneliness?') (15). I leave the feminine usage of 'seiner' in my translation since it is very definitely the condition of *her* 'heart,' *her* affections, *her* sensibilities that concerns Jameson in these first sections, as she views everything through the disappointment of her position as a wife, sorting through the problems of a troubled marriage. The conclusion of her negative description of Toronto is a hardly disguised comment on her personal situation: 'I did not expect much; but for this I was not prepared. Perhaps no preparation could have *prepared* me, or softened my present feelings. I will not be unjust if I can help it, nor querulous. If I look into my own heart, I find that it is regret for what I have left and lost – the – absent, not the present – which throws over all around me a chill, colder than that of the wintry day – a gloom, deeper than that of the wintry night' (16). The form of the epistolary dijournal allows the am-

biguity of the expression its full play, because its words could be
description of exile felt by the traveler in a strange land, a wife's
lament too well understood by the epistolary 'other' to need mention, or a heart exiled from relationship with the beloved correspondent. The 'left and lost' is also unspecified and allows a play
of meaning between place and person, between present and past
husband and absent intimate addressee of the epistle. In describing
her own helpless position, the 'I' of the text also makes a connection at a profound level with 'my own sex,' the 'good woman' (10),
she seeks as her readers. She asks: 'Is there most wisdom ... in
passively assimilating ourselves, our habits, and our feelings, to
external circumstances, or resisting and combating them, rather
to defend the integrity of our individual being ...?' (28). While
identifying this female dilemma, she also beings to answer it, and
in doing so slides out of her passive stance.

A self-mocking humour is Jameson's characteristic strategy in
moving from the foregrounding of one identity to the foregrounding of another. She tells us that 'I begin to be ashamed of recording
idle days and useless days, and to have a conception of what those
unfortunate wretches must suffer, who are habitually without an
interest and without an occupation ... To me it is something new,
for I have never yet been *ennuyée* to death – except in fiction'
(33–4). Recognizing the comic potential of her own situation while
simultaneously establishing her 'discursive authority' as a writer
of fiction (Jameson's first novel – 1825 – was *Diary of an Ennuyée*),
she begins the process of slippage between subject positions. Humour is particularly useful in this regard, for while the comic
moment distracts from the wretchedness of her condition it also
is a method of empowerment. What can be laughed at can be (is
being) changed, since comedy is a method of recognition and articulation of a problem.

For Jameson, as for many cultured women then and now, one
solution to the problem of action in a situation in which one is
disenfranchised is to turn to literary criticism. Using Olhlen-
schlager's study of Corregio as a way of commenting on her own
resources she examines the way in which it is possible to be the
artist who blends the 'purely natural with the purely ideal' (38) as
Corregio did. This is the same act she must accomplish if she is
to reconcile the vast natural world of Canada that surrounds her
with her idealism and blend the natural ground of her femaleness
with the idealistic ground of her emotional needs.

A trip to 'Niagara in Winter' proves to be the vehicle by which she can effect personal change while overcoming the sense of helpless passivity that her husband's place, Toronto, imposes on her. Anna, the traveling cultural critic, is introduced in the humorous moment of her encounter with one of the great wonders of the modern world: 'I am no longer Anna – I am metamorphosed – I am translated – I am an ass's head, a clod, a wooden spoon, a fat weed growing on Lethe's bank, a stock, a stone, a petrifaction, – for have I not seen Niagara, the wonder of wonders; and felt – no words can tell *what* disappointment!' (57). In terms of the multiple-identity Jameson is establishing she serves notice that she will not always accept the conventional view of things.

But at the same time that this more active, confident 'I' introduces itself, Jameson maintains the complaints, the viewpoints, the strategies of the subject positions she has already established. Anna, the unappreciated wife, is able to make an imaginative identification with the process by which trees are killed by settlers: 'a deep gash is cut through the bark into the stem, quite round the bole of the tree. This prevents the circulation of the vital juices, and by degrees the tree droops and dies ... Is not this like the ... [way] in which a woman's heart may be killed in this world of ours? (64–5). Anna, the neglected wife, complains that at the opening of the legislative assembly she takes her 'proper place ... among the wives of the officials' but that no one bothers 'to give me any necessary explanation, or to point out any remarkable or distinguished persons, if there were such' (93). Recognizing that she lives among these people 'branded with notoriety' (102), she constructs a subject position that recognizes both her imprisonment in the helplessness of her gendered place and her subversion of that prison: 'I have found a *file*' she announces, 'I shall take to translating' (103). The play on the word 'translating' (not to mention the punning on 'file') can be understood in the context of the epistolary dijournal form. Such aspects as travel, daily revisionist writing, the intimate diary voice, and the assumed sympathetic addressee allow for a continuing sense of 'translating,' of the self, the new experiences, the new settings, the new people, into a multiple of subject positions.

But to know also the character of the actual addressee(s) increases the possibilities of 'translation.' We already know that the text is explicitly addressed to women, but Thomas's exploration of Jameson's letters shows that she wrote directly to such contemporaries as Fanny Kremble, the actress, and Ottilie von Goethe, daughter-in-law to Goethe, women who knew what it was to have to make one's living in a world hostile to independent women, and oppressive to dependent women (the text is most overtly addressed to Ottilie as the continuing references to things German, and one direct address to Ottilie indicates). Translating, editing, reviewing, and writing for the popular market – the precarious life of the freelancer – was Anna Jameson's lifetime solution to the lact of place offered the educated woman in the nineteenth century. In the new setting of Canada, 'translation' will become, in all its possible meanings, the powerful subversive strategy of the multiple 'I' that Jameson is processing.

At the same time as Jameson establishes the 'sliding' subject position of her text she creates a narrative method that compliments the slippage from one subject stance to another. These 'fictions' of story, like the fictions of memory, the 'I' and the 'imagined reader,' are influenced by Jameson's consciousness of gender constructs. Her method of storytelling must be viewed through its gender consciousness and the contribution that makes to subject position, or else Jameson's text becomes the 'fragments' of a journal' (9), the 'mere unconnected, incongruous heap' (10) that Jameson feared it might to readers who discount the 'flimsy thread of sentiment' that is her self.

The way in which Jameson constructs narrative is a complex combination of embeddedness, associative shifts, and indirection. The sections entitled 'Niagara,' 'the Rapids,' 'Don Carlos,' 'Niagara,' and 'A Dream,' between pages 202 and 216 are illustrative. By a linear, rationalist, progressive reading, the passage would seem indeed a 'incongruous heap,' but in fact represents an important turning-point in Jameson's experience in Canada. She has, by this point in the text, explored and adventured somewhat into the countryside. More important, summer has come and with it the birth of Jameson's desire to know Canada on her own terms. Implicit in this change is the (extra-textual) fact that her husband has achieved the promotion he wanted to vice-chancellor (Thomas 113), and she feels she has behaved in a restrained enough manner to help in this regard. As well, she is fast realizing that she and he are destined to live apart after her visit to Canada is over (ibid. 115). Now, she offers her second assessment of Niagara.

The exploration begins with a visit to 'the only place I saw in Upper Canada combining our ideas of an elegant, well-furnished

English villa and ornamented grounds, with some of the grandest and wildest features of the forest scene' (202). It is fitting that it should begin in a house that in its double beauty represents Jameson's subject position of that moment, as she learns to bring together the old elegances of the European taste and the new values taught by the wilderness. Niagara in summer is to become the place where she first internalizes this joining. She describes the strange effect Niagara now has on her. While impressed by the visual impression of Niagara, she is conscious now of a sensual awareness beyond sight: 'there was ... no light but that reflected from the leaping, whirling foam; and in spite of the deep-voiced continuous thunder of the cataract, there was such a stillness that I could hear my own heart's pulse throb – or did I mistake feeling for hearing?' (203). This conflating of the senses, of feeling Niagara inside her, is the beginning of a fuller experience in Canada, in which Jameson's characteristic habit of mingling the object of study with her subject position will serve her well.

She wishes 'for some one who would share all this rapture of admiration and delight, without the necessity of speaking – for, after all, what are words? They express nothing, reveal nothing, avail nothing. So it all sinks back into my own heart, there to be kept quiet' (203). She ends the section with another description of the falls: 'in the midst of this tremendous velocity of motion and eternity of sound, there was a deep, deep repose, as in a dream. It impressed me for the time like something supernatural – a vision, not a reality' (203). By hinting that she must keep silent among her visitors from Toronto who will not approve of her 'projects,' she declares her separateness from those with her and this allows the associative shift of wishing to be in touch with a consciousness like her own, that will appreciate without words a view of the world that is more than natural. The effect is to include the reader as well as the assumed correspondent in the group of those more 'appreciative' souls. Her doubt of the efficacy of language to express feeling affirms her strategy to work towards expression through indirection, through strategies that will be recognized by those who are used to sharing her 'silence.' By implication, this desire looks backward to the 'friends' to whom this journal addresses itself and forward to her meeting with the Indian women who will be able to share some of her feeling of the internalization of the landscape.

Jameson offers a description that emphasizes the new effect Niagara has on her: 'It soothed, it melted, rather than excited' (212). However, she does not deny her past subject position vis-à-vis the Falls, that is, her opinion of Niagara formed the previous winter, when both the Falls and herself were in different modes of being, when she saw the object, but did not feel the force of it. Rather she builds the new subject position on the ground of the old, in the same way as the summer Niagara is created out of the winter Niagara.

At this important nexus of the text, Jameson includes a seemingly unrelated discussion of Schiller's *Don Carlos*. But what seems logically unrelated to the change that has occurred in her consciousness is in fact related in an associative sense because of Jameson's habit of reading the changes in herself through the new readings she makes of literature. Her critical tasks are a way of intellectually realizing what she has emotionally experienced, a way of illuminating the 'silence' that language's inadequacy forces on feeling. Her investigation of Don Carlos proceeds through a new appreciation of the hero Posa, while recognizing the impossibility that such a man could exist. Thus, she indirectly acknowledges that her own expectations of a certain kind of sensibility in men may be imagined, as Schiller has imagined it, but not exist in the world. In this way we are given notice that Jameson has grown out of the need for a particular male definition of herself that made her expect men to be what men have asked women to think men are.

After paying the prescribed attention to the hero of Schiller's work, she moves to a discussion of the character, Elizabeth of France, who she feels has been misinterpreted because people do not know how to understand such a 'cloudless, transparent, crystalline purity' (208). She tells us that we can sometimes see such a mind as 'shallow,' when in fact 'the mind of a woman, which should be wholly pure, simple and true, would produce this illusion [of water that appears more shallow than it is]: we see at once to the bottom, whether it be shining pebble or golden sands, and do not perceive the true depth till we try, and are made to feel and know it by getting beyond our own depth before we are aware' (208). This is the possibility she is discovering in herself, and will discover in the country and Natives, and especially the native women she will soon meet. One must get beyond one's depth to discover another, especially one who may seem simple, unsophisticated, on the surface. Indirectly, as readers we are asked to go 'beyond or beneath what is visible and spoken' (208) to discover the embedded stories, the associative connections, the subversive indirection of Jameson's text.

In the three-page section that follows this discussion of Schiller she manages to embed an important feminist statement concerning women's 'false position' (211) in society (one that is to become of primary importance during her Great Lakes voyage), while seeming to offer only a gossipy account of a visit to the American falls. As well, she allows this first overt mention of her feminist agenda to come from the mouth of her respectable male companion, Colonel Delatre, thus reassuring her less liberated readers of the acceptability of the radical views she will present later in the text.

The passage under consideration culminates in the recounting of a dream, not one she had at Niagara, but one she inserts as an interruption of the chronology of her travel journal. In her dream (framed by reading German folk tales that she feels she is still reading after she has fallen asleep) she sees a 'Being' that laments for all the miseries of the world. The Being rises towards heaven to escape the sight of suffering by drinking from 'a charmed cup.' But the transcendent position does not bring rapture since the Being is sad that 'the bond which had united the sympathizing with the suffering heart was broken for ever' (214). To dream of a transcendent experience that leads not to rapture but to separation, sadness, and incompleteness is to deconstruct the expected experience of the Romantic in nature. For transcendence implies a peace, a completion, an end to suffering. Jameson's narrative strategy in this portion of her text, which has concerned her experience of herself in community with nature, is not only interjected, at every point, by the words and events of people in the world, but is culminated by a refusal of Romantic detachment and by the acceptance of the necessary bond between sympathizer and sufferer. In fact, Jameson's travel account of her trip through the Great Lakes is to be no Romantic escape, but a continuing experience of the lives of people in nature.

She keeps the 'bond' between herself and her subject-matter from being broken by the use of the epistolary dijournal that mingles observation, study, intimate feeling, and relationship. A good example of this state of 'involvement' immediately follows the relating of her dream, when she tells her addressee: 'I do not mean to tell you that I dreamed all this to the sound of the Falls of Niagara; but I do aver that it was a real *bona fide* dream. Send me now the interpretation thereof – or look to be sphinx-devoured' (214). Not only does the passage renew the pleasant feeling that we are reading part of an exchange of letters between inmates, but it tells us that the dream is placed here, out of chronology, purposefully. We, like the intimate addressee, are asked to interpret this dream on pain of being 'sphinx-devoured.' Jameson, far from sanctioning the Romantic experience, is proposing quite a different experience of Canada and selfhood, one that we must recognize if our reading act is not to be riddled with confusion, 'sphinx-devoured.'

Of the features described in Smith's *Poetics*, I have foregrounded those of memory, of the 'I,' and of story, and shown how they operate in Jameson's text and how these autobiographical 'fictions' are affected by her position as woman in a patriarchal culture. I would now like to give more direct treatment of the fiction of the 'imagined reader' and the ways in which Jameson establishes her 'discursive authority' with that figure. Smith describes the difficult position that public autobiographical discourse presents for a woman in that she is 'attuned to the ways women have been dressed up for public exposure, attuned also to the price women pay for public self-disclosure ... As a result, the autobiographer, at least until the twentieth century, approaches her "fictive" reader as if "he" were the representative of the dominant order, the arbiter of the ideology of gender and its stories of selfhood' (49). As well, in establishing her 'discursive authority,' she must choose from the 'speaking postures' (55) available to her as a woman. Smith describes each of these and points to their limitations: she may speak as a public man (by definition in patriarchy only men can have public lives) and risk being condemned as an unnatural woman; she may speak as a private woman (since all womanly activities in patriarchy are private) and risk public notoriety by breaking the silence imposed on women's lives, or she may choose one of the 'life scripts' of privilege offered by patriarchy to a minority of women, for example, that of 'queen [or] female religious' (55). In Jameson's case, the position of 'scholar' is just beginning to become the privileged 'life-script' it has become for a minority of women today. Whatever position the woman autobiographer chooses, Smith emphasizes that, before the twentieth century, such a woman 'does not engage consciously the prevailing ideology of gender or challenge the authority of autobiography as a generic contract' (56).

I would argue that Smith is both right and wrong in her diagnoses when it comes to a woman like Jameson. She is correct in that Jameson is obviously aware in her text of how she may be perceived as a 'notorious' woman, or an unnatural woman. She is at great plains to show herself in consort with the most feminine of women in the persons of Mrs MacMurray and especially Mrs Schoolcraft, who have 'true ladylike simplicity' (377), and who by their mixed-blood heritage, represent all that is womanly by both Indian and white standards. At the same time, Anna Jameson is a public writer, a literary critic, a cultural analyst, roles that give her the position of 'man.' But, ironically, she uses this position to advocate an increasingly fervent feminism. We are never allowed to forget her privileged public status as she weaves her intellectual activity into the fabric of her journal. She even, slyly, takes a few opportunities to pose as 'queen,' as she is increasingly treated as visiting royalty in her tour of the Great Lakes, fêted and entertained, appealed to and deferred to, and like all queens gratefully thanked when she distributes presents to her obliging subjects. But I would argue that although she heeds these strictures on the woman autobiographer, Jameson both consciously 'engage[s]' the prevailing ideology of gender' and 'challenge[s] the authority of autobiography as a generic contract,' through the form of the epistolary dijournal, which offers her a way to overcome strictures on women autobiographers and write a 'dense kind of autorepresentation' (Kadar 8) that we find in contemporary postmodern texts.

By addressing herself to an intimate friend and to 'good women' she is able to speak openly about herself and her life in a way that could not be is she addressed herself only to the public (male) reader in traditional autobiographical discourse. In this way she both allows for the existence of the public reader and denies the validity of his generic assumptions by the adoption of the epistolary dijournal. In fact, Anna Jameson's 'challenge' to the genre of autobiographical is typical of the subversive literary acts that women writers have always engaged in: the use of marginalized genres (travel writing, journals, diaries, letters) to achieve what is not permitted to them in mainstream (malestream) genres (novel, autobiography, short story), so that generic contracts are deconstructed and reconstructed by these writing acts. Jameson is not limited by the 'confusion, the crampedness, the compromises, the ambivalences' (62) that damage the accounts of writers examined by Smith (for example Charlotte Charke and Harriet Martineau) because she refuses the male-defined generic contracts that these women accepted (and that Smith indirectly accepts by her traditional and profoundly patriarchal definition of what constitutes autobiography).

Despite the fact that the word auto/bio/graphy – the life written by the self – needs to be and is being re-examined for its radical implications for female experience, Smith's *Poetics* remains a useful investigative tool for women's accounts.[4] And nowhere is it more useful than in Smith's third marker of women's accounts: 'the relationship of that literary authority to her sexuality and its presence or absence as subject to her story.' Smith points out (and correctly so in the accounts she chooses for examination) that in the 'speaking postures ... the authority to speak as both "representative" man and "representative" woman derives from the erasure of female sexuality; for the male-identified fiction commands the repression of the mother, and the "good woman" fiction commands the suppression of female eroticism' (55). Anna Jameson's epistolary dijournal allows for the expression of her female sexuality in the 'eroticization' of the Canadian wilderness she travels through, and allows her to rescue the positive image and influence of the mother in women's lives through the figure of O,shah,gush, ko,-da,na,qua (Mrs Johnson) at the furthest western point of her symbolic and literal journey into the wilderness.

Marion Fowler has observed, 'Anna Jameson is the first Canadian – but not the last – to eroticize [the wilderness] ... Anna sees the wilderness as a passionate woman' (169). But Fowler's example might indicate that Jameson's eroticism is characteristic of a woman who takes the position of man in her writing act, seeing the land as woman awaiting (although not too passively in Jameson's case) the male embrace. Indeed, Jameson at times does take this 'representative man' stance. It is once again the formal arrangement of her text that converts the subject/object nature of male eroticism to the female experience of sexuality as a merging of self and other, of a breaking down of the barriers between Anna and the land that travels into her.

In fact Jameson's text is a feminized discourse, it is text as body, as erotic body of selfhood. Her text is filled with femaleness, her own and others.' From her first declaration that the text is 'particularly addressed to my own sex' (10) through her minute notice of the details of person of every woman she meets, from the daughter of Joseph Brant to her beloved surrogate mother,

O,shah,gush,ko,da,na,qua, femaleness is her subject. She examines her own sensual reactions to every experience and is able to turn any subject to a discussion of the place of women in culture (their 'false position'). In all these strategies this is a text of female sexuality. The culmination of that sexuality comes in the journey undertaken by canoe from Mackinaw to the Sault in the company of her new and admired friend Mrs Schoolcraft, daughter of the Indian mother Jameson will soon meet. They lie awake together talking and singing to keep their 'pilot and guardian' alert: 'Thus we floated on beneath that divine canopy "which love had spread to curtain the sleeping world"': it was a most lovely and blessed night, bright and calm and warm' (441), the now quieted and blissful Anna tells us. In fact, the experience of travelling on the water at night, covered by the stars and lulled by the soft Indian-inflected sounds of her female companion's voice as she sings, tells stories, is told to us in detail and culminates with this passage:

> I remember lying awake for some minutes, looking up at the quiet stars, and around upon the dark weltering waters, and the faint waning moon, just suspended on the very edge of the horizon. I saw it sink – sink into the bosom of the lake as if to rest, and then with a thought of far-off friends, and a most fervent thanksgiving, I dropped asleep. It is odd that I did not think of praying for protection and that no sense of fear came over me; it seemed as if the eye of God himself looked down upon me; that I *was* protected. I do not say I *thought* this any more than the unweaned child in its cradle; but I had some such feeling of unconscious trust and love, now I recall those moments. (443)

The detail of this passage, while acknowledging the reality of life within patriarchy (her male 'pilot and guardian' at the stern of the canoe, a male god in heaven), nevertheless speaks to the femaleness of her condition. She no longer feels yearning and emptiness when she thinks of absent women friends, only thankfulness for their existence. She is able to feel she is resting in their love, as the moon does in the 'bosom' of the lake. The female validation of her far-off friends that used to make her alive to her own womanhood and that she has often felt so bitterly in need of in Canada is now with her in a new context, her Canadian context. She has no need to pray, for she is already under the protection of that female voice that lulls her to sleep. Like Mrs Schoolcraft's real children around them in the canoe, Anna is the 'unweaned child,' 'cradled' by female plenitude, a plenitude felt as an 'unconscious' quality in the wilderness and its people that is now realized intellectually through the act of 'recall,' the act of writing the epistolary dijournal. Reading Jameson's words in any other context than the epistolary dijournal, for instance by the standards of the realist novel, or male autobiography, could make us question their sincerity, to judge them as overextended, forced, even sentimental (indeed, women's expressions of sentiment are often labelled as sentimentality by the standards of male generic contracts). But by this point in the text we are accustomed to the merging of the intimate confession of the diary, the assumed presence of the beloved other to whom the words are addressed, and the journey as metaphor for metamorphosis of selfhood.

For Jameson's text it is felicitous that this moment of female plenitude couches itself in maternal imagery, for she is about to embrace that experience that students of women's autobiography find to be archetypal for women in search of a language of selfhood: the experience of reunion with the mother.[5] At Sault Ste Marie she is introduced to her new friend's mother, who, despite her position as wife of a white man, is a full-blooded Indian and becomes the interpreter of a way of life and thinking that Jameson seeks. O,shah,gush,ko,da,na,qua is the female 'head of her large family' (454) who generously welcomes Anna, who recalls: 'she took me in her arms, laid me down on a couch, and began to rub my feet, soothing and caressing me. She called me Nindannis, daughter, and I called her Neengai, mother' (455). Mrs Johnson feeds her new daughter, introduces her to the family and like Mrs Schoolcraft, tells her stories that illustrate Indian life and belief, stories Jameson embeds in her text as part of the preparation for the political and personal subject positions described in the last sections of the text.

On a personal level, Jameson performs the empowering act of shooting the St Mary rapids, is christened into the Chipewyan tribe under the name Wah,sah,ge,wah,no,qua (woman of the bright foam) and is praised and admired by her Neengai. Jameson's characteristic humour keeps this moment from having too heroic a cast as she continues her narrative by observing: 'Now that I have been a Chippewa born, anytime these four hours, I must introduce you to some of my new relations' (462). Despite the self-deprecating tone (and the playful paraphrase of Shakespeare carefully noted by Jameson) there is, as always, a very serious intent behind Jameson's comment. She does intend to speak as a 'Chippewa born,' since she has painstakingly, like the good researcher she is, established her discursive authority by studying their culture and its stories, from white sources and Indian sources, she has built close and reciprocal relations with individuals Chipewyans, undergone ceremonies of her own devising and their sanctioning to mark her entry into this new selfhood, and shared meals and celebrations with them.

This personal internalization of identity is followed by a defence of Indian culture and her most overt and confident feminist statement of the text as she analyses the relationship of Indian females to males and compares their situation to white women, to find that 'however hard the lot of woman [in Indian society], she is in no *false* position. The two sexes are in their natural and true position relatively to the state of society, and the means of subsistence' (515). She notes their advantages over white women in the equal division of labour, the lack of class privilege, their usefulness in the economy of the tribe. Comparing the Indian woman to the English servant class she finds 'the condition of the squaw is gracious in comparison, dignified by domestic feelings, and by equality with all around her' (516). At the same time the Indian woman does not have to feel, as a white woman of leisure should, the guilt of a lifestyle purchased by the slavery and prostitution of other women.

For Jameson the political is the personal as she concludes that in all societies a woman is valued by her usefulness. Jameson has certainly proved her usefulness as literary critic, sociologist, political commentator, and so forth, and in her new stance as feminist intends to make herself additionally useful to 'her own sex,' that is, to her own sexuality as well as to female subjects, the imagined readers of this text. In establishing her femaleness on these feminist grounds she has also considerably broadened her 'discursive authority,' for no stance she has taken throughout the text, as wife, friend, literary critic, political commentator, sociologist, journeyer, natural woman (and she denies none of these in her changing self), speaks with quite so much confidence as this last stance of feminist.

In her discussion of what she calls 'epistolary autobiography,'

Katherine Goodman notes the irony of the fact that at the same
historical moment that produced one of the central texts of male
autobiography and the humanist ideal of the 'harmonious and naturally unfolding individual' (306 (Goethe's autobiography, *Dich-
tung und Wahrheit*), a German woman, Elizabeth von Stagemann,
was writing her autobiography, under the guise of a series of self-
revealing letters. As Goodman points out, such women began the
subversion of the humanist view of identity, long before doubts
about the 'authenticity of the subject' (306) were made central
philosophical concerns by writers such as Foucault and Barthes. I
find that at the same historical moment, an Englishwoman in Canada was creating her collage of journal/diary/letters, large portions
of which were inspired by her correspondence with Goethe's own
daughter-in-law, Ottilie, who represents, in her life and her relationship to Jameson, that dependent, but very subversive female
entity at the heart of European patriarchy.

   For literary critics such as myself and Goodman, accounts like
von Stagemann's and Jameson's are not only the alternative tradition to male autobiography, they are the corrective to the humanist view of the autobiographical enterprise that proposes the
formulation of the self as unique, unitary, and independent. But,
as well, they are the corrective to current poststructuralists' views
of the writing individual as merely a function of the text. Women's
texts offer formal strategies for the writing subject 'which both
credits individual experience and avoids harmonizing or unifying
the subject' (Goodman 311). Jameson's text is particularly note-
worthy because it conflates the roles of 'reader, writer and critic
in one school of self-reflexivity' (Kadar 9) in a way that finds res-
onances with contemporary autobiographical texts by postmodern
writers. In naming Jameson's usage of these formal strategies as
'epistolary dijournal' I do not intend to fix her text inside a prescriptive rigidity, or inside the 'overdetermined loci of contention
and conflict' (Schenck 292) that traditional generic contracts have
often become, but rather I wish to offer a conditional framework
(in the sense that one constructs – and here I hope I would have
Jameson's approval of my female-centered image – a framework
for the making of a tapestry or quilt), inside which many readings
may more fully stitch themselves.

NOTES

1 For example, Hallvard Dahlie's consideration of Jameson in a study primarily concerned with realist prose fiction finds that although *Studies and Rambles* is a rich text it is also uneven. Marion Fowler finds Jameson's book to be an example of a new Canadian genre, the feminist picaresque, but must concentrate on the 'Rambles' rather than the 'Studies' to justify her naming.

2 Bina Friewald is also concerned with the epistolary features in *Studies and Rambles*, but in terms of how these features shape selfhood in what she calls Jameson's 'novel.'

3 In contrast, the pre-twentieth-century accounts dealt with in Smith's text, women's accounts imitating male autobiographical discourses, do, because of their formal structures, set up an expectancy of resolution that can never be fulfilled given the competing natures of the fictions of the 'I' in these accounts.

4 For the current re-examination of the genre of autobiography in terms of women's experience see, for example, Domna Stanton's arguments in her introduction to *The Female Autograph* and the variety of female autobiographical acts examined in that text, as well as in texts such as *Life/Lines* (see Brodzki and Schenck), *The Private Self* (see Benstock), and *Interpreting Women's Lives* (see Personal Narratives Group).

5 Critics from Stephanie A. Demetrakopoulos, who explores the mythic manifestations of this archetypal urge, to Lynn Z. Bloom, who examines the cultural aspects of the complex, point out the centrality of the experience of a need for maternal acceptance, even if only of a surrogate kind, in women's accounts. Bella Brodzki and Celeste Schenck devote an entire section (four essays) of *Life/Lines* to maternal issues.

WORKS CITED

Benstock, Shari, ed. *The Private Self: Theory and Practice of Women's Autobiographical Writings.* Chapel Hill: U of North Carolina P 1988

Bloom, Lynn Z. 'Heritages: The Tradition of Mother/Daughter Relationships in Women's Autobiography.' In *The Lost Tradition: Mothers and Daughters in Literature*, 291–303. Ed. Cathy N. Davidson and E.M. Broner. New York: Frederick Unger 1980

Brodzki, Bella, and Celeste Schenck, eds. *Life/Lines: Theorizing Women's Autobiography.* Ithaca: Cornell UP 1988

Buss, Helen M. 'Canadian Women's Autobiography: Some Critical Directions.' In *A Mazing Space: Writing Canadian Women Writing*, 154–66. Ed. Shirley Neuman and Smaro Kamboureli. Edmonton: Longspoon-NeWest 1986

Dahlie, Hallvard. *Varieties of Exile*. Vancouver: U of British Columbia P 1986

Demetrakopoulos, Stephanie A. 'The Metaphysics of Matrilinearism in Women's Autobiography: Studies of Mead's *Blackberry Winter*, Hellman's *Pentimento*, Angelou's *I Know Why the Caged Bird Sings* and Kingston's *The Woman Warrior*.' In *Women's Autobiography: Essays in Criticism*, 180–205. Ed. Estelle Jelinek. Bloomington: Indiana UP 1980

Fowler, Marion. *The Embroidered Tent: Five Gentlewomen in Upper Canada*. Toronto: Anansi 1982

Friewald, Bina. 'Femininely Speaking: Anna Jameson's *Winter Studies and Summer Rambles in Canada*.' In *A Mazing Space*, 61–73 (see Buss)

Goodman, Katherine R. 'Elisabeth to Meta: Epistolary Autobiography and the Postulation of the Self.' In *Life/Lines*, 306–19 (see Brodzki and Schenck)

Jameson, Anna. *Winter Studies and Summer Rambles in Canada*. 1838. Toronto: McClelland and Stewart 1990.

Kadar, Marlene. 'Whose Life Is It Anyway? Some Preliminary Remarks on Life-Writing.' In *Essays in Life-Writing*. Robarts Centre for Canadian Studies Working Paper 89-WO3, North York, Ont.: York U. 1989

Personal Narratives Group, ed. *Interpreting Women's Lives: Feminist Theory and Personal Narratives*. Bloomington: Indiana UP 1989

Schenck, Celeste. 'All of a Piece: Women's Poetry and Autobiography.' In *Life/Lines*, 281–305 (see Brodzki and Schenck)

Smith, Sidonie. *A Poetics of Women's Autobiography: Marginality and the Fictions of Self-Representation*. Bloomington: Indiana UP 1987

Stanton, Domna. 'Autogynography: Is the Subject Different?' In *The Female Autograph: Theory and Practice of Autobiography from the Tenth to the Twentieth Century*, 3–21. Ed. Domna C. Stanton. Chicago: U of Chicago P. 1987

Thomas, Clara. *Love and Work Enough: The Life of Anna Jameson*. Toronto: U of Toronto P 1967, 1978

❦ 4 ❧
Writing as a Daughter:
Autobiography in
Wollstonecraft's Travelogue

ELEANOR TY

Mary Wollstonecraft's *Letters Written during a Short Residence in Sweden, Norway, and Denmark* (1796), which one critic calls a 'generic hybrid, a kind of subjective autobiography superimposed on a travelogue' (Myers 166),[1] is most obvious as an epistolary narrative, as its title suggests. The twenty-five letters were written to Wollstonecraft's lover Gilbert Imlay, during a business trip to three Scandinavian countries in the summer of 1795. However, though it was intended as a travelogue, the work is more interesting today for the way in which it reveals how one woman writer dealt with some of the difficulties encountered in eighteenth-century female autobiography. That Wollstonecraft needed to express herself in this covert fashion – generically disguised in a travel book structured through a series of letters – is a significant indication of the problems of self-expression faced by a woman who is not wholly at ease with her own subjectivity and subject position in the male-dominated literary sphere of the 1790s.

I want to argue that part of the quandary stems from the fact that, based on Jacques Lacan's account of language, Wollstonecraft is writing from the perspective of the daughter rather than from that of the son, the son who is able to fully embrace the symbolic world of the law of the Father. Because of a daughter's lack of the phallus, the mark of sexual difference for Lacan, she is excluded from the complex signifying system and laws that make up Western culture. Nancy Chodorow, revising Freudian and Lacanian theories, argues that because of women's mothering, a mother tends to identify more closely with a daughter than with a son, which accounts for crucial differences in feminine and masculine personality. Girls do not renounce the mother and her pre-Oedipal world in the way that sons do, thereby retaining the pre-symbolic, pre-verbal language, or what Julia Kristeva calls the 'semiotic,' at the same time as they adopt the rational, linguistic language of the Father. The consequences of this retention of the earliest language has varied and fascinating implications for life writing. Instead of a polished product, the autobiographical texts produced by daughters tend to record a 'subject in process' (*Kristeva Reader* 91), tend to reveal fluctuations in tone, voice, subject-matter, and even genre as in Wollstonecraft's case. In her attempts to write as a daughter, Wollstonecraft often wavers between the discourse of the symbolic and what Margaret Homans calls the 'literal.'

The construct of self, the subject, and subjectivity has been rendered more complex by the work of such theorists as Althusser and Lacan (see Belsey 56–84). According to these thinkers, both women and men are products of diverse sets of ideologies and specific reading practices. But for the female life writer the problem of selfhood and self-inscription within literary conventions is particularly acute. In the first place, her very existence is questioned to the point where Jacques Lacan can say, 'Woman does not exist' (qtd. by Jones 83). Similarly, Luce Irigaray echoes: 'Woman ... remains in unrealized potentiality ... She can *never* achieve the *wholeness* of her form' (*Speculum* 165). Irigaray indicates that 'theoretically there would be no such thing as woman. She would not exist. The best that can be said is that she does *not exist yet*' (ibid. 166). Formless and indescribable except through the negative side of the binary opposition, women cannot write themselves (see Cixous, 'Sorties'). Hélène Cixous laments that 'with a few rare exceptions, there has not yet been any writing that inscribes femininity' ('Medusa' 248). Hence, female autobiographers resort to different ways of expressing their subjectivity. Because, historically, women have not fulfilled the kind of public roles their male counterparts have, they may not have seen themselves as 'responsible agents,' as autonomous entities who leave a mark in the world, a condition that Georges Gusdorf thinks is necessary before the writing of autobiography occurs (see 29–31). Often more covert methods such as subterfuge, disguise, double-voiced discourse, role-playing, and projection are adopted when females engage in the interpretation of their lives.[2] The reader of women's *bios* has to creatively decipher between the lines to discover the hidden *autos*, the sometimes multiple selves and subjects struggling to escape from textual confinement.3

I am not suggesting that all women's texts can be read as forms of autobiography, because there is much writing by females that is not from or of the self. However, since women's lives have traditionally and historically been regarded as less worthy of examination than men's, women frequently do employ more circuitous means to write about their lives. In this particular case, since Wollstonecraft's travelogue originated as actual personal letters, there is naturally a strong confessional tendency in the work that many modern critics have noted (see Myers, 'Letters' 165–6). The element of self-revelation present in a public genre such as a travelogue leads one to consider the question of gender difference in life writing, as it is virtually impossible in this instance to discuss one without the other.

Wollstonecraft's situation is an interesting one because although she never attempted formal autobiography, so much of her life was public, and made public, either through her fiction, her various treatises – political and educational – or through the *Memoirs*, which was a kind of tribute or 'love offering' written and published posthumously by her husband, William Godwin (Tomalin 231).4 As a female intellectual living at the end of the eighteenth century, Wollstonecraft can be understood as Irigaray's 'non-subjective subjectum,' as that 'which can never achieve the status of subject, at least for/by herself' (*Speculum* 165). Using a masculinist discourse that is unable to specify feminity, 'a woman can ... only speak ... either *as if* a man (miming the discourse of patriarchy), or as a "subject" without specificity, without her own language' (S. Smith 144). Interestingly enough, both contemporary and present-day critics of Wollstonecraft seem to have perceived the 'masculinist' quality in her writings. The Reverend Richard Polwhele's attack on Wollstonecraft and her followers suggest this loss of 'femininity' by the very title of his satiric poem *The Unsex'd Females* (1798). Mary Poovey, by contrast, describes Wollstonecraft's two *Vindications* as 'man's discourse, woman's heart' (48). What these labels point to, in fact, is Wollstonecraft's polarized subjectivity and gender-related difficulties. In order to succeed and make a living as a writer, she knew she had to adopt the language, the stance, the subjectivity of a male author, to enter the symbolic world of the Law of the Father. She had to check or repress her feminine sensibility, her sense of the discontinuous, emotional, and bodily world of the pre-symbolic or the semiotic[5] (see *Kristeva Reader* 92; Moi 161).

I would like to show that this polarity accounts for much of the ambiguous and contradictory tendencies in her literary productions. As exemplified in *Letters Written ... in Sweden* Wollstonecraft's writing is often characterized by ambivalence and inconsistency, in terms of both content and style. Wollstonecraft's uneasiness with the masculine or Lacanian symbolic world can, in part, be seen in her distrust of conventional literary forms. *Letters* borrows from at least three genres: letters, the travelogue, and autobiography or diary. Wollstonecraft's use of all and, simultaneously, none of these genres can be viewed as an effort not to be written by and into a specific text and its pre-existent structure.

While *Letters* is most obvious as a narrative in a series of letters, it does not, strictly speaking, conform to the epistolary mode. Though the work has an implied reader or narratee, that being Imlay, there is no reciprocity or exchange between letter writers and readers. Janet Gurkin Altman says, for example: 'What distinguishes epistolary narrative from these diary novels ... is the desire for exchange. In epistolary writing the reader is called upon to respond as a writer and to contribute as such to the narrative' (89). Since the addressee plays no role in the narrative, nor do we see him initiating 'his own utterance' (Altman 117), *Letters* does not entirely correspond to conventional conceptions of epistolary form. We do not see Wollstonecraft answering Imlay's queries, nor do we see his comments included in the text. Instead, critics have noted that the work has a 'quality of poetic reverie' and that it is 'organized through a very personal version of associationism' (qtd. in Myers, 'Letters' 166).

As a travelogue, *Letters* is also an anomaly because of its intrusive personal voice.[6] Wollstonecraft herself was conscious of this as she says in her Advertisement: 'In writing these desultory letters, I found I could not avoid being continually the first person – "the little hero of each tale"' (5). As a critic for the *Analytical Review* Wollstonecraft had read many travelogues and had formulated her own aesthetics on the genre (see Myers, *Letters* 167, 183). She had many eighteenth-century models by male writers to choose from, such as John Locke in *Travels in France*, Daniel Defoe, *A Tour Thro' the Whole Island of Great Britain* (1724), James Boswell, *Tour to the Hebrides with Samuel Johnson* (1785), and Samuel Johnson, *Journey to the Western Islands of Scotland* (1775), as well as one by a female writer, Lady Mary Wortley Montagu, whose letters from Turkey were published as *Travels in Europe, Asia, and Africa*. While a typical travelogue would describe the country in terms of climate, flora and fauna, and its natives' customs (see Reviews of travelogues, and Adams, ch. 2 & 4), Wollstonecraft's 'pervasive self-emphasis goes far beyond the incidental personal references common in travel literature' (Myers *Letters* 165). In her work, reflections on the self become as important as the travel writing; the expression of her personal anxieties competes with her commentaries about the countries she visits.

In fact, in Wollstonecraft's *Letters* there is little or no distinction between the public and private sphere. As Mitzi Myers has noted, 'There are no rigid separations in the *Letters*: personal and social themes, rational assessments and emotional epiphanies, flow one into another joined by a use of associationism quite subtle and sophisticated' (*Letters* 181). While I agree with Myers that the personal and the social 'flow one into another' I see this quality not so much as sophisticated artistry as a revelation of Wollstonecraft's divided subjectivity. For instance, few descriptions of the physical, geographical, or social scene remain purely factual and external accounts. Instead Wollstonecraft usually begins with the concrete and the visible world, but ends up by extemporizing on her own psychological and spiritual condition. In my view her narrative demonstrates the eruption of what Kristeva calls the semiotic into the symbolic order as it is often characterized by ruptures, discontinuity, emotional and bodily drives, and heterogeneity (see *Kristeva Reader*, ch. 5). If Wollstonecraft speaks from what Kristeva calls the 'thetic' phase, she perches on a rather precarious and marginal threshold between the two heterogeneous realms (*Kristeva Reader* 102). Her repressed 'chora' often intrudes and breaks into the order of symbolic language.

A few excerpts will demonstrate my point. On entering St Mary's church in Tonsberg, for example, Wollstonecraft remarks on its catacombs:

> There is a little recess full of coffins, which contains bodies embalmed long since ...
> A desire of preserving the body seems to have prevailed in most countries of the world, futile as it is to term it a preservation ... When I was shewn these human petrifac-

tions, I shrunk back with disgust and horror. 'Ashes to
ashes!' thought I – 'Dust to dust!' ... The contemplation of
noble ruins produces a melancholy that exalts the mind ...
Our very soul expands, and we forget our littleness; ...
Life, what art thou? Where goes this breath? this I, so
much alive? (71)

Notice that we see little of the actual interior of the church as
Wollstonecraft's disturbing reaction to death is outlined instead.
The text is a virtual failure as a travel guide, as we get a stronger
sense of Wollstonecraft's fear of mortality, the tension between
her life and her death drive, than of the scenery or of the actual
tombs. Without warning the passage moves from an impersonal
description to a philosophical comment to a personal reflection to
an apostrophe to life itself. The third-person voice of the social
or symbolic language is assimilated by the overwhelming emotional drive and mental flux of the first-person subject, who sees
the dead bodies as extensions and a sign of the inevitable extinction
of self.
    Similarly in the next passage, a discussion of the corrupt justices
of Norway ends with a poetic metaphor about her own condition:

[In Norway] I saw the cloven foot of despotism ... these
grand bailiffs, particularly the superior one, who resides
at Christiania, are political monsters of the same species.
Needy sycophants are provided for by their relations and
connexions at Copenhagen ... I can scarcely say why, my
friend, but in this city, thoughtfulness seemed to be sliding into melancholy, or rather dulness. – The fire of
fancy, which had been kept alive in the country, was almost extinguished by reflections on the ills that harass
such a large portion of mankind. – I felt like a bird flut-
tering on the ground unable to mount; yet unwilling to
crawl tranquilly like a reptile, whilst still conscious it had
wings. (121–2)

Wollstonecraft's efforts to maintain a public or symbolic discourse, distanced from the subject, are again thwarted by her
semiotic or psychical energies. While the writing continues in
the verbal-signifying system, her use of the metaphor of the helpless bird makes the end of the passage closer to dream logic or the

pre-symbolic than to the rational linguistic world of the Father. As in the first passage, the descriptions of the external world, in this case that of tyrannical politicians, do not remain objectified and remote but become literalized into a personal sense of power-lessness.

I am not suggesting that the whole of *Letters* manages to 'cover the infinity of the [signifying] process, ... reach the semiotic *chora*,' (*Kristeva Reader* 122) that is, imitate that non-verbal rhythmic articulation of the *chora*, in the same way as Kristeva believes the avant-garde texts of Mallarmé and Joyce do. But sections of the work exhibit the subject's struggle in its efforts to enter into the symbolic world of the Father. While Kristeva, who is anti-essentialist (see Moi 164), does not emphasize the role the female sex plays in the constitution of the subject, I believe that gender and traditional mothering customs do influence self-representation. Using Nancy Chodorow's feminist revisions of the Freudian myth to supplement Kristeva's (and Lacan's) theories, I wish to propose another explanation of Wollstonecraft's seemingly generically, thematically, and stylistically contradictory writing practices.

In *The Reproduction of Mothering* Chodorow demonstrates that the psychic maturation of a young girl neither repeats nor simply reverses the Oedipal configuration that Freud identified in young boys. Because they are of the same gender, the mother's 'primary identification and symbiosis with daughters tend to be stronger,' and this identification is likely based 'on experiencing a daughter as an extension or double' (109). When the father's phallus inter-rupts the mother-and-child dyad, the effect on the daughter is not that of rejection of the mother as it is with the son who fears castration, but rather the girl develops 'important oedipal attach-ments to her mother *as well as* to her father' (127). There is no absolute 'change of object' (127), as the daughter continues to love the mother. When she does enter into the symbolic order, she embraces the law of the Father much less enthusiastically than the son. Based on Chodorow's findings, Margaret Homans concludes that because the daughter does not 'perceive the mother as lost or renounced, she does not need the compensation the father's law offers as much as does the son ... [She] therefore speaks two lan-guages at once. Along with symbolic language, she retains the lit-eral or presymbolic language that the son represses at the time of his renunciation of his mother' (13).

In relation to *Letters*, this ability to negotiate between the two languages may account for Wollstonecraft's conflation of the public and private, of the symbolic and the semiotic discourse. Writing as a daughter she shows her uneasy sense of self and divided subjectivity, as she attempts to repress her sense of the emotional or bodily world of the pre-symbolic, and adopts a conventionally acceptable, rational discourse of travel literature. In many instances her running commentary about Scandinavian customs are covert revelations about her own insecurities and anxieties. For instance, her distaste of the indiscriminate pushing about of 'the bottle' at tables either too early in the day or too often in Sweden (20, 21) and of the fact that 'the churlish pleasure of drinking drams takes the place of social enjoyments amongst the poor' (25) can be attributed to her negative childhood experience and perhaps almost semiotic fear of her father's excessive drinking habits. As Virginia Woolf suggests, Wollstonecraft may have 'lain as a child on the landing to prevent her father from thrashing her mother' (97). Another seemingly public or philosophical commentary about marriage and divorce customs in Sweden culminates with this moral: 'Affection requires a firmer foundation than sympathy; and few people have a principle of action sufficiently stable to produce rectitude of feeling' (145–6). This statement about weak principles and feeling may be an unconscious expression of her inexpressed dread of being unwanted and unloved. It is probably directed at Imlay, whom Wollstonecraft discovered was unfaithful to her more than once (Tomalin, ch. 15).

Margaret Homans postulates that another effect of the daughter's retention of the pre-symbolic language is the 'differential valuations of literal and figurative' for male and female writers (13). Homans associates representational language with the figurative, as it is 'symbolic language alone that can approximate the bridging of the gap between child and mother opened up by the ... prohibition of incest' (7). According to Homans, because of the mother's association with nature, and with the Other, the son tends to 'view the mother as literal, she whose absence makes language both necessary and possible' (13). For the daughter, however, who is 'only partially within the symbolic order, the whole question of the literal and figurative will be more complex' (13). The daughter 'will perhaps prefer the literal that her brother devalues' (13), or she 'might simply not find the opposition of literal and figurative as telling and important as the son might, for it maintains a boundary not sacred to her – the boundary of the prohibition of incest with the mother' (14).

In *Bearing the Word* Homans shows how some nineteenth-century women writers 'articulate thematically a daughter's bond to an identification with a ... vanished mother (often figured as Mother Nature),' and how in their texts the 'literal is sometimes preferred' (16). For my concluding point, I want to illustrate how Wollstonecraft is similarly 'writing and practising myths' of a daughter's 'relations to symbolic language, working out through [her] writing the conflicts between being a daughter and being a writer' (Homans 16). Frequently, Wollstonecraft's text demonstrates an inability to transcend the literal, which may explain why her *Letters*, though exhibiting many of the same concerns as the works by male Romantic poets of the same period, is not read as art. As Homans suggests, 'to write "literature" is to write within the symbolic order' (20), and Wollstonecraft does not always remain strictly within this order.

As Wollstonecraft advances toward Quistram, for example, she describes a particularly splendid scene where the road 'was on the declivity of a rocky mountain, slightly covered with a mossy herbage and vagrant firs' (40). At the bottom, she sees a river 'amongst the recesses of stone, ... hastening forward to the ocean' on one side and stealing 'peacefully forward into the meadow' on the other (40). Drawing near, she views the 'loveliest banks of wild flowers' that 'variegated the prospect' (40). However, this almost perfect combination of the sublime and the beautiful is shattered when, instead of inhaling the sweet odours of the flowers, she describes the odour of 'putrifying herrings, which they use as manure, after the oil has been extracted' (40). Even the train of her thoughts is affected, as she 'could not escape from the detestable evaporation of the herrings, which poisoned all [her] pleasure' (41). Compare the passage to Wordsworth's 'Lines Written in Early Spring,' for example, where the male poet, seeing the 'primrose tufts,' the periwinkle's wreaths, asserts, albeit with some uncertainty: 'And 'tis my faith that every flower / Enjoys the air it breathes' (lines 11–12).[7] In Wollstonecraft's text, unlike Wordsworth's, the natural landscape resists symbolic representation. The identification with nature, the literal smell of the herrings here, prevents Wollstonecraft from imaginatively recreating a figurative signification for the scene. She is unable to withdraw sufficiently

away from the non-symbolic to lament philosophically, as Wordsworth does, 'What man has made of man' (8, 24).

Again in the next passage Wollstonecraft attempts a figurative
representation of the beauties of harvest time through symbolic
language, but finds that she cannot forget the literal.

> How interesting are the varied beauties of nature; and
> what peculiar charms characterize each season! The pur-
> ple hue which the heath now assumed, gave it a degree of
> richness, that almost exceeded the lustre of the young
> green of spring – and harmonized exquisitely with the
> rays of the ripening corn. The weather was uninterrupt-
> edly fine, and the people busy in the fields cutting down
> the corn, or binding up the sheaves, continually varied
> the prospect ... The women and children were cutting off
> branches from the beech, birch, oak, & c, and leaving
> them to dry – This way of helping out their foddder, in-
> jures the trees. But the winters are so long, that the poor
> cannot afford to lay in a sufficient stock of hay. By such
> means they just keep life in the poor cows, for little milk
> can be expected when they are so miserably fed. (140–1)

The richness of Wollstonecraft's imagery at the beginning of the
passage can be compared to Keats's famous ode 'To Autumn,' with
its lush and mellow descriptions, but by the end of the paragraph
the practical needs of the poor, the literal concerns, displace the
figurative language. Wollstonecraft's subjectivity in process, her
attempts to write as a daughter, can be seen here in her vacillation
between the discourse of the symbolic and the literal. It is as if
she is unable to sustain for any great length of time symbolization,
which entails a disregard or even death of the literal.

While Keats's 'To Autumn' has been praised not merely for 'the
degree of resolution' it provides, but also for the fact that 'in this
short space, so many different kinds of resolution are attained'
(Bate 156), Wollstonecraft's abortive 'ode' to autumn supplies no
satisfying conclusion. Wollstonecraft was familiar with Shakespeare and Milton (see Wardle, 'Introduction' to *Collected Letters*
30, 38), two of the many poets whom critics cite as influential
sources for Keats's ode,[8] but does not draw upon their traditions
or beliefs here. For instance, she does not use 'the connection
between natural creation and the naming which is the proper work

of poetry, ... the relation of mutability to inception and growth;
the assertion that all aspects of the world are equally beautiful, ...
the notion that the mind projects its own mood on the essentially
neutral world' or the perennial parallel 'between the seasons of
man's life and the seasons of the earth' (Vendler 235). Instead,
Wollstonecraft's text, which begins with poetic symbolization –
the richness of the 'purple hue' of the heath, the 'lustre of the
young greed of spring' – descends to the lowly and literal – the
'poor cows' that produce 'little milk' because they are so 'miserably
fed.' Unlike Keats's ode, the passage does not end with the music
of nature: the 'wailful choir' of the gnats, the bleat of 'full-grown
lambs,' the song of the hedge-crickets, or the 'twitter' of the swal-
lows gathering in the skies (27, 30, 33). The harvest scene does not
lead Wollstonecraft to conceive of a figurative 'Edenic harvest,' a
'paradisal fruitfulness,' or a 'prelapsarian dream' (Vendler 247); it
becomes grounded solidly in the quotidian, literal realm.

Wollstonecraft's feelings about nature are more ambivalent than
her male Romantic counterparts'. She says: 'Nature is the nurse
of sentiment, – the true source of taste; – yet what misery, as well
as rapture, is produced by a quick perception of the beautiful and
sublime, ... how dangerous is it to foster these sentiments in such
an imperfect state of existence' (58). And again: 'Why has nature
so many charms for me – calling forth and cherishing refined sentiments, only to wound the breast that fosters them?' (109). Compared to Wordsworth's confident belief that 'Nature never did
betray / The heart that loved her' ('Tintern Abbey' 122–3) Wollstonecraft's conception of nature is unsentimentalized. Her relationship with nature is not that of the son's to an idealized (m)other,
a figurative creation originating from desire, but that of the daughter's more literal, non-symbolic one. Because women are usually
identified with a vanished mother, often figured as Mother Nature, female writers do not share male authors' valuation of the
transcendent figure or their need to mythologize the Other.

One final example of Wollstonecraft's vacillation between the
symbolic and the semiotic realms occurs towards the end of her
journey. After being frustrated by the difficulties of obtaining
lodgings, Wollstonecraft comments: 'After a long journey, with
our eyes directed to some particular spot, to arrive and find nothing as it should be, is vexatious, and sinks the agitated spirits'
(184). In *Idler* no. 58 Samuel Johnson had expressed similar sentiments: 'Pleasure is very seldom found where it is sought,' he

begins his 26 May 1759 essay, and concludes, 'It is seldom that we
find either men or places such as we expect them ... Yet it is necessary to hope, though hope should always be deluded, for hope
itself is happiness, and its frustrations, however frequent, are yet
less dreadful than its extinction.' Wollstonecraft, by contrast, does
not finish her letter with such philosophic complacency about the
values of hope. Instead, the epistle terminates with her memory
of the 'cruellest of disappointments' (184), with a desire to relinquish the adult, rational world of the symbolic order altogether:
'Know you of what materials some hearts are made? I play the
child, and weep at the recollection – for the grief is still fresh that
stunned as well as wounded me – yet never did drops of anguish
like these bedew the cheeks of infantine innocence – and why
should they mine, that never were stained by a blush of guilt?
Innocent and credulous as a child, why have I not the same happy
thoughtlessness?' (184). Her grief at Imlay's infidelity makes her
long for a literal return to the world of childhood innocence, to
the realm of the semiotic. Wollstonecraft's admission that she
'play[s] the child' and her depiction of herself as an 'innocent and
credulous' child reveal an unmediated merging with the pre-symbolic domain that suggests that her attachment to the semiotic was
never fully rejected, only suppressed. A tragic occurrence, such as
the discovery of Imlay's mistress, upsets the balance of her pre-
cariously constructed subjectivity.

Viewed in terms of conventional notions of genre – whether the
autobiographical memoirs, the travelogue, or the epistolary form
– *Letters Written ... in Sweden* can be classified as a failure. Wollstonecraft has not adhered to the requirements of the three genres,
liberally borrowing from each enough only to create what she desired. Nevertheless I would hesitate to call the *Letters* an *oeuvre
manquée*. Its non-conformity, its originality, its multilevelled dis-
cursivity are attestations and a celebration of what Irigaray calls
the 'plural' in women ('Ce sexe' 102). As an autobiography, it not
only illustrates vividly some of the difficulties encountered by
daughters as they attempt to write about their constructed selves,
but can be read positively as an example of how women, though
often silenced and marginalized, nevertheless find creative and
unorthodox means to write about their lives. Perhaps the fault lies
not in the text, but in its readers. As Irigaray points out, 'Contradictory words seem a little crazy to the logic of reason, and in-

audible for him who listens with ready-made grids, a code prepared in advance' ('Ce sexe' 103).

NOTES

1 In 'Mary Wollstonecraft's *Letters Written ... in Sweden*: Toward Romantic Autobiography' Mitzi Myers argues that 'Wollstonecraft's travels constitute a metaphoric as well as an actual journey; her readers participate in a romantic quest, a complex search for identity,' and that the account 'in some ways resembles Wordsworth's later pilgrimage in search of reintegration of self, nature, and society' (170, 166).
2 Some recent studies of women's autobiography include those by Sidonie Smith, Mason, and the essays collected in Benstock. Most critics view female life writing as different from the masculine form, though they do not agree on how they are different. Smith, for example, discusses the way in which female autobiographers situate themselves and their stories 'in relation to cultural ideologies and figures of selfhood' (*A Poetics of Women's Autobiography* 47). 'Often, projecting multiple readers with multiple sets of expectations, [the autobiographer] responds in a complex double-voicedness, a fragile heteroglossia of her own, which calls forth charged dramatic exchanges and narrative strategies' (50).
   In 'Eighteenth-century Women's Autobiographical Commonplaces' Felicity A. Nussbaum explores the way in which the self-writing of someone like Hester Thrale 'ventriloquates male ideologies of gender while it allows alternative discourses of "experience" to erupt at the margins of meanings' (149).
3 Feminist critics point out that one way women break out of textual confinement or silence is through madness. Mary Jacobus, for example, reads 'madness imagined as revolution, or the articulation of Utopian desire' in Wollstonecraft's *The Wrongs of Woman* ('Difference of View' 16). She believes that because women are marginalized, 'the language of feeling can only ally itself with insanity – an insanity which, displaced into writing, produces a moment of imaginative and linguistic excess over-brimming the container of fiction, and swamping the distinction between author and character' (15).
   Like Janet Todd, I am not entirely satisfied with this reading, as it tends to depict and emphasize Wollstonecraft in a posture of insanity when she was so concerned in *Mary, A Fiction*, and in *Vindication of the Rights of Woman* with striking a balance between reason and feeling. In response to Jacobus's view, Todd says: 'Jaco-

bus has ignored the surface of history, of class and politics, for example, to find critical excess and turn her subject into a kind of
shadowy Virginia Woolf' (*Feminist Literary History* 106).

4 Both *Mary* and *The Wrongs of Woman* have many autobiographical
elements as pointed out by Gary Kelly in his introduction, x. In a
theoretical essay Sara Harasym reads Wollstonecraft's fictions as a
failure to construct a unified self. On the other side of the debate is
Mitzi Myers, who demonstrates that *Letters* can be read as romantic
autobiography (1979) and that, similarly, each of *Thoughts on the
Education of Daughters* (1787), *Mary, A Fiction* (1788), and *Original
Stories from Real Life* (1788) is, in effect, 'a stock-taking response to
[Wollstonecraft's] own traumatic history' ('Pedagogy' 195). Myers's
reading implicitly views Wollstonecraft as a coherent unified subject, which I am questioning in my essay.

5 For an alternative view see Poovey, who believes that in *Letters*
Wollstonecraft endorses feeling in 'direct antithesis of her adoles-
cent religious renunciation' (*The Proper Lady and the Woman
Writer* 84). Poovey writes: 'Perhaps because [Wollstonecraft] no
longer dreads the vulnerability attendant on feeling, she no longer
argues for a defensive self-control that requires the imagination to
be shackled to the warden reason. Instead, in the *Letters*, reason and
the imagination play equally important roles in educating the individual' (85). I do not see Wollstonecraft embracing feeling as whole-
heartedly as Poovey seems to suggest. For me Wollstonecraft's
attitude to sensibility and feeling remains complex, even confused,
throughout her life. The *Letters* betray her hesitation and her unwillingness to cross over to either reason, which I link with the
symbolic order, or feeling, which I associate with the semiotic and
the literal.

6 This intrusive autobiographical voice is found in her fiction as well.
Todd points out that 'in *The Wrongs of Woman* Wollstonecraft is
writing out of a constructed character of the compassionate female
... a feature of the female novel of sensibility' *Feminist Literary History* (107). While *Letters* is not a novel, the voice of this compassionate female construct also emerges.

7 Mary Jacobus is an example of a critic who points out that while,
'on the face of it, this is the lyric that contains some of Wordsworth's most astonishing assertions,' such 'claims are made in a
context of uncertainty' (*Tradition and Experiment* 97). She sees
Wordsworth's 'expressions of optimism' increasingly 'qualified by a
tone of puzzled, pained doubt' (97). This uncertainty may exist but
it does not take away from my point, because Wordsworth is still
able to make his assertions in spite of his doubts, while Wollstonecraft cannot and does not.

8 See, for example, Helen Vendler who says: 'The essential anteced-
ents of *To Autumn* include, besides *When I have fears*, Shakespeare's sonnets "That time of year" and "How like a winter";
Spenser's Mutability Cantos; Milton's *Il Penseroso* and the Eve and
Eden of *Paradise Lost*; Wordsworth's Intimations Ode; Coleridge's
Frost at Midnight; and Keats's own *La Belle Dame sans Merci*, as
well as his sonnets on the human seasons and the poetry of the
earth' (*The Odes of John Keats* 234).

WORKS CITED

Adams, Percy G. *Travel Literature and the Evolution of the Novel.* Lexington: UP of Kentucky 1983

Altman, Janet Gurkin. *Epistolarity: Approaches to a Form.* Columbus:
Ohio State UP 1982

Bate, Walter Jackson. 'The Ode To Autumn.' In *Keats*, 155–60. Ed. Walter Jackson Bates. Englewood Cliffs, NJ: Prentice-Hall 1964

Belsey, Catherine. *Critical Practice.* London and New York: Methuen
1980

Benstock, Shari, ed. *The Private Self: Theory and Practice of Women's
Autobiographical Writings.* Chapel Hill: U of North Carolina P 1988

Chodorow, Nancy. *The Reproduction of Mothering: Psychoanalysis
and the Sociology of Gender.* Berkeley: U of California P 1978

Cixous, Hélène. 'The Laugh of the Medusa.' In *New French Feminisms*, 245–64 (*See* Marks and de Courtivron)

– 'Sorties.' In *New French Feminisms*, 90–8 (*see* Marks and de Courtivron)

Gusdorf, Georges. 'Conditions and Limits of Autobiography.' In *Autobiography*, 28–48 (*see* Olney)

Harasym, Sara D. 'Ideology and Self: A Theoretical Discussion of the
'Self' in Mary Wollstonecraft's Fiction.' *English Studies in Canada*
12.2 (June 1986): 163–77

Homans, Margaret. *Bearing the Word: Language and Female Experience in Nineteenth-Century Women's Writing.* Chicago: U of Chicago P 1986

Irigaray, Luce. *Speculum of the Other Woman.* Trans. Gillian C. Gill.
Ithaca: Cornell UP 1985

– 'Ce sexe qui n'en est pas un' [This sex which is not one]. In *New
French Feminisms*, 99–106 (*see* Marks and de Courtivron)

Jacobus, Mary. 'The Difference of View.' In *Women Writing and Writing about Women.* Ed. Mary Jacobus. London: Croom Helm 1979

– *Tradition and Experiment in Wordsworth's* Lyrical Ballads *(1798).*
Oxford: Clarendon 1976

Jones, Ann Rosalind. 'Inscribing Femininity: French Theories of the Feminine.' In *Making a Difference: Feminist Literary Criticism*. Ed. Gayle Greene and Coppelia Kahn. London: Routledge 1985

Kristeva, Julia. *The Kristeva Reader*. Ed. Toril Moi. New York: Columbia UP 1986

Marks, Elaine, and Isabelle de Courtivron, eds. *New French Feminisms*. New York: Schocken Books 1981

Mason, Mary G. 'The Other Voice: Autobiographies of Women Writers.' In *Autobiography*, 207–35 (*see* Olney)

Moi, Toril. *Sexual/Textual Politics: Feminist Literary Theory*. London and New York: Methuen 1985

Myers, Mitzi. 'Mary Wollstonecraft's *Letters Written ... in Sweden*: Toward Romantic Autobiography.' *Studies in Eighteenth Century Culture* 8 (1979): 165–86

– 'Pedagogy as Self-Expression in Mary Wollstonecraft: Exorcising the Past, Finding a Voice.' In *The Private Self*, 192–210 (*see* Benstock)

Nussbaum, Felicity A. 'Eighteenth-Century Women's Autobiographical Commonplaces.' In *The Private Self*, 147–76 (*see* Benstock)

Olney, James, ed. *Autobiography: Essays Theoretical and Critical*. Princeton: Princeton UP 1980

Polwhele, Richard. *The Unsex'd Females*. Intro. Gina Luria. New York: Garland 1974

Poovey, Mary. *The Proper Lady and the Woman Writer: Ideology as Style in the Works of Mary Wollstonecraft, Mary Shelley and Jane Austen*. Chicago: U of Chicago P 1984

'Review of Cousett's *A Tour Through Sweden, Swedish Lapland, Finland & Denmark*.' *Analytical Review*, 1789: 14–19

'Review of Imlay's *A Topographical Description of the Western Territory of North America*.' *Critical Review*, Sept. 1794: 53–8

'Review of Meare's *Voyages to the North West Coast of America*.' *Critical Review*, Jan. 1791: 1–10

'Review of Radcliffe's *Journey Made in the Summer of 1794, through Holland & the Western Frontier of Germany*.' *Critical Review*, July 1795: 241–7

'Review of White's *Journal of a Voyage to New South Wales*.' *Critical Review*, Jan. 1791: 10–18

Smith, Paul. *Discerning the Subject*. Theory and History of Literature 55. Minneapolis: U of Minnesota P 1988

Smith, Sidonie. *A Poetics of Women's Autobiography: Marginality and the Fictions of Self-Representation*. Bloomington: Indiana UP 1987

Todd, Janet. *Feminist Literary History*. New York: Routledge 1988

Tomalin, Claire. *The Life and Death of Mary Wollstonecraft*. New York and London: Harcourt Brace Jovanovich 1974

Vendler, Helen. *The Odes of John Keats*. Cambridge: Harvard Belknap 1983

Wollstonecraft, Mary. *Collected Letters of Mary Wollstonecraft*. Ed. Ralph M. Wardle. Ithaca: Cornell UP 1979

– *Letters Written during a Short Residence in Sweden, Norway, and Denmark*. 1796. Ed. Carol H. Poston. Lincoln: U of Nebraska P 1976

– *Mary, A Fiction and The Wrongs of Woman, or Maria*. Ed. Gary Kelly. London: Oxford UP 1976

– *Original Stories* (1788). Intro. E.V. Lucas. London: Henry Frowde 1906

– *Thoughts on the Education of Daughters* (1787). Intro. Gina Luria. New York: Garland 1974

– *A Vindication of the Rights of Woman: With Strictures on Political and Moral Subjects*. Ed. Ulrich H. Hardt. Troy, NY: Whitson 1982

Woolf, Virginia. *Women and Writing*. Intro. Michele Barrett. London: The Women's Press 1979

PART TWO

RECORDING A LIFE AND THE CONSTRUCTION OF SELF

Non-Literary Life Narratives
as Life Writing
Personal Oral Narratives,
Life Histories, and Testimonials

IN THIS SECTION life writing is used to incorporate 'the recorded life' (James Cummings, in Hoffman and Culley, *Women's Personal Narratives*, 14; see p. 15, above) as it is represented in the vernacular – personal narratives, oral narratives, and life testimonies or testimonials; that is, documents that are composed by ordinary people, and that are not considered of equal 'literary' merit with either the life writing of literary persons or with published autobiographies. At the same time, however, these documents are observed to find a home in the genus of life writing where a previously silenced self has been rendered into text at the margins of an otherwise hegemonic discourse, and are therefore often referred to by literary critics as 'nontraditional' literature (see Hoffman and Culley 1–3). Thus, the contributors focus on both the nature of this particular kind of life-writing document, and on the problematic of sub-jecting the 'subject' to his or her construction of an already neglected 'self.'

Here life narratives – sometimes called life stories – may be defended as 'alternative' (to-the-canon) texts within the over-determined or canon-reliant contexts and disciplines. The self-conscious scholar, historian, anthropologist then uses life writing in order to voice complaints and observations about various theories that have been used in their disciplines, and that have pre-determined the status and voice of the 'subject' who is not viewed as an individual. As illusory as the construct of the individual may be, he or she is generally assumed to be doing the determining on his or her life, or text, as in published autobiography.

The life-writing documents discussed here are originally oral and/or archival documents. We can see how life writing can be used not only to privilege previously neglected selves, but also to constitute a rallying post or reader position from which to see the constructed self in the text. This reader position is crucial to our later exploration of life writing as both a genre that includes certain kinds of fiction, and a critical practice.

~§ 5 §~
Court Testimony from the Past: Self and Culture in the Making of Text

ELIZABETH S. COHEN

For understanding other places and times, reading the 'life' of someone who lived there has long been a favourite means. The enduringly popular genres of biography and autobiography gratify the appetite to see into the experience, the mind, the sensibility of another. It may be difficult, however, to satisfy such curiosity about the many men and women of earlier eras who could not read and write. While historians can reconstruct much about the circumstances of their lives, we can rarely see directly into their minds and feelings. Before modern times only a very few, non-élite people have represented themselves to us in somewhat auto-biographical form.[1] From the sixteenth and seventeenth centuries, however, there are other sources that, if we are willing to read them as self-representation, deliver what we crave. Judicial records from this early modern period, particularly testimonies and complaints uttered and transcribed in the first person, offer a gallery of vivid, animated images of self. If not the only, certainly a very fruitful reading of court testimony is as life writing.[2]

For students of literature this proposal to read court records as a form of text raises the problem of genre. As self-representation, judicial testimonies do not conform to the conventions of auto-biography; therefore, at least by construction, they are not strictly literature. A great gift of the concept of life writing is the per-mission to read these and many other kinds of texts as expressive of the person who made them. Thus, as we see in this anthology, we find self-representation in a diversity of writings – for example, letters, journals, and fictional or poetic fragments – that have often been undervalued because they lack formal generic character. Ad-

vocates of thus opening and redefining the turf of literary scholarship face the challenge of setting up guide-ropes through the
diversity. Nevertheless, the moment to lengthen the range of our
literary sights is ripe; thus, at a forum on Renaissance women,
staged recently amidst the cacophony of the meetings of the Modern Language Association, feminists and others called frequently
for the incorporation of 'alternative' texts into the study and teaching of literature. Court testimonies provide one rich source for
such novel texts.

Since, previously, other disciplines, particularly history, have
been the principal exploiters of some of these lodes of alternative
texts, literature's expansion invites exchange across disciplinary
boundaries. Such a welcome enterprise, however, must address the
different preoccupations of scholars on two sides of the frontier.
Heated controversies among literary scholars over the definition
of genres and the classification of texts within or without the
'canon' may baffle innocent historians. 'What is all the fuss?' they
think. Any sort or form of source can feed the mill of historical
truth. Historians, however, have preferences and those who study
politics, economies, and societies commonly have favoured non-
literary texts over identifiably literary ones. While literary scholars
have delighted in the artful fashioning of their corpus, many historians, for the same reason, have distrusted those texts. Art itself
may be a gratifying subject of study, but those historians whose
interests lie in what the art represents suspect distortion, even
lying. With a disparaging 'there's only literary evidence,' a historian has often discounted a colleague's point. When the sources
do not speak 'truth' about what was, historians are often at a loss.

The systematic study of life writing forces us to confront a theoretical conundrum that bedevils the boundary between the disciplines of history and literature. The problem: what, if any, is the
relationship between the text and the world that produced it, that
is, between the text and the individual creator, the culture, and
the historical circumstances that may have shaped it? While historians and literary critics alike pore over texts, they frequently
disagree over what they are seeking. Some currents in literary study
have contended that text is all there is. To critics who are of this
mind-set, texts speak to other texts, through genre and structure
and rhetoric, through conformity to such conventions and their
violation. The process of creating texts must be put aside as elusive, even irrelevant. People cease to have much to do with writing.

What matters is how texts are received, and that response bears little connection to how they originally came to be. So, as readers too, people tend to disappear from the discussion, for the reception of a text resides only in other texts. Often linked to this approach to literature has been an enthusiasm for symbolic interpretation, which generates a pullulating multiplicity of meanings. Detached from the nuts and bolts of earthly life, one meaning may be as good as another, and several meanings resonating together are better yet. Bread, sweat, and blood, inaccessible as material experience, transcend as metaphor.

Historians, especially those considerable numbers among them now open to trying out ideas from other disciplines, have found these developments among their literary colleagues both challenging and disquieting.[3] Recent articles in the flagship journal of the American Historical Association bring to the forefront the debate over the place of such currents of thinking in historical research.[4] Certainly, the literary scholars' presentation of text as a largely independent artefact, as neither a photograph of the world it describes nor a simple expression of its author's views, offers a valuable corrective to wishful literalism in some historical reading. The injunction to take account of how a text's impact may depart radically from its generator's intentions also highlights a dimension of communication sometimes overlooked.[5] Nevertheless, an insistence that text represents only itself poses fundamental problems for most historians. The study of history aspires to see not only the sources, but the past behind them. Manuscripts and newspapers, as well as ruins, paintings, coins, old machinery, and the like, all of which may be read as texts, are interesting as vehicles for the reconstruction of the world in which they were made. Only a naïve historian would claim that the past itself may be recovered by these means, but more sophisticated peers would still maintain that their goal is a conceptual whole, the best possible vision of what maybe was, distinct from the textual fragments from which it is derived. This exercise, while it defies the assertion that text cannot be read to reveal its origins, must none the less respond to the notion that text refracts meaning and does not yield truth straightforwardly. Yet to build a picture of the past, historians need to assess and select certain among multiple meanings as of greater consequence to the unfolding of the canvas through time.

The construction of life writing as an object of scholarly examination necessarily occupies a middle ground and seeks an accommodation between the study of text and of world. Life writing presumes some meaningful connection between the words and the writer and her or his context of experience. In permitting us to focus on one or a few individuals, the study of life writings provides a laboratory on a manageable scale in which to experiment with the problems of interpretation inherent in the relationship between text and its makers.

In particular, life writing offers one forum for exploring the process by which culture, or what some historians have called *mentalité*, intervenes between the writer and the text. This medium of culture has attracted lively attention from numbers of historians, including those who, through their interest in the minds and behaviour of ordinary people, have turned to anthropology for models.[6] Culture defines the words, the gestures, the units of meaning, the patterns of arrangement, through which people, among them writers, package their experience both for themselves – in consciousness and memory – and for others – in text. In important, though probably variable measure, culture shapes text. Thus, as historians read texts to discover the past, much of what they encounter is this cultural mediation that smoothes out and conventionalizes the uniqueness of particular experience. This interest in culture requires the scholar of the past to adjust the focal length of his lens.

Exemplars of this new 'cultural history' have adopted several different approaches to text. Some studies have pursued the traditional historians' recourse to many documents, where multiple texts of varying origins and genres are compared in order to distil a collective meaning. Others, seeking an image of culture that renders the complex texture of experience, have followed the Italian innovators into the domain of 'microhistory.'[7] This form takes a small subject – a minor incident or the opinions of a nobody – and probes the details to discern the subtle, but potent habits of consciousness and act. But such inquiries, which usually must depend on a single clutch of records, always risk charges that the results represent nothing beyond themselves. Even avant-garde historians may become uncomfortable resting the credibility of their infant history of culture on unique and, likely, idiosyncratic examples. Defenders of microhistory counter by asserting that, for all its shortcomings, their method reveals things otherwise unknowable. Anomalies can teach profitably about the more normal state of affairs.

This vision of culture as a powerful, if amorphous, force mediating between a person and her or his world has mobilized the efforts of students of literature and anthropology as well as history. One problem with the perspective is that a notion of individuality tends to disappear. Certainly, the recent scholarly enthusiasm for culture as an analytical category has not imposed a model of determinism; rather culture has appeared as an engine spinning off marvelous multiplicities of meanings and symbols. The question of how one particular person or another navigates among the vast array of choices has, however, been left mostly to common sense or to what the observer finds psychologically plausible. The idea of life writing proposes one approach with which to investigate this somewhat murky zone. From this point of view the maker of text has a measure of consciousness and autonomy. The writer is here not only the object of cultural mediation, but also a subject practising it.

The challenges – both literary and historical – of reading court testimonies reflect these general problems on the disciplinary boundaries. The expansive scope of life writing can provide the theoretical frame for the exploration of these texts that, while preserved in written words, were in some real sense not written at all. These are the records of oral testimony of various sorts; they are valuable because they allow us to 'read' the selves not only of the literate, but also of some members of that majority of humanity, past as well as present, who could not write. For those who seek to understand the lives and minds of people neither élite nor dominant and, in particular, of women, this notion that validates unconventional texts is especially welcome.

Oral testimonies from the early modern period have survived in the archives of judicial investigations, conducted by both secular and religious authorities. Among the richest of such records, notably for the study of self-representation, are the discursive, first-person depositions preserved in various cities of Italy. I have worked in particular with complaints and interrogations in the criminal courts of the city of Rome in the later sixteenth and early seventeenth centuries.[8] While, like every body of texts, this one has idiosyncrasies, it nevertheless offers a good example with which to illustrate the steps in reading this one form of life writing.[9] Still, what I suggest here about interpreting trial records as one version of self-representation does not mean that all court documents either can or should be read this way.

When early modern people spoke to their magistrates, they often incorporated statements about who they were. More accurately, they created images of whom they wished to be in that particular situation. In so concocting their self-presentation they were not, however, different from the courtier seeking favour or the auto-biographer justifying her or his life. In all these cases – even the last – the representation of self is a public, social exercise shaped by values, conventions of expression, and the political circum-stances of the moment. Thus, to understand the process of the construction of self in court testimonies, we need to look at the several ranges of institutional, cultural, and social constraints that shaped their words.

The first step in reading testimonies is to trace the creation of the text as a physical object. Here I will describe what happened in Rome as an example of the issues that a sensitive reader must consider. There, accusers, defendants, and witnesses alike were questioned by the pope's officials, not in the public forum of a court, but individually, in private – sometimes in their own homes, sometimes in the offices of the authorities. While preparation of a story, sometimes with the advice of a lawyer, and collusion among several witnesses could and did happen, no other parties to the case were present to hear exactly what someone actually did say. Those words were transcribed verbatim by a notary and became the record of evidence on which judges based their decisions. Men and women testified under oath, and some, not only the accused, faced the threat of torture to validate their tales. The magistrates, who, unlike the witnesses, did have the benefit of hearing or read-ing all the testimonies, could re-call and reinterrogate, using their superior information to press the speaker for a better story. Some-times the court's strategy demanded a formal confrontation be-tween the tellers of contradictory tales, but these bits of judicial drama seldom produced the rich self-declarations that emerged in private inquiry.

Manifestly, the circumstances that generated these testimonial texts offered several ways in which distortion could enter the transmission of the words. The notary could mistake both what he heard and what he wrote. (If the documents were recopied, further error could creep in.) More serious damage occurred if the notary, occasionally or consistently, transformed the words from the colloquial or dialectical discourse of the witness into the more proper, Tuscanized version of the vernacular. Certainly, the notaries were not altogether passive or mechanical recorders, if the scrawl into which their penmanship sometimes declined during torture sessions is any indication. Yet, while caution is always healthy, there is enough variety in the language of the records to be confident that the discourse of the witnesses has not been systematically standardized. Indeed, the purposes that the written documents were to serve may have ensured that they were little altered. And, however flawed by such, mostly minor, technical lapses in accuracy, these testimonies are still too precious an entrée into the self-perceptions of otherwise inaccessible men and women to discard.

Much more profoundly, the law and its enforcers shaped these texts by defining the subject-matter, the rhetoric, and the genre. To deal in the courts, men and women had to frame their predicaments to fit what the law permitted and prohibited. They had to speak a language that could be understood to cohere with the discourse of statutes and legal practice; sometimes they had to recognize and use specialized terminology. And they had to tailor what they wanted to say into forms set by the authorities. The predominant format was a dialogue, specifically a hierarchically structured exchange in which officials posed questions and people had to answer. Thus, these texts appear, in large part, as a disclosure in two voices: on the one hand, the terse, formulaic Latin of the magistrates, often neutral in tone, but sometimes pointedly sceptical; on the other, the often sprightly vernacular of a plaintiff, a defendant, or witness, sensitive to the weight of the law, but keen to present a personal point of view. The interrogators' questions at times set a very broad scope and asked the respondent to speak about himself and what he knew 'from beginning to end.' Such a demand was inserted into the dialogue episodes of more extended narrative, in which the speaker could with some freedom choose how to paint a picture of self. While the court imposed heavily on the shape the dialogue took, the respondents could have a high stake in turning every opportunity of expressive convention to their advantage. Consequently, though officials held institutional power in these exchanges, the ordinary Romans frequently commanded the greater literary force.

Beyond the courts themselves, women and men who testified had to contend with a welter of additional social and cultural constraints. In presenting an image of themselves they had to take account of what society prescribed as desirable and plausible for a person of their gender, age, rank, and familial position.[10] Thus, a speaker chose words depending upon what others would deem appropriate. This definition of the options touched both the content of the image and the language that presented it. To the various niches in society, culture made familiar different glossaries and forms of expression – dialogic, narrative, polemic, poetic, and so on. While the law framed testimonial discourse in important ways, it did not determine everything. Witnesses had considerable leeway to draw on whatever among their customs of speech suited their purposes.

The personal politics of the speaker's situation also moulded self-presentation. The magistrate's interrogation took place within the context of complex social and economic relationships that impinged on the specific dispute. Indeed, hauling someone into court, even over an extraneous issue, could serve as a ploy in some larger conflict. In other circumstances, the role in which the court proceedings cast a person – for example, as antagonist or supporter – might well be at odds with her or his stance in other dealings with the same people. Thus, a testimony may try to thread a tricky course between implicating and exonerating either one's self or someone else.

The textual vitality of such court records has made them very popular in the historical reconstruction of the lives and minds of ordinary Europeans. Some historians, however, have strong doubts about how much these documents can in fact tell about what happened or how people thought.[11] These critics, much impressed by the heavy influence of the various forces shaping the texts that I have just discussed, believe that any image of people or events produced in a trial will be so distorted as to be useless to a historian. In addition to the presumption that many folk lied in court to protect themselves or to make micropolitics, the legal processing of a conflict so transformed its nature that any truth of the original situation becomes obliterated. According to these historians, testimonies can therefore serve as evidence only of judicial realities; one can write the story of the trial, not of the experience that initiated it. This position sees the institutions of the law as so powerful as to constitute a world unto themselves, largely impervious to the wider culture in which the courts were situated or to the manipulations of people who used, but were not of, them. This view anticipates the achievement of only a rather limited truth.

If, however, I cast the courts as in some ways distinct, but none the less part of an early modern cultural universe, court testimonies can bring us to a different kind of truth. If people are dishonest before the magistrates, culture mediates their lies as well as their verities; interpretation can wring meaning from either. If the people who appear in court are abnormal – which for many of the testifiers appears unlikely – and thus unrepresentative of their society, they are none the less members of it and, even if in unusual ways, reflect its preoccupations. (The great achievers, standardly read as the epitomes of their culture, are hardly typical either.) If the law and its discourse leans heavily on the people who testify, it is not the only power with which they have to contend. The very necessity of juggling among a variety of constraints imposes the opportunity to construct a representation of themselves.

There is an interesting analogy between some historians' assertion that court testimony speaks only about courts and some literary scholars' argument that all one can study profitably is the text itself. Both seek radically to restrict examination of the context and of the persons who made the text. The response to both these contentions is similar. Indeed, the study of texts, and trials, as autonomous, parthenogenetic entities may yield valuable insight. Yet both have to be also the creation of people. Even if the process of creation is elusive, and the links between the makers and the products difficult to discern, those are compelling matters for inquiry. If some methods begrudge the task and prefer to exclude the enterprise rather than to embrace change, then new manners of study deserve exploration. As I understand it, life writing seeks to define one space in which this inquiry may evolve. It embraces the study of once-neglected texts. It tolerates a model of making text that extends beyond old-fashioned notions of conscious authorship. There we can talk about many kinds of speakers, not just conventionally literary ones, as both shaped by their culture and shaping new expression with it. In this domain scholars of both literature and history can work to mutual benefit.

NOTES

1 There are, for example, the autobiographies of the goldsmith Benvenuto Cellini, the printer Thomas Platter, and the city wife Margery Kempe.

2 This essay explores some of the methodological challenges posed by such a reading; while the paper touches on several very current and rich controversies, it does not pretend to be definitive.

3 Toews, 'Intellectual History,' reviews these developments in the context specifically of intellectual history, but his comments have relevance for other types of historical study as well. See also Kramer, 'Literature, Criticism.'

4 Besides Toews's review article, see the *AHR* Forum in *American Historical Review* 94:3 (June 1989).

5 A historian who alerts his colleagues to be mindful of a text's varying reception is Chartier, 'Text, Printing, Readings.'

6 An anthology usefully describing and exemplifying this scholarship is Hunt, *New Cultural History*. The interest in cultural history is not limited to those investigating the minds of common people; intellectual historians, among whom are those most outspoken about the applications of literary thinking to historical questions, have undertaken cultural analyses of élite texts.

7 The classic example is Ginzburg, *Cheese and the Worms*. Works in this form by North Americans include Davis, *Return of Martin Guerre*, Brucker, *Giovanni and Lusanna*, and Brown, *Immodest Acts*. All these studies depend on records of trials.

8 Archivio di Stato in Roma, Tribunale criminale del Governatore, Processi

9 To examine the application to particular texts of the approach described here, see Cohen, 'Agostino Bonamore and the Secret Pigeon' in this volume. Other examples are Cohen and Cohen, 'Camilla the Go-Between' and Cohen, 'No Longer Virgins.'

10 Regarding another type of judicial document, Davis, *Fiction in the Archives*, addresses the question of who can speak in what way.

11 A sharp, thoughtful example of this type of critique is Kuehn, 'Reading Microhistory.'

WORKS CITED

Brown, Judith C. *Immodest Acts: The Life of a Lesbian Nun in Renaissance Italy*. New York: Oxford UP 1986

Brucker, Gene. *Giovanni and Lusanna: Love and Marriage in Renaissance Florence*. Berkeley: U of California P 1986

Chartier, Roger. 'Texts, Printing, Readings.' In *The New Cultural History*, 154–75 (*see* Hunt)

Cohen, Elizabeth S. 'No Longer Virgins: Self-Presentation by Young Women in Late Renaissance Rome.' In *Refiguring Woman: Gender*

Studies and the Italian Renaissance. Ed. Marilyn Migiel and Juliana Schiesari. Ithaca: Cornell UP 1991

Cohen, Elizabeth S., and Cohen, Thomas V. 'Camilla the Go-Between: The Politics of Gender in a Roman Household (1559).' *Continuity and Change* 4 (1989): 53–77

Davis, Natalie Z. *The Return of Martin Guerre.* Cambridge: Harvard UP 1983

– *Fiction in the Archives: Pardon Tales and Their Tellers in Sixteenth Century France.* Stanford: Stanford UP 1987

Ginzburg, Carlo. *The Cheese and the Worms: The Cosmos of a Sixteenth-Century Miller.* Trans. John and Anne Tedeschi. Baltimore: Johns Hopkins UP 1980

Hunt, Lynn, ed. *The New Cultural History.* Berkeley: U of California P 1989

Kramer, Louis. 'Literature, Criticism, and Historical Imagination: The Literary Challenge of Hayden White and Dominick LaCapra.' In *The New Cultural History,* 97–128 (see Hunt)

Kuehn, Thomas. 'Reading Microhistory: The Example of *Giovanni and Lusanna.' Journal of Modern History* 61 (1989): 512–34

Toews, John. 'Intellectual History after the Linguistic Turn: The Autonomy of Meaning and the Irreducibility of Experience.' *American Historical Review* 92 (1987): 879–907

❦ 6 ❧
Agostino Bonamore
and the Secret Pigeon

THOMAS V. COHEN

It has been some years since historians could say with any justice that the minds and hearts of the men and women of the European lower classes, in early modern times, must remain beyond our ken. We now enjoy a growing literature, which sometimes browses on scattered diaries and letters, tales, songs, and proverbs, but most often battens on well-heaped court records, a new scholarship that brings us almost face to face with the no longer forgotten masses.[1] We are beginning to learn how the common people spoke, thought, and felt, how they did business and negotiated the delicate politics of daily life. Thus, we now know much of what to look for and how to find it, but our ignorance is still vast. We need not only to chart the countless facts but, especially, to pose new questions appropriate to the quirky, nuanced records in which the forgotten people speak.

Full as they are of self-serving half-truths and guileful lies, trial records are tricky documents. Only with care can the historian try to reconstruct the events at issue. At the same time, even where mendacious, court testimony bears honest witness to narrative conventions, to language, and, if not to true deeds, to what a witness's world would swallow as plausible. For historians, both the elusive fact and the more palpable fiction that veils it have their worth, use, and charm. Our goal in this essay is first to study a single inconclusive trial, piecing together the domestic quarrel that provoked it to lay out one small fact, that is, the tug of tensions in one artisanal household in mid-sixteenth-century Rome. But, second, in the fashion of cultural history, we anatomize a fiction, for we hope not only to stake out deeds and relationships but also to show how perception, memory, guile, and narrative convention refracted social facts into words and stories. Thus, we turn first to the crime and its roots and bitter fruit and then to the language in which the victim, the perpetrators, and the witnesses described, explained, and justified what had happened. Thus, moral vocabularies and narrative styles catch the eye no less than the tactics of the domestic strife that brought them forth. We will argue that in both deeds and in the later life writing of testimony, we can discern the flickering, but calculated interplay of competing moral codes.

Since a lone event can suggest much but prove little, our arguments must be modest, for we can offer no single lesson and no conclusive finding.[2] We can suggest, if, even though it may be false, this single tale does represent its world, that the small merchants and artisans of Rome, like their social betters, often chose and explained their actions with an eye to honour. Although, unlike those betters, they seldom cited *onore*, the politics of daily life often turned on it. By honour we mean not the moralist's intrinsic virtue, but the anthropologist's extrinsic social reputation, individual or collective, which must be conserved and vigilantly protected from those eager to steal or damage it. Italian honour, for all its sometimes preaching virtue, was very much a respecter of persons; its strictures attached men and women to their social allies: family, kin, patrons, clients, profession, neighbourhood, and town. At the same time as they dealt in honour, we will argue, Romans could avail themselves of other, more universalistic ethical idioms opposed to the particularistic claims of honour, idioms that took their terms from the law or from religion, and could pursue other strategies that in their goals and basic suppositions opposed honour's dictates. There was thus no unanimity as to moral codes. Rather, in this story of the secret pigeon, we see several disputes about how to define the ethics of a situation. Such wranglings, we maintain, were far from rare in the daily life of Rome, for there, as in many societies, no language of right and wrong was either sovereign or even autonomous; although men and women were sometimes constrained by moral strictures, they could still campaign to put them to tactical and strategic use.[3]

The fragment of a trial that leads us to our story is sadly one-sided, for we hear only three witnesses: Giulio, a man-servant, Bartolomea, a woman-servant, and a victim of assault, an apothecary name Agostino Bonamore.⁴ Bartolomea and Agostino were allies, while Giulio struggled for neutrality. Like many other Romans, Agostino, who did most of the talking, told stories well. Though his words were plain, he had a good sense of setting and an ear for dramatic tension. We can use Agostino's own words to lay out some of the events. To reconstruct the whole story of the 'secret pigeon,' we have had to cut and paste the testimony to juxtapose and assay fragments of what he and the other witnesses deposed. Like the casual viewer of a rebuilt fresco or a repieced vase in a museum of antiquities, the reader may more readily discern the handsome lineaments of the whole than the labour and the sometimes dubious guesswork that went into the reconstruction. Like such salvaged artefacts, our story is but a work of historical archaeology, that is, of informed interpretation. Let us now turn to Agostino and listen to what, on 14 July 1558, he told a notary of the governor's court about an evening in the middle of May.⁵

> I believe that as of this Friday it will have been eight weeks ago that, in the evening, around seven, I was in the shop, at a desk, dispensing a rhubarb medicine. When I had dispensed it, I fell asleep on the desk-top. Just then, along came a lad all wrapped in his cape. He said, 'Where is messer Agostino?' And Virgilio, my serving boy, answered, 'And so what do You want?' The lad replied that messer Agostino Paloni and Madonna Giulia want him to come to them right now. Then, Virgilio called me, saying, 'Messer! Messer Agostino has sent for You. He wants You there right away!' I said, 'Messer Agostino who?' He answered, 'Agostino Paloni and Madonna Giulia.'
>
> I was wearing my doublet at the time because I intended to go to dinner. I fetched my cape and left for Messer Agostino's. When I got to the corner of the Santa Croces', by the shop of Cecco Fracasso the goldsmith, I saw someone at the corner all bundled up, with a naked sword under his clothes. I steered clear because I hadn't arms of any sort, and that man there with the naked sword asked, 'Bonamore Agostino?' I said yes and went on, walking fast because I saw him move. And as I went toward the house of Messer Agostino, at his house, there was someone leaning there, with a naked sword. When I

arrived, he lunged at my thighs with his right hand. I parried with the box and jumped into the middle of the street. At that point, the one who had called me back at the Santa Croce house caught up, and another one too, who came from the alley of Messer Agostino Paloni. The one who came from the alley gave me a blow in this left leg and cut the bone short, as you can see. And all the while they laid into me, they were shouting, 'To the ground! To the ground!' I pulled myself over to the pharmacy on the corner of Via dei Catinari, and out came an employee of the pharmacy with a pike and they went off saying, 'He won't make it another four hours.' 'He can't hold out any longer.' 'Away, away!,' said one of them.

I believe they thought I had armor on because they hit me only on the legs and on the head. And there is a son of Tarquinio the stocking-maker, who lives behind Santa Maria dell' Anima, who says that when one of them was hitting me he said to another, 'Hit him in the legs. Bring him to the ground.' And this boy saw when they were hitting me, and when they ran away, and everything.[6]

Agostino's rescuers had him carried home in a chair, all but dead. For seven or eight days he lay unconscious. He awoke, he told the court, shorter in one leg and quite baffled as to who had hit him, and why. Enlightenment was to come far sooner than health, for his mother, coming to the side of the bed to which he would be confined for another month, told him enough to start him on an investigation. Let us see what he told the court about that inquiry and what it taught him, remembering that, for the most part, we have only his word to go on.

Some time around Christmas 1557, Agostino had married Margherita, one of two daughters in the house of Ferdiano Lucchese. As the name suggests, Ferdiano's family came from Lucca.[7] We do not know his trade. When Agostino first slept with Margherita, she did not bleed, or, as the apothecary said, she did not 'make a sign the way other virgins do.'[8] This lack of blood surprised and riled Agostino.[9] Margherita's lack of a hymen brought dishonour both to her and to her kinfolk and, if he accepted her, to her new husband in that, like the others earlier, he had let himself be tricked. We do not know if Ferdiano had been a party to the fraud, but others of the household surely were, for Agostino

found in the bag of the serving woman Bartolomea the secret pigeon – whether dead or alive he does not say – whose blood had
been meant to counterfeit the nuptial stain.[10]

Agostino's discovery put everything askew; he protested to Ferdiano, who, the apothecary said, retorted only that the girl was
'pretty and good.' Agostino did not take Margherita home with
him.[11] Most likely, her father would not let her go, for, as Agostino
told the court, 'Because of this [i.e., because I told the father what
I knew] they didn't trust me, and they didn't want Margherita to
come to my house because her father had told her that I would
kill her.'[12] On the other hand, the servant Giulio, whose self-
interested and less-informed testimony we would rather discount,
could be construed as saying that Agostino himself had refused to
take her.[13] Whatever the cause, Margherita stayed in her father's
house, in conspicuous violation of the customs of a virilocal society, and her new husband, Agostino, sometimes ate there and
slept with her.[14] Ferdiano seems to have wanted the apothecary
to make this odd arrangement permanent. Adding yet another snarl
to this tangle, Ferdiano failed to come forth with the promised
dowry. In that world, the father's default was in itself nothing
extraordinary, but here it took on added resonance. Ferdiano and
Agostino wrangled continually, ostensibly about the money and
the new husband's frequent absence from the Lucchese bed and
board and, covertly, about the whole affair. The servant, Bartolomea, heard only the surface quarrel, or so she said, for she told
the court that Ferdiano 'was always complaining about Messer
Agostino because he would have liked Messer Agostino to come
to his house more often. And Messer Agostino didn't come because
they were all in a confusion because Messer Agostino wanted the
dowry and messer Ferdiano said he didn't have it.'[15]

Before long, unable to have his way, Ferdiano summoned re-
inforcements. He called in his brother from Lucca, Francesco, who
was made of sterner stuff. Bartolomea reported, 'Many times, I
heard Messer Ferdiano say, "If Francesco, my brother, came, things
would come to a finish."'[16] But when Francesco arrived some time
in March or April to set matters right, things did not at all come
to a finish, for neither his threats nor his clumsy blandishments
could dislodge the apothecary from his campaign to extract both
his wife and his money from Ferdiano's house. Agostino told the
court:

Then there came to Rome this messer Francesco, his [Fer-
diano's] brother, who said he wanted to know why I
didn't go see my wife. I said because they hadn't given
me the dowry they had promised. I didn't want to tell
him why it really was. Francesco said I would have to
deal with him himself and not with his brother, that he
wanted me to tell him for what reason I wouldn't go see
my wife. In the end, I told him, and Francesco then
changed his tune and said, 'It doesn't matter. I want us to
go have fun in Lucca. You will carry one hundred *scudi*, I
will carry one hundred, and we will put them into some
commercial venture. We will stay there enjoying ourselves. You won't spend a thing. And that way this whim
of yours will pass.' I answered him, in no way would I go
out of Rome because I was afraid he would do me
harm.[17]

Even before this impasse, the choleric Ferdiano had taken to
growling threats against Agostino in the earshot of the servants,
saying things like, 'I wish he'd get killed!' and muttering that 'a
pair of *scudi* would do everything and that he'd done bigger things
and that he'd had things to do and had them done.'[18] Then, about
a week before the attempted murder, Agostino and Francesco came
to heated words that may well have triggered the attack. As Agostino told the court: 'Perhaps eight or nine days before I was
wounded, I had words with messer Francesco. He said that I did
not deserve to be their [the Lucchesi's] kinsman, and that there
was no one in my kin-group who was equal to his. I said that you
judged things by their effects, and I said about Margherita what I
told in my other examination, that I knew all about that business.
They wanted to trick me. I talked to the father about it, because
I myself saw the pigeon that they had brought to cut its throat in
the bed. Bartolomea brought it in the sack.'[19] By these words,
Agostino gave his in-laws the lie. Let us examine the logic of the
exchange.

By the logic of Mediterranean culture, the Lucchesi's trick on
Agostino was a lie half-sanctioned by their power. As the anthropologist Pitt-Rivers observed about southern Spain, although the
Mediterranean honour code claims to require truthfulness of men
of honour, in fact it allows the strong who have the more honour

to lie with impunity to their inferiors, who have less.[20] We can consider Ferdiano Lucchese's attempt to marry off Margherita to Agostino as a minor case of *prepotenza* (proud man's contumely), analogous to the bouts of bullying lords often inflicted on their lesser neighbours. The parents of a damaged bride like Margherita had several options. They could take her seducer or her richest lover to court to try to extort a marriage or a repentant dowry.[21] Or they could lay on a small monastic dowry to make a nun of her. Or, if they could not go to court but wished to see her married, they could raise her dowry above the usual to counterbalance her depreciated hymen and cast about for a social underling willing to trade his honour against her economic worth. Or, like Ferdiano, parents could try fraud, always hoping, if detected, to bully the groom into acquiescence.

The logic of the honour code argued against Agostino's protest, for he was the weaker player. We cannot prove that the apothecary was of lower station than his in-laws, but what we see of him suggests that he might have seemed liable to intimidation, for he had fewer social resources than had Ferdiano.[22] Certainly, though he had a mother and a sister in Rome, he had neither father nor male kin to come to his defence. When he failed to refuse Margherita on the spot, he betrayed a weakness, a lack of honour, that left him open to Ferdiano's bullying. But Agostino was only half-cowed by his in-laws; while he lacked the nerve to call things what they were, he was unwilling to accept a bride with an unpaid dowry who remained in her father's house. Then, when taunted by Francesco's insults to the honour of his kinfolk, he retorted not by vaunting his lineage but, more tellingly, by uttering the truth his in-laws knew he knew, and so called into question that superior honour with which Francesco had just assailed him. Agostino's was a double-bladed retort, for it at once branded the bride and gave the lie to the Luccheses' trick, and so questioned that very honour that Francesco had just brandished in his face. Unluckily for him, Agostino seems not to have reckoned on the dire consequences of his counterchallenge.

Agostino had never lacked for warnings. Even before Francesco came to Rome, Bartolomea had cautioned him not to go out at night.[23] And, then, the apothecary said, 'one day, when I went to the house of messer Ferdiano to see my wife, I lay down on the bed and I fell asleep. Messer Ferdiano was in the house, and my wife, who had to go to Santa Cecilia with my mother and my sister, came to the bed and woke me up, saying that I should not stay in the house but should go with them. When I asked why, she said to me, "Come, come! I don't want you to stay in the house!"'[24] Ferdiano seems to have taken no pains to hide from any of his household his itch for violence. The very night of the *attentat*, Agostino's mother told her son, while she was in Ferdiano's kitchen, Francesco and Ferdiano had said at table, 'It won't be tomorrow night that Agostino will have a wound in the head, and he won't even be able to say, "Help me!"' and 'As for the wife, I will make her eat with the dogs!'[25] At this, Caterina, Margherita's sister, had run crying into the kitchen to Agostino's mother, saying, 'My father wants to have Messer Agostino killed! My father wants to have Messer Agostino killed!'[26] The mother set off to warn her son, but arrived too late.

Let us step back and reflect on the logic of Ferdiano's resolve to kill his son-in-law. His actions may have had in them more irrational passion than calculating sense, for, as Bartolomea said, he was an impulsive man, 'who governs himself by his own will.'[27] But even the coolest reflection might have recommended murder as the solution to a painful dilemma. If, as Ferdiano said, he really feared Agostino would kill his wife, he could let her go only at the risk of losing both girl and dowry. An apothecary, after all, could easily mask poisoning as a wasting illness. Since keeping the girl at home would set ever-present 'bad tongues' a-wag, at cost to his family's honour, why not have the man ambushed, shrug off his death as just another of those violent events that routinely punctuated the Roman night, and then pass Margherita off as a young, chaste, sad widow?[28]

Agostino's lucky survival both scotched these plans and posed Ferdiano the two-pronged threat of *vendetta* and the law. His first riposte was bribery; he sent a nephew to the man's bedside with offers of the assailant's plea for forgiveness, a hefty twenty-five or thirty *scudi* for the cure, and a proffered welcome to return to bed and board.[29] Agostino angrily spurned the bribe and the dubious invitation and hobbled off to seek not *vendetta* but justice. He never told the court what he would have done with it. Did he want his wife, his money, or the punishment of his tormentors? On hearing his tale, the apothecary said, some magistrates of the governor had told him that if he could produce witnesses to Ferdiano's menacing words, they would punish him.[30] But good witnesses were hard to snare. As for Francesco and for Vincenzo, a servant who was said to know of the threats, Ferdiano had spirited both off to Lucca. Fearing blood revenge, he had also armed his serving men and brought in other, less guilty kin as bodyguards.[31] Agostino's other best witnesses, the two daughters, were in their father's house, out of easy reach. In their absence, his best ally turned out to be the ex-servant, Bartolomea, who, though she knew less than some of the others, was quick to offer aid.[32] Agostino told the court how he persuaded her to help:

> I was going toward my house and I met Bartolomea just past the house of messer Ludovico Matthei, in front of a tree at the dyers', and she said to me, 'How are you, messer Agostino?' I said, 'Well, a bit better! There's nothing wrong except that I have two fingers gone to sleep; I don't feel anything in them.' She said to me, 'God knows, it went badly with you!' I asked her if she knew anything about what had happened. She said, 'Find Giulio, because I've talked to him and he says he knows who attacked you.' I asked where I could find Giulio and she said she had met him around Rome and told me the place, but I don't remember where, and said, 'Let me take care of it. When I encounter him, I'll make a note of where he lives, and everything.' She went off, and there were no other words between us. Then I went back home. I told my mother about this. She begged me to let the matter drop, because God had given me my life. About two or three evenings later, one Saturday evening, I went toward Piazza Montanara. There I ran into some men dressed like sailors, in ambush for me in some corners. I went to madonna Bartlomea saying to myself, 'They're going to attack me again.' I asked her if she was willing to be examined. She said, 'In the examination, have the notary come here.' So I said, 'I'll see. I'll have him come.'[33]

Even before Bartolomea gave evidence, Agostino had succeeded, with some pains, in tracking down the elusive Giulio. Some fifteen days before the crime, he too had left the service of Ferdiano and had moved to a cutler's shop in the Rione Ponte.[34] Even with Bartolomea's help, it had taken Agostino several days to find the man.

Agostino's tale of how he found Giulio and convinced him to

testify is interesting for its complexity of theme and voice. Because the magistrates were keen to ascertain how the apothecary had made his witness testify, they led him through the story twice. The two accounts differ slightly in their words, but agree, overall, in their artistry. Here, we give the second version, with interpellations from the first in brackets.

> I said to him, 'Giulio, I've been out looking for you for three or four days. I've never found you.' He asked me how I was getting over the wound. I told him I wanted him to be examined. Otherwise, I would have him sent to jail. He said to me, 'What do You want me to know about these things? I don't want to get in the middle between you. You are all kinsmen and friends and I will be thought ill of.' ['I don't know if I will be useful to one side or the other. I have eaten the bread of messer Ferdiano. I wouldn't want to do him harm, nor be useful to You. I wouldn't want to get mixed up in this.'] I said to him, 'I don't want you to say anything except what you told madonna Bartolomea, and the truth.' So we went towards the house of the Governor and there were no further words between us.
>
> He came along conversing with that young man who came with him, whose name is Francesco [the fishmonger who lives by (the statue of) Marforio].
>
> *He was asked about the words between Giulio and Francesco as they went along.*
>
> *He answered:* Giulio said, 'I am certain that messer Ferdiano will be angry that I am being examined.' So we walked on and Francesco said, 'Don't screw around.'[35] ['Don't get fancy ideas. Even if it had been your brother, you should take neither one side nor the other! And tell what you heard with your ears.'] and told him to tell the truth, and that he would always be considered a worthy man.[36]

To unravel the artistry of this passage, we must jump ahead to the end of August. Then, we find in prison not the resourceful Ferdiano, but hapless Agostino. He was there on the charge of suborning Giulio. For Ferdiano had in the meantime succeeded in extorting from his former servant a sworn retraction, proffered

kneeling to a magistrate, and the avowal that Agostino had fed
him his testimony. Thus, the intuitive strategy of Agostino's latter
testimony was to validate himself in the suspicious judge's eyes
as a law-abiding man.

All Italians lived with several conflicting moralities. They were
all Christians, unless Jews, and thus subscribers to a universalistic
morality of sacrifice and love that in theory made no respect of
persons. At the same time, in general, they often used a discourse
of honour that, unlike Christianity, prized particular loyalties, to
oneself as well as others, at the expense of the common good. This
latter code raised up the family, the quarter, the city, the friend,
the patron, and the client, for a man of honour was held to protect
his own.[37] Alongside these two vernacular vocabularies was a third,
bookish in origin but readily available to a litigious populace, that
looked to the law as a mainstay of the *bonum publicum*.[38] In
theory, law, like religion, brooked no respect of persons.[39] ·

Agostino, eager to fend off the charge against him, wished to
show the magistrate how attentive he was to truth, to just dealing,
and to the law and, by sharp contrast, how mendacious, how un-
fair, and how scornful of the law were his adversaries, bound as
they were by honour to a moral particularism that paid heed to
blood and a patron's bread. In his testimony, then, the craven
Giulio, who was soon to sell or surrender the truth to his ex-
master, appeared as the respecter of persons. By extension, he served
as a *figura* for all the men of the Lucchese clan. For, like Giulio,
they put the interests of family and household ahead of the claims
of truthfulness and fair dealing and of the law itself. Against him
Agostino the storyteller ranged both his own voice and above all
that of the man he made his chorus, Francesco the fishmonger. In
Agostino's telling, it fell to Francesco to make the strongest af-
firmation, that even a brother's claim to loyalty must cede to the
demands of impartial justice. In offering Giulio the chance to be
considered a worthy man (*homo da bene*) because he told the truth,
Agostino the storyteller in fact hoped to wrap that mantle of respectable, law-abiding honesty around his own shoulders.[40]

There is some justice in Agostino's attempt to portray himself
as a man less entwined in calculations of honour than were his in-
laws and their entourage. He was less violent then they; so far as
we can tell, neither the initial affront of the fobbed-off bride, nor
the ensuing threats and slights stirred him to violent retribution.
After the assault, where another man might have chosen the vio-

lence the Lucchese must have feared, for they armed their servants, Agostino picked the more timorous recourse of the law. Honour, clearly, neither always bound nor suited everyone of his station.

Nor was Agostino alone in spurning honour, for, in his telling, the four women of this story all subverted honour as the men understood it. Bartolomea, Agostino's mother, and Ferdiano's daughters all did their best to keep peace, to protect the weak, and to thwart male plans for vengeance. Agostino's mother opposed even his wish to turn to the law for satisfaction, urging him to be content with the life God had spared him. In her plea we hear some of the very few overtly Christian words in Agostino's testimony; in his tale, pious sentiments come from the mouths of others: his mother, Bartolomea, Giulio. There terms were never strictly ethical, for they referred more to Providence than to virtue.[41] Nevertheless, they were not without their moral resonance, for God's overarching justice and power argued against honour's yen to redress every adverse tilt of the social balance. Bartolomea, as Agostino showed her, succoured honour's underdogs. So, when Margherita needed a pigeon-carrier, she obliged. But when danger threatened, she warned the apothecary. When Agostino needed witnesses, she offered both her word and her eye for Giulio's haunts.

Most striking are the actions of the two daughters of Ferdiano, who went to great lengths to allay the effects of their impetuous, violent father's wrath and guile, first by warning Agostino not to sleep in the house, then by alerting his mother to the impending attack. Agostino told the court that later Caterina had gone even further, telling his mother how Francesco paid Vincenzo to slip out of town and even threatening, if she could get out, to take the whole story to the Duke of Paliano, a papal nephew and one of the great men of the state.[42] It is hard to imagine an unmarried daughter ever denouncing her father to the regime. But if she ever spoke such words to Agostino's mother, even as mere empty angry threats, they show how sedulously the women could oppose their menfolk's bent for ruthless self-interest and spiteful violence. If Agostino merely made these stories up, they still show how men saw women as peacemakers and subverters of the bloodthirsty claims of honour.

Like most trials, this one ends with a question mark. At the bottom of the last surviving page, Agostino was sent back to jail 'with a mind to continue.'[43] We have no sentence, but, since the sentences are often lost, its absence does not mean he went free. We suspect he did, for the evidence against him was flimsy. But if he did escape punishment, what could have come of his marriage to Margherita, who seems to have been fond of him, as was he of her?44 How could he ever safely reclaim her from so obdurate a father? When it comes to larger matters, we can be surer of conclusions; we have seen how in family politics men and women could have different priorities, how men of the shopkeeper class could observe the strictures of honour without much talking about it, or how they could sometimes dodge them. And we have observed the artistry of some of the testimony of one good witness, the apothecary who, to make a point, could set rival moral codes nose to nose.

NOTES

1 The following are examples of some of the more influential and more subtle works: Davis, *Martin Guerre*; Sabean, *Power in the Blood*; Brown, *Immodest Acts*; Ginzburg, *Cheese and the Worms*.
2 Ginzburg, 'Morelli, Freud and Sherlock Holmes,' makes an interesting and now famous argument for doing historical detective work very different from classical induction. The clue invites surmise. Surmise suggests a tale that at last invites comparisons and Humean induction. But Ginzburg stops at the tale, leaving induction to others. So, here, in fact, do we.
3 Rosen, 'The Negotiation of Reality,' gives an example of an anthropologist's studying the negotiations that determine what definition one can lay on an event. He views morality as subject to the politics of daily life.
4 Archivo di Stato, Roma (henceforth ASR), Governatore, Tribunale Criminale, Processi, busta 38, caso 8, fols. 119r–30v (1558). Henceforth, I will only give folio numbers. This trial, like most in the archive of the Governor of Rome, is the transcript of a judicial inquiry, not the record of the proper trial, with defence and prosecution, for which such an *inquisitio* prepared. The cover page merely says 'contra' Agostino Bonamore and Ferdiano Lucchese and, as sometimes happens, does not name a charge. The procedures of such a court required a faithful scribal transcription of the answers of every witness, which later would furnish both prosecution and defence a record from which to argue and plead. The interrogations in this case date from the middle of July and the end of August.
A grant in aid from the American Council of Learned Societies

supported some of the research in Rome. All the undergraduate students in History 1000A and History 4250 contributed to this analysis. Among them, David Harris deserves special thanks.

5 English cannot replicate the alternative of *voi* and *tu*, the formal
and the intimate familiar pronouns. I have tried to indicate the distinction by capitalizing 'You' where the Italian has *voi*.

6 fol. 119r–v. 14 July

7 Our manuscript, a good copy from a short-hand original, calls Margherita's father Frediano (28 times), Ferdiano (13 times), Fiodiano
(six times), and Fradiano (six times). The scribe must have seen an
over-lined 'F' on the earlier draft.

8 fol. 119v. 14 July

9 fols. 119v–120r. 14 July: 'Io la sposai et che dormi con lei non fece
segno secondo fanno le altre zitelle et io non la potevo vedere
perche per questa causa mi casco d'adosso.' A difficult passage. Professor Rita Belladonna, an expert on sixteenth-century Italian literature, suggested, 'and I couldn't stand her because, on account of
this, I no longer cared about her.' Overhearing our conversation, a
busy clerk in Ferlisi's supermarket stopped stacking *bietina* and *rap-
ini* to confirm the professor's reading.

10 fol. 129v. 30 August. We cannot tell by what ruse the conspirators
hoped to bloody the sheet without alerting the groom.

11 fol. 129v. 14 July

12 fol. 129v. 30 August

13 fol. 120v. 14 July. 'messer fiordiano diceva che Agostino non faceva
bene a lassar la moglie ...' Giulio's words may also mean merely
that Agostino was not visiting Margherita at her father's house.

14 fol. 129v. 30 August

15 fol. 122r–v. 14 July. '[Frediano] sempre se lamentava de mr Agostino
perche harebbe voluto che Mr Agostino fusse venuto spesso a casa
sua et mr Agostino non ci capitava perche siano in confusione che
mr Agostino voleva la dote et mr Frediano diceva che non la hav-
eva.' Bartolomea, the pigeon carrier, of course knew the bride had
been no virgin. Here she passed over the fact in silence.

16 fol. 122v. 14 July. 'Piu volte sentii dire da mr Frediano se venisse
francesco mio fratello le cose se finirebbono.'

17 fol. 120r. 14 July. 'Dopoi venne a Roma questo mr francesco suo
fratello et disse che voleva intendere perche non andavo da mia
moglie. Io dissi perche non mi havevon data la dote che me havevon promesso et non le volsi dire la cosa come passava et detto
francesco me diceva che io harei havuto a far con lui et non con suo
fratello che voleva li dicessi per che causa io non andavo da mia
moglie. Al fine gli lo dissi et detto francesco alhora se cambio et mi
disse non importa voglio che andiamo a spasso a Lucca. Portarete

cento scudi voi et cento io et metteremo in qualche mercantia star-
emo lli a spasso non spenderete niente. Cosi passera questa fantasia.
Io li resposi che for di Roma non volevo andar per nessun conto
perche dubitavo non mi facesse dispiacer.'

18 fol. 122v. Bartolomea, 14 July. She quoted and paraphrased Ferdiano: 'Vorrei che fusse amazzato' ... Messer Frediano diceva che un
par di scudi faceva ogni cosa et che havea fatte maggior cose et che
ne havea fatte far et fatte lui.'

19 fol. 129r–v. 30 August. 'Io forsi otto o 9 giorni inanzi che io fusse
ferito venni a parole con detto mr. francesco et venne a dir che io
non meritavo esser parente a loro et che non vi era alcuno del mio
parentato che fusse uguale al suo. Io li dissi che se vedeva per ef-
fetto la cosa et li dissi della margherita quel che ho detto nel altro
mio examine per che me ero accorto de quella facenda. Costoro vol-
evon gabbarme. Io ne parlai al padre che io medesimo veddi il pic-
cione che havevon portato per scannarlo nel letto che la Bar.a lo
porto lei in la sacoccio.'

20 Pitt-Rivers, 'Honour and Social Status' 19–78, esp. 32–4. 'The anomaly is therefore this: while to lie in order to deceive is quite honourable, to be called a liar in public is a grave affront ... To lie is to
deny the truth to someone who has the right to be told it and this
right exists only where respect is due.'

21 Cavallo and Cerrutti, 'Onore Femminile'; Cohen, 'La Verginità Perduta'; Ruggiero, *Boundaries of Eros* 16–44; Brucker, *Society of Renaissance Florence* 118–22, shows how, in private negotiations, a
pregnant servant could win a dowry from her seducer. For a Roman
case, see ASR, Governatore, Tribunale Criminale, Processo 135, for a
prosecution for 'rape' that really aimed to clinch matrimony without paying a dowry.

22 The Lucchese family had at least three servants: Vincenzo, Giulio,
and Bartolomea. We can detect only one in Agostino's house. Both
men went by the respectful title of *Messer*. This honorific had once
attached to notaries, but had come to characterize men in the lower
and higher professions. Agostino, as an apothecary, would be called
messer because he worked with written materials.

23 fol. 120r. 14 July. Bartolomea had left Ferdiano's service on the first
day of Lent, before Francesco came.

24 fol. 129v. 30 August. 'Un giorno essendo andato in casa de mr frediano da mia moglie me buttai sopra il letto me adormentai et essendo detto mr francesco in casa et mia moglie havendo d'andar a
santa Cicilia con mia madre et mia sorella venne al letto et me sveg-
lio con dir che io non restasse in casa che andasse con loro. Dicendo
io perche lei me disse vieni vieni non voglio tu resti in casa.'

25 fol. 124v. 30 August: 'La sera medesima che io fui ferito dissero a

tavola non e domane a sera che Agostino havera una ferita in testa
che non potra dire mo aiutame'; fol. 120r–v: 'Et la moglie voglio far
magnare con li cani.'

26 fol. 120v. 14 July. 'Catherine ... ando in cucina da mia madre pian-
gendo et le disse mio patre vol far amazzar mio patre vol far amazzar mr Agostino.' Here, as in the incident of the warning at the bed,
we find the women of the two families acting in concert.

27 fol. 123r. 14 July. 'E un homo che se governa secondo la sua vol-
unta.'

28 Bad tongues: *male lingue*. The expression, common in Mediterranean societies, is ubiquitous in Roman trials. In a society sensitive
to honour and reputation, gossips represented a danger.

29 fol. 121r–v. 14 July. 'Quando io stavo nel letto venne il nepote de
detto mr fiordiano del quale non so il nome et me offerse dinari poi
me disse se colui che te ha dato te venisse a domandar perdonanza
et te refacessi le spese che faresti tu Io li dissi vorrei sapere perche
mi ha dato non fo le mie cose a questo modo et me levai in colera
et lui non mi disse altro.' The scudo was a coin of considerable
value.

30 fol. 124r. 30 August

31 fol. 125r. 30 August

32 Bartolomea was married to the drinking-glass merchant Pasquino, a
Florentine. She had been only two months in the service of Ferdiano, where she had been in charge of the daughters. She claimed to
have parted on good terms with her employers.

33 fol. 127r–v. 30 August. 'Andando io verso casa mia incontrai la
Barth.a passata casa de mr ludovico Mathei inanzi ad un arbore alli
tintori et me disse come stai Agostino Io dissi orsu un poco meglio
non c'e altro senon che ho dui deti adormentati che non nelli sento
lei mi disse dio il sa me ne ... [haga?] male l'adomandai se li sapea
niente che fusse stato lei mi disse trova Julio perche io l'ho parlato
et mi ha detto che lui sa chi ti a dato Io domandai dove possi trovar
giulio lei me disse che lo havea incontrato per Roma et me disse il
loco ma non mi vien a memoria et me dise lassa far a me come li
incontrero me farro insegnar dove habita et ogni cosa lei se parti et
non ci fur altre parole fra noi allhora tornai a casa referii questo a
mia madre le me preghava che io lasasse andare poi che dio me
havea data la vita Dopoi questa de li a due o tre sere un sabbato a
sera andai verso piazza montanara trovai certi lli che me havevon
apostati in certi cantoni vestiti da marinaro et io andai da madonna
Bartholomea dicendo fra me in ogni modo Costoro me farrano dare
un altra volta et li dissi se lei se voleva examinare lei mi disse nel
examinare fate venire il notario qua cosi io dissi vedro farlo venire
et non dissemo per allhora altre parole.'

34 fol. 121r–v. 14 July. Giulio was from Nice. He had worked for Ferdiano as a house-boy for nine months at the pay of nine *giulii* a month. There were roughly ten silver giulii per gold scudo.

35 Non se ghabare [gabbare] niente.

36 fol. 128r: 'li dissi, Iulio Te son andato cercando tre o quattro di mai te ho trovato me domando come Io stesse della ferita Io li dissi che volevo se examinasse altrimente lo farria mandare pregione lui me disse che volete sapia cose Io non mi voglio intromittere tra voi voi serete parenti et amici et io serro mal voluto Io li dissi non voglio tu dichi altro se non quel che hai detto a madonna Bartholomea et la verita Cosi andamo verso casa del governatore et non ci fur altre parole tra noi et lui veniva ragionando con quel giovine che veniva con me chiamato francesco Interrogatus de verbis que in itinere habuerint inter dictus Julius et francisco Respondit Julio diceva io son certo che mr frediano lo havera per male se io me examino cosi caminavamo et francesco disse che no se ghabare niente che dicesse la verita et che serebbe sempre tenuto homo da bene'; also 125r–v. 30 August. 'Io son stato a magnar il pane de mr frediano non vorrei far danno a lui na far utile a voi non me vorrei impacciare.' ... 'non te incantar l'anima se fusse tuo fratello ne per luno ne per laltro di quel che tu sai et che habbi inteso con le orechie.'

37 For a clear statement about the conflict between Christian and vernacular moralities and about some of the ways of living at once with both, see Weissman, *Ritual Brotherhood* ch. 1–2. The historical and anthropological literature on honour is very large. For an anthology of classic articles, see Peristiany, *Honour and Shame*. For two recent works on the subject that treat of early modern Europe, see Farr, *Hands of Honour* 150–95, and Burke, *Historical Anthropology*. For a discussion of the implications of honour for a single household in sixteeth-century Rome, see Cohen and Cohen, 'Camilla the Go-Between.'

38 Kagan, 'Golden Age of Litigation' 145–66, makes an argument for the easy familiarity of the Spanish lower classes of the sixteenth century with the workings of the courts. The same was clearly true of the Romans; even the illiterate knew legal formulae.

39 In practice, and in its rules of evidence and its assessment of crimes, the law in fact was quick to distinguish sex and social station.

40 The very common expression *da bene* could fit the discourse of honour as readily as that of law, for it summed up one's standing in the eyes of the community.

41 fol. 127v. 'Le me preghava che io lassassa andare poi che dio me havea data la vita.' Only in Vincenzo's instance do we find Christian words attributed to a male speaker, and even there, a woman conveys them (fol. 125r. 30 August). Agostino said Vincenzo had

told his mother that he didn't want to get involved in these matters and that he would pray to God that he get well and that things would work out. Here, Vincenzo seems to be ducking behind the divinity in hopes of avoiding a quarrel.

42 fol. 129v–30r. 30 August
43 Most of the *processi* in the Governatore's fund are not texts of proper trials, but rather transcriptions of the proceedings of courts of a judicial inquiry, whose job it was to decide whether to lay a charge. A good copy would then serve the prosecution, and another, with the names deleted, would go to the defence. One seldom finds the pleadings of advocates attached to these records of interrogation. Sentences appear in two other archival series riddled with lacunae. Thus, the subsequent fate of a suspect is not easy to determine.
44 fol. 129v. 30 August. Agostino told the court, 'I believe I slept with my wife some twenty-five times, being very sweet to her and she even more so to me.' 'Credo esser dormito con mia mogliere da 25 volte mostrando bona ciera a mia mogliera et lei facendo molto piu a me.'

WORKS CITED

Brown, Judith C. *Immodest Acts: The Life of a Lesbian Nun in Renaissance Italy*. New York: Oxford UP 1986
Brucker, Gene. *The Society of Renaissance Florence: A Documentary Study*. New York: Harper and Row 1971
Burke, Peter. *The Historical Anthropology of Early Modern Italy*. Cambridge: Cambridge UP 1987
Cavallo, Sandra, and Simona Cerrutti. 'Onore Femminile e Controllo Sociale della Riproduzione in Piemonte tra Sei e Settecento.' *Quaderni Storici* 44 (1980): 346–83
Cohen, Elizabeth S. 'La Verginità Perduta: Autorappresentazione di Giovani Donne nella Roma Barocca.' *Quaderni Storici* 67 (1988)
Cohen, Elizabeth S., and Thomas V. 'Camilla the Go-Between: The Politics of Gender in a Roman Household (1559).' *Continuity and Change* 4 (1989): 53–77
Davis, Natalie Z. *The Return of Martin Guerre*. Cambridge: Harvard UP 1983
Farr, James R. *Hands of Honor: Artisans and Their World in Dijon, 1550–1650*. Ithaca: Cornell UP 1988
Ginzburg, Carlo. *The Cheese and the Worms: The Cosmos of a Sixteenth-Century Miller*. Trans. John and Anne Tedeschi. Baltimore: Johns Hopkins UP 1980
– 'Morelli, Freud and Sherlock Holmes: Clues and Scientific Method.'

History Workshop 9 (Spring 1980): 5–36

Kagan, Richard. 'A Golden Age of Litigation.' In *Disputes and Settlements: Law and Human Relations in the West*. Ed. John Bossy. Cambridge: Cambridge UP 1983

Peristiany, J.G., ed. *Honour and Shame: The Values of Mediterranean Society*. Chicago: U of Chicago P 1974

Pitt-Rivers, Julian. 'Honour and Social Status.' In *Honour and Shame*, 19–78 (*see* Peristiany)

Rosen, Lawrence. 'The Negotiation of Reality: Male-Female Relations in Sefrou, Morocco.' In *Women in the Muslim World*, 561–84. Ed. L. Berk and N. Keddie. Cambridge: Harvard UP 1978

Ruggiero, Guido. *The Boundaries of Eros: Sex, Crime and Sexuality in Renaissance Venice*. New York and Oxford: Oxford UP 1985

Sabean, David W. *Power in the Blood: Popular Culture and Village Discourse in Early Modern Germany*. Cambridge: Cambridge UP 1984

Weissman, Ronald F.E. *Ritual Brotherhood in Renaissance Florence*. New York and London: Academic Press 1982

ঙ 7 ঙ
Anthropological Lives:
The Reflexive Tradition in
a Social Science

SALLY COLE

'My life is no secret. My life is a romance (*um romance*). But it is only I who can give it value. Telling the story doesn't do it justice.'

Alvina, a Portuguese fisherwoman, to the author

'Whose life is it anyway?' our editor asks and goes to the heart of the current interest in reflexivity in anthropology. The question also evokes traditional concerns within the discipline. My purpose in this essay is to explore the history of reflexivity in anthropology and to suggest that the contemporary concerns of postmodern and feminist practitioners may be traced to a long tradition of personal narrative that comprises a subgenre in anthropological writing.

Anthropologists travel (generally alone) to places (that today include the inner cores of our cities) usually far away from their university offices, where they share the daily lives of people whose culture, history, and material conditions tend to be different from their own, and expose themselves to physical discomfort, loneliness, and other emotional constraints for prolonged periods of time. They then return to their offices, families, and social and intellectual circles to write about the lives they have seen, participated in, and come to understand. The 'doing' is called 'fieldwork'; the writing is called 'ethnography.' Why do anthropologists do fieldwork? Whose lives do they think they have come to know? What is it that they hope to communicate through ethnographic writing? These questions are current within the discipline but they are also age-old ones for anthropologists.

Conventional responses would argue that anthropologists do fieldwork in order to 'experience' the life of the 'Other,' and that ethnographic authority rests on the practice of fieldwork. Anthropologists study the life of the Other in order to illuminate the diversity of human social forms and at the same time in order to reveal the shared bases of human experience, no matter how diverse in form and appearance. Those in pursuit of the scientific goals of anthropology call this the search for 'general laws' of human behaviour. Those who pursue the hermeneutic or interpretive goals of ethnography say that anthropologists study and write about the lives of others in order to reach a higher understanding of their own lives and of their own societies – the comprehension of the Self through the detour of the Other. We 'encounter aborigines' in order to encounter ourselves, Burridge says. The anthropological Other, then – as Burridge so bluntly puts it – historically has also been a non-Western and/or non-white Other. Curiously, contemporary responses to these questions are essentially the same.

It is in the different methods and language used – the rhetoric of ethnography – that we can oppose conventional and contemporary ways of writing about lives in anthropology. In this essay I speak of 'conventional' and 'contemporary' ethnography rather than using other oppositions such as 'modernist' and 'postmodernist' or 'scientific' and 'anti-scientific' or 'naturalist' and 'interpretive' or 'objective' and 'subjective' because I believe that when we look at anthropology in terms of life writing we find a greater continuity than these oppositions allow. In other words, I believe that conventional ethnography often can be found to be quite contemporary, and that contemporary ethnography can be seen to be, in fact, quite conventional. Exploring the history of life writing in anthropology enables us to appreciate this continuity.

Kadar describes life writing as 'a genre of documents or fragments of documents written out of a life, or unabashedly out of a personal experience of a writer,' and includes 'narratives which tell a story in their own right, even though they may not be fiction' (5). In anthropology life writing includes (a) the different ways that anthropologists conventionally have written about the life of the Other, whether it be an individual 'life history' or an ethnographic monograph that describes the life of an entire society or 'culture'; (b) the memoirs, letters, diaries, novels, prefaces, and so on written by anthropologists that describe their personal experiences in the field as they went about finding out about the lives of others; and (c) contemporary ethnography wherein anthropologists self-consciously attempt to acknowledge their presence and integrate their personal experience or political consciousness in the writing of ethnography itself.

My awareness of the importance of life writing as a kind of anthropological writing began in graduate school. Reading ethnography after ethnography in preparation to undertake my own fieldwork I found myself like Pratt, asking, 'How ... could such interesting people doing such interesting things produce such dull books? What did they have to do to themselves?' (33). I was particularly concerned with how the people being studied seemed to recede into the background as abstract, scientific analysis appropriated their lives. As an apprentice I was also puzzled by the invisibility of the anthropologist in the ethnography. Our professors had taught us that the relationship between the anthropologist and the people was a special one, that the anthropologist's relationship with his or her subject was different from that in the other social sciences. Anthropologists developed a special rapport that came from living among people – they became 'like natives,' 'almost kin,' 'our professors said – and this special relationship gave them access to privileged information and a more intimate knowledge of other lives, other cultures. But in the finished monograph there was no evidence of this special relationship; the anthropologist wrote about people's lives in language that is used to describe natural scientific phenomena, in a style that Spencer has called 'ethnographic naturalism.' Besides my concern about the nature of the relationship, I was heading off to the field myself and I wanted to learn about the mechanics of fieldwork: I wanted to know *how* it's done. But that, too, was mystified in ethnographic writing.

I was going to live in a village in northern Portugal to study the lives and work of women over three generations, and as a feminist I had additional concerns about undertaking research. I was conscious of the assumptions about race and class that are part of the history of the discipline: anthropologists are traditionally privileged, white, Westerners who study non-privileged, non-Western, and usually non-white peoples and cultures. I wanted to minimize the resultant hierarchical nature of the traditional relationship between the anthropological researcher and the subject. I wanted rural Portuguese women to share in defining the research problems. I wanted the work to represent a collaboration between the women and myself. And, I hoped that the women I was writing about would be able to identify themselves in the finished ethnography and feel that the ethnography represented and validated their lives.

One form of anthropological writing presented portraits of real people and suggested for me the possibility of conducting democratic research at the same time. This was the traditional life history. The life history, as defined by Geiger, is 'an *extensive* record of a person's life told to and recorded by another, who then edits and writes the life as though it were autobiography' (336). A classic would be Simmons's *Sun Chief: The Autobiography of a Hopi Indian*. A contemporary example would be Shostak's *Nisa: The Life and Words of a !Kung Woman*. Life histories are also portraits of individuals or groups of individuals that are presented as 'case studies' and that are part of a larger study of a whole *way of life*. Conventional would be the work of Oscar Lewis, for example, in *The Children of Sánchez: Autobiography of a Mexican Family*. A contemporary classic would be *Number Our Days*, Barbara Myerhoff's study of elderly American Jews. In both of these kinds of life histories – the extensive life history and the case history – the use of first-person narration is a hallmark, whether or not the text is the product of transcription of a tape-recorded oral narrative or is highly edited and takes the form of autobiography.

The opening lines of the narratives of *Sun Chief* and *Nisa* show us the power of this form of anthropological life-writing. Both begin with birth:

When we were within our mother's womb, we happened to hurt her. She has told me how she went to a medicine man in her pain. He worked on her, felt her breasts and belly, and told her that we were twins. She was surprised and afraid. She said, 'But I want only one baby.' 'Then I will put them together,' replied the doctor. He took some corn meal outside the door and sprinkled it to the sun. Then he spun some black and white wool, twisted the threads into a string, and tied it around my mother's left wrist. It is a powerful way to unite babies. We twins began, likewise, to twist ourselves together into one child.

My mother also helped to bring us together by her strong
wish for only one baby. (*Sun Chief* 25)

I lay there and felt the pains as they came, over and
over again. Then I felt something wet, the beginning of
the childbirth. I thought, 'Eh hey, maybe it is the child.' I
got up, took a blanket and covered Tashay with it; he was
still sleeping. Then I took another blanket and my smaller
duiker skin covering and I left. Was I not the only one?
The only other woman was Tashay's grandmother, and
she was asleep in her hut. So, just as I was, I left.

I walked a short distance from the village and sat down
beside a tree. I sat there and waited; she wasn't ready to
be born. I lay down, but she still didn't come out. I sat
up again. I leaned against the tree and began to feel the
labor. The pains came over and over, again and again.
(*Nisa* 1)

I avidly read all the life histories I could find and learned that
the life history as a form of ethnographic writing dates to at least
the 1920s and comprises a rich and large body of literature within
anthropology. However, when I suggested to my professors that
I would like to collect life histories in the field they discouraged
me and indicated that I would have to do 'more than' life histories
in order to do anthropology. Life histories, they said, are too individual, idiosyncratic, subjective, anecdotal; the data they represent is non-comparable, non-generalizable, non-scientific. I could
collect life histories if I wanted but I would also have to collect
all other kinds of standard ethnographic data using standard field
methods. And this I attempted to do.

One-and-a-half years later when I returned from Portugal and
began to write up my results, I started first with the life histories.
I gave a few of them to my professors to read. While they admitted
that the stories were 'interesting' they told me that 'if I insisted
on using them' they should go in an appendix. That first year back
from the field, I was trained to write in the more acceptable style
of ethnographic naturalism – the style that Spencer has described
as involving 'the creation of a taken-for-granted representation of
reality through the use of certain standard devices such as free
indirect speech and the absence of any tangible point of view' (152).
Ethnographic naturalism was the kind of writing I had tried to

escape when I had turned to life histories. In contrast to the rich descriptions of life events such as those Sun Chief and Nisa offer us of birth, ethnographic naturalism produces barren descriptions like Radcliffe-Brown's in *The Andaman Islanders*: 'In childbirth the woman is assisted by the matrons of the camp. She is seated in her hut in the village on fresh leaves, and a piece of wood is placed at her back for her to lean against. Her legs are flexed so that her knees may be clasped by her arms. The only manipulation is pressure exerted on the upper part of the abdomen by one of the attendant women. The umbilical cord is severed with a knife, formerly of cane or bamboo, but in these days of iron. The after-birth is buried in the jungle. The infant is washed and then scraped with a *Cyrena* shell' (89).

The invisibility and omniscience of the narrator in this passage is the hallmark of 'scientific,' 'professional' ethnography. The reason most often put forward for the habit of ethnographic effacement is that without it ethnography would descend into subjectivity and autobiography. But the devices of ethnographic naturalism do not serve as one more-or-less adequate way among others to represent a chosen subject. Rather they serve to eliminate other possible understandings of the ethnographer's material. Furthermore, the anthropologist's apparent ability to speak authoritatively of 'The Andaman Islanders' (or of any other group of people) universalizes Andaman Islanders and implies a homogeneity (of gender, age, and class) that often rests on the words of a few unspecified (but, traditionally elder male) Andaman Islanders. The ethnography reproduces a style of nineteenth-century natural-history writing and has the appearance of being factual, authoritative, and 'objective.' However, when we remember the subject-matter – people's lives – the effect upon the reader is alienating, and the reader questions the validity of the description. As Spencer has said, 'Ethnographic naturalism, while working with ostensibly unproblematic literary devices, in fact constructs a kind of object – a world robbed of its idiosyncrasies and foibles – which is foreign to the experience of its readers' (153–4).

I felt the alienation from the subject and from my own experience as I went about the task of producing an ethnography that would pass the examining board that would licence me as a professional anthropologist. I searched the literature again for possible models that would show me how to integrate the subjective experience of the anthropologist with the formal ethnographic de-

scription. This time I found that the writing and publication of
the personal narratives of anthropologists in fact constitutes a second anthropological subgenre that has existed parallel to the ob-
jectifying description of scientific ethnography and despite
concerted efforts to 'professionalize' ethnographic writing.

There is a long tradition of personal narrative in anthropology,
but this life writing conventionally has been located in certain
predictable places, most commonly in the preface or introduction
to the scientific ethnography (see, for example, Evans-Pritchard
'The Nuer, or Firth' We, the Tikopia) but also in diaries like Malinowski's posthumously published A Diary in the Strict Sense of
the Term; memoirs of fieldwork published separately from the
scientific monograph like Maybury-Lewis's The Savage and the
Innocent; and novels like Return to Laughter, Bohannan's fictionalized account of her West African fieldwork published under the
pseudonym of Elenore Smith Bowen. In these writings the anthropologist is the subject. Return to Laughter is a classic. Typical
of Bohannan's narrative style is her description of attempting to
practise the anthropological 'scientific method' of 'participant-ob-
servation' at an African friend's wedding:

> Now it was Ihugh's wedding ... I was her shadow. I had
> determined to record this wedding in detail ... We [went
> to] Udama's hut. There the bride was handed to her
> mother-in-law. The women scrambled into the hut after
> them. I tried to follow. Udama herself stopped me. 'You
> must make up your mind,' she announced loudly, so all
> could hear, 'whether you wish to be an important guest
> or one of the senior women of the homestead. If you are
> an important guest, we will again lead out the bride, so
> you may see her. If you are one of us, you may come in-
> side, but then you must dance with us.' I had longed to
> be accepted, but I had meant something rather different
> by it: the privilege of going my own way with their full
> confidence. Udama now pointed out that I could not at
> the same time claim the guest's privilege of doing more
> or less as I wished and the family privilege of going be-
> hind the scenes ...
> I went inside the hut ... 'Dance,' [Udama] ordered me.
> 'Teach me then,' I retorted. Duly, she and the other
> senior women began my instruction: my hands and feet

were to keep time with the gongs, my hips with the first
drum, my back and shoulders with the second. If I were
to dance at all, I had to concentrate on the music and my
muscles, but while I danced, my anthropological conscience nagged that I was missing something. In response to
my conscience, I craned my neck to watch the younger
matrons decorate the bride. Whenever I looked, my feet
subsided into an absent-minded shuffle, and then I was
poked by indignant old women: 'Dance!' ...
After an hour, 'Sing!' I was ordered ... (124)

As the following conversation between Bohannan and her friend
Udama exemplifies, Bohannan's writing is also 'dialogical' in the
contemporary sense. Bohannan lived as a member of Udama's
household during her year of fieldwork and Udama is reminding
Bohannan that their grandchild, Udama's son Ihugh's child, will
soon be born. Bohannan is trying to understand how it is that she
herself could become a grandmother in the village:

I thanked Udama for her lecture. Meekly I said, 'Thus
Ihugh's children are born and begotten and you are
Ihugh's mother. But I am not. How then ...'
Udama bristled, 'Because my son has married and no
longer sleeps in your kitchen, do you deny him?'
'Huh? Well ... You mean?' I am not coherent in my own
language when I am besieged by gradual realization; in a
foreign language I twitter feeble-mindedly. 'No! I don't.
You mean Ihugh called me mother ...'
'You feed Ihugh, therefore you *are* his mother.' Udama
corrected me firmly but quite patiently now that she saw
I meant no insult. 'Listen, Redwoman, if a woman dies,
do her children become motherless? Is not the woman
who feeds them and cares for them their mother? Therefore these are not merely matters of birth. They are matters of deed as well. You and I, we are both Ihugh's
mother; therefore his children are *our* grandchildren ...
Udama meditated into her pipe. I wrestled with the implications of this dual aspect of kinship, by birth and by
deed. She was the first to rouse herself. 'You must learn
more of these matters, Redwoman, or you will be like a
child among us, a child who knows nothing of life, nor of

death, nor of birth.' She scrabbled among the ashes looking for a coal to relight her pipe. (126–7)

Ironically, it is fieldwork itself, the scientific method of anthropology and a required rite de passage for the apprentice, that
produces an alternative kind of authority based upon the personal,
subjective, and sensual experience of the scientist. The scientist
immerses herself in another culture, participates in the everyday
lives of people, observes with her own eyes their customs and
values, comes in her own way to know and understand their history. Invariably, she also undergoes personal transformation because fieldwork is also a period of growth toward greater self-
knowledge. Yet, the professional text – the ethnography – that is
supposed to result from this encounter is required to conform to
the norms of a scientific discourse whose authority 'resides in the
absolute effacement of the speaking and experiencing subject' (Pratt
32). As I found, to convert fieldwork into formal ethnography
requires a difficult discursive shift from the position of subjective
experience face-to-face with the 'Other' to the scientific position
of observer looking in and/or down upon the 'Other.' Personal
narrative has persisted alongside ethnographic naturalism (in which
narrative is subordinated to description) because of this contradiction between the personal experience of the field and the post-
field experience of producing a scientific monograph. Personal narrative, as Pratt writes, 'mediates this contradiction between the
engagement called for in fieldwork and the self-effacement called
for in formal ethnographic description, or at least mitigates some
of its anguish by inserting into the ethnographic text the authority
of the personal experience out of which the ethnography was made.
It thus recuperates at least a few shreds of what was exorcised in
the conversion from the face-to-face field encounter to objectified
science' (33).

Two groups of contemporary anthropologists are addressing these
issues of reflexivity in anthropology: feminists and postmodernists. Both are interested in difference and experiential knowledge.
Both are reflexive and multivocal. Both endeavour to be intersubjective. Both recognize that objectivity is a relative concept, that
what one sees or experiences depends upon who one is, individually, socially, and historically. Both consider that much of what
was formerly considered irrelevant (anecdotal, self-indulgent, subjective, personal, and idiosyncratic) about doing fieldwork – the

122 Sally Cole

experience of fieldwork – and that was exorcised in the writing of 'scientific,' ethnography, is now highly relevant. And, both are attempting in their writing to resolve the contradictions inherent in the anthropological study of lives.

Differences between the two groups, however, have defined the relationship between them to be at best 'awkward' (Strathern) and at worst openly antagonistic (Clifford 20–1; Mascia-Lees et al.). Their greatest difference lies in their perception of the purpose of reflexivity. Their different perceptions result in a different relationship between text and context. Postmodernists are concerned with reflexivity in the text. They are concerned with the constitution of ethnographic authority and the interpretation and meaning of texts (see Clifford; Geertz; Marcus and Fischer). Feminists are concerned with the context within which we conduct research and the context within which we produce cultural texts. They are reflexive about context (see Behar; Caplan; Personal Narratives Group; Roberts; Mascia-Lees et al.).

A postmodern ethnography, according to Tyler, is 'a cooperatively evolved text consisting of fragments of discourse' (123), 'the mutual, dialogical production of a discourse, a story of sorts' (126). It is 'anti-genre, anti-form' (137). Metaphorically, it is 'polyphonic' because 'it evokes sound and hearing and simultaneity and harmony, not pictures and seeing and sequence and line' (137). According to Clifford the 'new' ethnography rests upon 'new' modes of authority that are either 'experiential,' 'interpretive,' 'dialogical,' 'intersubjective,' or 'polyphonic.' Tyler defines ethnography as 'evocation' – 'for the world that made science and that science made, has disappeared, and scientific thought is now an archaic mode of consciousness' (123). He writes: 'The post-modern world is a post-scientific world. Post-modern ethnography captures this mood of the post-modern world, for it, too, does not move toward abstraction, away from life, but back to experience. It aims not to foster the growth of knowledge but to restructure experience; not to understand objective reality, for that is already established by common sense, not to explain how we understand, for that is impossible, but to reassimilate, to reintegrate the self in society, and to restructure the conduct of everyday life' (134–5). Frequently cited examples of postmodernist ethnography are Rabinow's *Reflections on Fieldwork in Morocco*, a series of encounters with informants in which anthropologist Rabinow figures as amiable companion and participant in various social and ritual events; Crapanzano's *Tuhami: Portrait of a Moroccan Tilemaker*, an extended, stream-of-consciousness, psychoanalytic type of interview; and Dwyer's *Moroccan Dialogues*, a question-and-answer extended interview in which the anthropologist encourages the subject to talk about his life by leading him through standard ethnographic topical areas (childhood, puberty, marriage, work, migration, and so on).

For their part, feminists have been less concerned with text. The objective of feminist anthropology instead may be understood to be the exploration of the subjective experience of women, within the analytical context of sociopolitical relations and ideological constructions of dominance and oppression. This exploration is achieved through democratic research and the creation of texts that give women a voice and that both respect women's past decisions and illuminate their utopian agendas. Feminist ethnography, then, is largely a by-product of efforts to transform the conditions, methods, and goals of the research process itself. As a result, the texts of feminist anthropologists are not generally considered in discussion about experimentation in ethnographic writing.

Feminists, however, early recognized the life history to be central to the conduct of their research and have employed two approaches to integrating life writing in their ethnography. The first and most common approach has been to integrate text and context by presenting narratives within a larger analysis of the social and historical constraints and conditions under which individuals define themselves, their agendas, and their strategies. In some cases, the subjects are named and the reader comes to know them as individuals through a series of passages. Examples are Bourque and Warren's study of Peruvian women and economic development, *Women of the Andes*; Ginsburg's study of pro-choice and pro-life activists, *Contested Lives: The Abortion Debate in an American Community*; and Zavella's *Women's Work and Chicano Families*, a study of Chicano cannery workers in California. In other cases, individuals are unnamed but through a sequence of quotations the substance of individual lives emerges. An example is Luxton's *More Than a Labour of Love*, a study of three generations of women's work in the home in Flin Flon, Manitoba.

The second approach has been, like Shostak and Myerhoff, to elaborate the nature of the relationship between the anthropologist and the subject of the life story, to incorporate the anthropologist's experience in the telling of the story, and to make the stories

central to the text. Although the prior concern is the research
process and illumination of the historical context of lives, the resultant texts resemble postmodernist ethnography.

Shostak, who in *Nisa* has recorded the extended life story of a
woman of the !Kung hunter-gatherers of the Kalahari Desert of
Botswana, describes how she and Nisa worked together: 'We often
joked about how I (her "niece") was a child and she (my "aunt")
was a woman of vast experience whose task it was to teach me
about life' (40–1). Shostak describes how she had first approached
!Kung women and asked them if they would like to participate in
the research: 'At the outset, I told each woman that I wanted to
spend a number of days talking with her about her life. I explained
that I wanted to learn what it meant to be a woman in their culture
so I could better understand what it meant in my own. With older
women, I went further, presenting myself as a child in need of
help in preparing for what life might yet have to offer. In all cases,
the women were talking specifically to me, as a person and as a
woman' (21). 'I presented myself to them pretty much as I saw
myself at the time: a girl-woman, recently married, struggling with
the issues of love, marriage, sexuality, work, and identity – basi-
cally, with what womanhood meant to me. I asked the !Kung
women what being a woman meant to them and what events had
been important in their lives' (7).

Myerhoff is also reflexive about the reasons and conditions under which she conducts anthropological research and about her
relationship with her subjects. In the following excerpt she is describing her developing relationship with Shmuel, an elderly Jew-
ish-American immigrant. Her subsequent interviews with Shmuel
led to the creation of a rich and moving life story 'Needle and
Thread: The Life and Death of a Tailor' (*Number Our Days* 40–78).
Myerhoff developed her particular style of conducting research
and of writing ethnography in the context of her self-identification
as a feminist. In this excerpt, however, she reflects on her own
ignorance and gradual realization of the importance of also identifying herself as a Jew. In this regard, she tells us, Shmuel is
infinitely more knowledgeable and aware. Myerhoff describes her
thoughts as she walked with Shmuel to his house one late afternoon:

> Shmuel had agreed to let me record his life history. But
> clearly he was full of doubts about revealing himself to

me and about my ability to understand him. I shared his fears but was prepared to put doubts aside and try. The differences between us seemed less formidable as I contemplated our long shadows running before us in the clear afternoon light. Many people believe taking their pictures captures their soul, and taking a life story is even more threatening ... Our shadows were exactly the same size – small, compact, heads, enlarged by wiry curls. Despite forty years that set us apart, despite our differences in sex, history, knowledge, belief, and experience, we resembled each other. Same big nose, dark eyes, sharp vaulted cheekbones. It could be seen that we were of the same racial stock. Shmuel had a way of reckoning all differences between us in his favor, mocking but without cruelty, yet in a way that always made me feel somewhat apologetic. I was grateful for all our similarities and read them as signs of hope in the validity of my attempt to comprehend him. It didn't help that I was a professor with a Ph.D., for both of us were aware that his self-directed education was much broader than mine, not to mention his greater experience.' (41–2)

Life writing in anthropology, like all ethnography, is but one stage in a complex process of cultural production. Culture is *both* 'experience' *and* text and as such is an area of contest or dispute. In this contest, power and politics – context – affect the way in which people (including both anthropologist and the 'Other') make sense of their world and represent it to others. A truly reflexive ethnography is one that is reflexive not only about the anthropological self but also about context – about the subjectivity and historical specificity of the field experience as well as the social and political realities of the lives of anthropological subjects, the traditional Other. Reflexive ethnography involves the 'Other' as an integral part of the definition of research problems, the representation of historical contexts, and the production and interpretation of texts. The integration of epistemology and politics – text and context – produces ethnography that is both truly reflexive *and* consciously political. A new generation of anthropologists will be central to the development of a truly reflexive and *new* ethnography. These are the anthropologists coming out of social and historical conditions that formerly defined them as subjects or objects of study – as the 'Other.' As well, the writing of the increasing number of anthropologists who are working at home in their own societies will be critical to this new ethnography. When the 'Other' is not exotic but is oneself, ethnography – anthropological life writing – can only be both reflexive and political and the question 'Whose life is it anyway?' will be answered.

WORKS CITED

Behar, R. 'Rage and Redemption: Reading the Life Story of a Mexican Marketing Woman.' *Feminist Studies* 16 (1990): 223–58

Bourque, S.C., and K.B. Warren. *Women of the Andes: Patriarchy and Social Change in Two Peruvian Towns.* Ann Arbor: U of Michigan P 1981

Bowen, E.S. *Return to Laughter: An Anthropological Novel.* New York: Anchor Books 1954

Burridge, K. *Encountering Aborigines. A Case Study: Anthropology and the Australian Aboriginal.* New York: Pergamon Press 1973

Caplan, P. 'Engendering Knowledge: The Politics of Ethnography.' *Anthropology Today* (1988): 8–12

Clifford, J. 'On Ethnographic Allegory.' In *Writing Culture: The Poetics and Politics of Ethnography.* Ed. James Clifford and George Marcus. Berkeley: U of California P 1986

Crapanzano, V. *Tuhami: Portrait of a Moroccan Tilemaker.* Chicago: U of Chicago P 1980

Dwyer, K. *Moroccan Dialogues.* Baltimore: Johns Hopkins UP 1982

Evans-Pritchard, E.E. *The Nuer.* Oxford: Oxford UP 1940

Firth, R. *We, the Tikopia.* Boston: Beacon Press 1936

Geertz, C. *Works and Lives: The Anthropologist as Author.* Stanford, Cal.: Stanford UP 1988

Geiger, S. 'Women's Life Histories: Method and Content.' *Signs* 11 (1986): 334–51

Ginsburg, F. *Contested Lives: The Abortion Debate in an American Community.* Berkeley: U of California P 1988

Kadar, M. 'Whose Life Is It Anyway? Some Preliminary Remarks on Life-Writing.' In *Essays in Life-Writing.* Ed. Marlene Kadar. Robarts Centre for Canadian Studies Working Paper 89-WO3. North York, Ont.: York University 1989

Lewis, O. *The Children of Sánchez: The Autobiography of a Mexican Family.* New York: Random House 1961

Luxton, M. *More Than a Labour of Love: Three Generations of Women's Work in the Home.* Toronto: Women's Press 1980

Malinowski, B. *A Diary in the Strict Sense of the Term*. London: Routledge and Kegan Paul 1967

Marcus, G.E., and M.J. Fischer. *Anthropology as Cultural Critique: An Experimental Moment in the Human Sciences*. Chicago: U of Chicago P 1986

Mascia-Lees, F.E., P. Sharpe, and C.B. Cohen. 'The Postmodernist Turn in Anthropology: Cautions from a Feminist Perspective.' *Signs* 15 (1989): 7–33

Maybury-Lewis, D. *The Savage and the Innocent*. Cleveland: World Publishing Co. 1965

Myerhoff, B. *Number Our Days*. New York: Simon and Shuster 1978

Personal Narratives Group, ed. *Interpreting Women's Lives: Feminist Theory and Personal Narratives*. Bloomington: Indiana UP 1989

Pratt, M.L. 'Fieldwork in Common Places.' In *Writing Culture* (see Clifford)

Rabinow, P. *Reflections on Fieldwork in Morocco*. Chicago: U of Chicago P 1979

Radcliffe-Brown, A.R. *The Andaman Islanders*. New York: The Free Press 1922

Roberts, H. *Doing Feminist Research*. London: Routledge and Kegan Paul 1981

Shostak, M. *Nisa: The Life and Words of a !Kung Woman*. New York: Vintage Books 1981

Simmons, Leo, ed. *Sun Chief: The Autobiography of a Hopi Indian*. New Haven: Yale UP 1942

Spencer, J. 'Anthropology as a Kind of Writing.' *Man* 24 (1989): 145–64

Strathern, M. 'An Awkward Relationship: The Case of Feminism and Anthropology.' *Signs* 12 (1987): 276–92

Tyler, Stephen A. 'Post-Modern Ethnography: From Document of the Occult to Occult Document.' In *Writing Culture* (see Clifford)

Zavella, P. *Women's Work and Chicano Families: Cannery Workers of the Santa Clara Valley*. Ithaca: Cornell UP 1987

PART THREE

❧ § ❧

FICTION AND AUTOFICTION AS LIFE WRITING

Reading as Emancipating the Subject

PART THREE EXPLORES life writing in its postmodernist aspect as a way of reading certain kinds of fiction, metafiction, and 'auto-fiction'. Here life writing can enhance and politicize reading as a strategic way in which to emancipate the overdetermined 'subject.' In question is the epistemological assumption that human beings – both the subjects-in-the-text and the subject-readers – are free and self-determining agents. Instead, life writing is attached to various inversions of that assumption. Thus, life writing is used here as if it were a critical practice that incorporates the supposed contradiction between the individual who determines on his/her world (as in formal autobiography) and the passive subject who/which is fully determined and determinable. The fictional life writing text is seen to manifest various subject-locations for the self to inhabit.

Viewing both canonical and non-canoncial published (meta)fictional texts as life writing offers the opportunity for new representations of what we have variously called the 'subject' in the past – that which has come to stand for a host of indistinct autobiographical-like qualities: the person, the (psychological) self, subjectivity, the individual, or even the object of other social and historical forces.

There is a distinct progression among the four papers included here, from the market writing of the self to an allegorical mani-festation of the self or a life or some other construct of subjectivity. The section moves on naturally from the testimonial writing dis-cussed in the previous section, and so begins with an analysis of the overtly autobiographical, *Don't: A Woman's Word*. Following this, autobiography and fiction are mixed, as in the reading of *Heroine*; and then (only) the allusion to autobiography as it is used in fiction is discussed in *Cat's Eye*. It is appropriate that the section ends with the allegorical working out of the 'personal' and the fictive in the presentation of *Don Quixote*.

❧ 8 ❧
'I Peel Myself
out of My Own Skin':
Reading *Don't: A Woman's Word*

JANICE WILLIAMSON

13.6 Survival. Dreaming with a pen in my hand. Writing. Writing. Writing. Who will hear me?

Elly Danica

Our power does not lie in hope (we can learn to live without it), but in our invincible power to remember and to warn.

Mary Meigs, 'Memories of Age' 57

Institutional/Textual Borders

To write a body in pain, a particular historical body that has suffered particularly damaging abuse, is to articulate one of our culture's unspeakable secrets. To read a daughter's interpretive account of incestuous relations with her father is to experience how feminist writing rattles canonical and textual borders. In her analysis *Beyond Feminist Aesthetics: Feminist Literature and Social Change*, Rita Felski argues that 'the politics of feminist reading or writing is not a question which can be resolved at an aesthetic level alone; it is inextricably linked to the fate of the women's movement as a whole ... Writing should be grasped as a social practice which *creates* meaning rather than merely communicating it' (182). Women's life writing that exposes incest experiences makes possible new subject positions in that it potentially liberates the woman writer or reader, transforming her from silent victim to engaged 'survivor.'

My reading of Elly Danica's *Don't: A Woman's Word* is informed by the assumption that children are disempowered. Judith Herman writes: 'Because a child is powerless in relation to an adult, she is not free to refuse a sexual advance ... The question of whether force is involved is largely irrelevant, since force is rarely necessary to obtain compliance. The parent's authority over the child is usually sufficient to compel obedience. Similarly, the question of the child's 'consent' is irrevelant. Because the child does not have the power to withhold consent, she does not have the power to grant it' (27). Any useful analysis of child sexual abuse acknowledges not only the disempowerment and vulnerability of children but the structures of male domination and the organization of male sexuality in order to account for statistics that 'show that men – fathers, stepfathers, boyfriends, and other males – are the culprits in more than 90 per cent of child sexual-abuse cases' (Underwood 56). Many fathers rationalize their behaviour, insist on its normative character, and refuse to assume responsibility for their actions. A sexually abusive father might assert his paternal authority – 'I was just teaching her the facts of life.' Or he might accuse the victim – 'She seduced me' (Herman 27). Increasingly, there is documentation about sexually abusive mothers.[1]

While women's life writing about incestuous experiences circulates within the literary institution, it not only intersects but is central to feminist social practice in other disciplines. In a review of Sylvia Fraser's *My Father's House*, another autobiographical account of father/daughter incest, Jill Johnston notes that the narrative suggests 'what could be done to change society through the affecting, self-observing, literary enterprises of victims' (50). And indeed, these narratives both enable and are enabled by feminist interventions in both psychology and the law; they play an important role in the development of adequate treatment *for* and analysis *of* sexual abuse experienced by children.

There are too many stories. It wasn't until the mid-1960s that researchers asked the incest survivors for their responses; before this, they simply inferred what the effects would be. In 1984, American sociologist Diane Russell found that 54 per cent of the women interviewed reported an experience of incestuous or extrafamilial sexual abuse in childhood before the age of eighteen.[2] Other studies suggest that one in three boys are sexually abused. Therapists point out that the impact on the child does not necessarily correlate with the level of violence, since many cases of incest are with 'willing' children who do not 'object.'[3] Lori Haskell's critique of 'Research on the Effects of Child Sexual Abuse' ends with her ideal projection of future research. Central to this projected research are stories of the survivors themselves, their tell-tale signs, which describe 'what they believe is most aversive about the abuse, ... [and which lead] to important insights regarding the variables associated with differential effects.' (17).

What is at stake in telling the secret stories? In her incest narrative, *walking inside circles*, Angela Hryniuck outlines the terms of speaking out:

> *Dissuasion*. Write about it, but don't publish it. It would heal the family more if you didn't go public. Keeping silent will heal you? We did that for centuries and look where that has taken us. In a handbasket.

> The silence is broken. This time the story is told. She is aware. And she remembers. No one can tell her her memories are wrong. Or she didn't feel what she did. She knows. And she remembers. (44)[4]

In their courageous telling, survivors clarify the structures of authority that made their submission almost inevitable. They also often identify their own wounds and damage as life-long without remission were it not for their memories, disclosure, and healing. For many women survivors, the cost of silence is high. They often have symptoms of sexual disfunction or substance abuse, or they are unable to acknowledge boundaries between themselves and others. All these symptoms can be experienced by those who have not been abused, but feminist therapists and sexual-abuse centres identify this clustering of symptoms as specific to child sexual abuse.

While the sexual trauma for women 'does not necessarily lead to any permanent emotional damage, ... for too many, childhood sexual abuse is an introduction to a life of repeated victimization, an early and indelible lesson in woman's degraded condition' (Herman 33–4). In a study of adult women's responses to their own childhood sexual abuse, Mavis Tsai and her colleagues found that women who escaped permanent suffering, 'most frequently cited ... supportive friends and family members, who assured these women that they were not at fault' (Herman 33). Those incest survivors who communicate their experience to others through writing re-create this community of understanding and release many readers from silent collaboration in their own secreted guilt and shame.

Beyond this significant reading effect, life writing about incest intersects in very concrete ways with feminist social practice in the non-literary sphere of feminist psychotherapy and jurisprudence. In 1976, Louise Armstrong published her popular paperback 'pioneering book' *Kiss Daddy Goodnight*. Ten years later, in a foreword to its republication, Armstrong responded to the current rhetoric of 'disease and cure' that has medicalized incest and participated in a legal tangle of court decisions which have not led to the effective protection of the child. She addresses the proliferation of discussions about incest: 'At least we're talking about it now ... Yes. But it was not our intention merely to start a long conversation. Nor did we intend simply to offer up one more topic for talk shows, or one more plot option for ongoing dramatic series. What we raised, it would seem, was discourse. And a sizable problem-management industry ... It was not in our minds, ... ten years ago, that incest would become a career option' (ix).

In light of this cautionary note, the role of the cultural critic of incest narratives becomes problematic. Elaine Scarry has written that 'the turn to history and the body – the attempt to restore the material world to literature – has been in part inspired by a kind of collective regret at the very weightlessness, the inconsequentiality of conversation about literature' ('Introduction' xxvi). However, the apparent restoration of the body in feminist criticism can occur in potentially reductive and relativizing discourses about sexual abuse. In her reading of 'sexual violence and literary history,' Christine Froula replays psychoanalytic accounts of Freud's diminishment of 'the crucial role played in neurosis of the abuse of paternal power' (630). Analysing the controversy, Froula notes how 'metaphysically, the woman reader of a literary tradition that inscribes violence against women is an abused daughter' (631). This figurative repositioning of the incestuous female body from her bed of pain to the library is a rhetorical sleight of hand. It retraces with a difference Freud's own substitution of fantasy for truth in his notorious repudiation of the seduction theory during the development of his analysis of female hysteria. In Froula's economy, literary history and the female victim of patriarchal textuality stand in for Freud's insistence that women's accounts of incestuous sexual abuse were 'emotionally charged fiction' (631).

Reading Don't

Elly Danica wrote *Don't: A Woman's Word* after ten years of trying
to write *Don't* while living in a drafty church in Marquis, Saskatchewan, a few miles from where she grew up with a pornog-
rapher father who beat her, raped her, and photographed her with
other Moose Jaw men who paid to rape her. After Danica published
her book, other neighbourhood women her age came forward to
confess that as girls they too had been abused by her father. Some
had what came to be known as 'happy pictures.' After her father
humiliated and abused neighbourhood girls, he sent them home
with photographic portraits of their unsettling 'happy' smile for
their mothers.

Danica wrote 2200 pages before she sat down and wrote *Don't*
in two weeks, revising it for another four weeks. She sent the
manuscript to Nicole Brossard, who was teaching at the fifth summer women's writing workshop, West Word, a two-week retreat
sponsored by the West Coast Women and Words Society. When
Danica was accepted into the workshop, she assumed her writing
was simply notes towards a book. She had numbered all of her
paragraphs so she could remember how her memory had structured her story and revised her long repressed history. Brossard,
astonished by the content and writerly innovation, assured Danica
her manuscript was not only complete but 'postmodern.' Prince
Edward Island publisher and writer Libby Oughton, another student at West Word, published *Don't* through her feminist Gynergy
Press.[5] Danica published the book without prior publicity and called
it 'autofiction' in order to discourage attempts by others to dis-
suade her from publication. They also hoped to avoid possible law
suits. Immediately following the publication of *Don't*, Gynergy
Press received one hundred unsolicited poetry and prose manuscripts of autobiographical incest narratives. Since then *Don't* has
sold more than 10,000 copies in Canada and was republished in a
mass-market paperback. It has been translated into German, Dutch,
and Italian and is forthcoming in French.

Danica's work can be read in relation to several other father-
daughter incest accounts written recently by Canadian women.
Charlotte Vale Allen's *Daddy's Girl: A Very Personal Memoir* was
published in 1980 by McClelland and Stewart and Sylvia Fraser's
autobiographical account *My Father's House* was released for the
North American paperback mass market in 1987. While both books

trace the process of remembering and reconstructing a lost history of sexual abuse, the narrative resolution of each is specific. In a review of Charlotte Vale Allen's *Daddy's Girl*, Eleanor Wachtel describes how Allen constructs a counter-narrative to deflect the pain of her own history, a story of compensation with 'tributes to her saviours' and the promise of a happy ending. Wachtel interprets this as 'an exercise with which we are all familiar: when feeling discouraged, make a list of those things we do have – friends, family, home, whatever' (14).[6] Sylvia Fraser's narrative enacts her own splitting into a multiple personality, the 'Girl Who Knows' and the 'Girl Who Doesn't Know,' during the period she suffered her father's sexual abuse between the ages of $2^1/_2$ and 17. This split female subject is reconciled finally in a version of the 'happy ending,' an epiphanic scene of forgiveness where the child imagines the father as victim also.

Danica's narrative differs from both of these accounts in its refusal of compensatory narratives involving family or father. In discussing these incest stories, I do not wish to construct a comparative ranking. Each writer required great courage to write her story; however, a different set of reading effects is created by each text. Charlotte Vale Allen posits an ideal nuclear family as the utopian space for recuperation outside father-daughter incest. Sylvia Fraser implicitly identifies both child and father as 'co-victims' of the incestuous encounter, commenting that 'coming to grips with this [incest] has to involve acceptance and forgiveness ... I feel very deeply sorry for my parents' (MacKay 3). However, for Danica, any forgiveness is out of the question: 'I think there are things that human beings do to each other that are not forgivable and I put child abuse in that category ... If you consider power imbalances, as you *must* in this issue, there's no such thing as adults and children being co-victims in this scenario' (Williamson 'once I remembered'). Danica's writing and painting are compensation for childhood wounding; her imaginative repetition helps propel her through healing and recovery.

Don't is also focalized through the dissociation of the narrator, but the split subject is not named or personified as character as in Sylvia Fraser. In a particularly grotesque section that describes how her father arranged for her to be raped by a group of men, Danica communicates the abjection of her body by dissolving the first-person voice into the third; the eleven-year-old self becomes other: 'The panties come off. He doesn't notice that my skin comes off with them. I peel myself out of my own skin. I am no longer myself. I am someone else. Someone I don't want to be. Someone I don't want ever to remember having been. Someone I used to know sits on a white brocaded bench, under photo lamps, in front of a camera. A body sits here naked. The body tries to cover itself. Its hands move automatically. It clenches its thighs ... The body is no longer capable of response. The voice was peeled away with the skin' (53–4).

Danica's feminist account is an enactment in a language of a woman's pain; this embodied tortured knowledge is unmediated by a comfortable framing narrative that would provide the reader with a safe critical distance. Language is at the centre of Danica's remembering. Boundaries of language are exceeded by writerly suffering and the reader's horror. The perceiving subject 'peels' herself out of her first-person skin, sliding away from both agency and subjective insight. The narrative performs a psychological zoom from 'I' to an anonymous spectacular body. This process of dis-embodiment replicates one-half of the procedure that occurs in a medical examination, where the 'dual attention to the body as incarnate and discerned, self and object, is handled by a delicate manipulation of frames and boundaries which might be called the etiquette of touch.' In Danica's case, the 'etiquette of touch' is not operative in the 'manipulation of frames and boundaries.' However, in both case 'the dislodgement of the self from the body is designed to preserve the social persona from the trespasses.'(Young 63).

This psychological splitting initiates Danica's amnesia and provides her with the narrative distance to retell her story. Her book begins at the outer edges of memory where her consciousness first glimmers with the realization that her hatred for her father has an actual abusive genealogy.

> 1.1 DON'T. I only know this word. This is the only word I have ever learned. Don't. I can not write with only this word. A woman's vocabulary: Don't.
> 1.2 Don't tell. Don't think. Don't, what ever else you do, don't feel. If you feel, the pain will be there again. Don't.
> 1.3 But the pain is there anyway. It exists even when I don't. See? I warned you. You can't afford to feel. Pain will reach out of your belly and grap you by the throat. Choking. His hands around my throat. It is only pain.

Old friend. I thought it was him. Again. Only pain. I can
stand the pain. I can drown it in words or wine or smoke.
Something can be done. If it was him again, that would
be different.(7)

Don't: A Woman's Word begins at the beginning of a survivor's
lexicon. The birth into language of her savage abuse is marked by
the imperative assertion of her own agency, 'don't' – the survivor's
Cartesian revision, 'You do not, therefore I am.' 'A woman's word'
is part of a language not authorized by the father, a difficult language beyond collaborative silence.

An Inappropriate Response

Australian feminist critic Meaghan Morris discusses how 'a "feminist speaking-position" ... is a problem of rhetoric, of developing
enunciative strategies (or ways of "play-acting" ...) precisely in
relation to the cultural and social conventions that make speaking
difficult or impossible for *women*' (7). The problem of establishing
a speaking position in relation to *Don't* collapses into the problem
of establishing a reading position.

Danica's narrative interpellates the reader as one who will not
misread. Early on she recounts her childhood attempt to tell her
story. In Holland at four years of age, she told her story of her
father's abuse to her mother and grandmother. While the grandmother heard her words, Danica's mother denied them and refused
decisive action. The revelation did nothing to deter the abuse and
simply initiated the father's decision to bring his wife and children
to Canada. Later Danica would tell her story to priests, to nuns,
to teachers. All of them refused to hear Danica's words and did
nothing. Their denial stands as a warning to the reader who is
asked to not only believe her story but to vicariously participate
in a shadow of Danica's tortured pain.

On reading *Don't*, the reader herself is unbounded; we are the
speaker's witness inside a body that does not lie. The speaker is
birthed into the sound of nothingness; 'Nothing is born of pain
... Pain like a mountain (7). Birth is the coming into being of an
absence which has annihilated selfhood. The narrator/the reader
is dispersed in a shattering of words: 'The woman made of potsh-
erds. Pieces. Not herself. Never herself. Who is herself? Only broken pieces' (13).

In the case of sexual abuse, the child experience feelings of betrayal and powerlessness, often enacting the perpetrator's view; if he tells her she is bad, she tells herself she is bad.[7] In Danica's case – the child has sinned. The child is responsible or guilty; any affection is sexualized. Danica writes that when the father asks whether she wants to have intercourse, 'he'll get a yes. Now it is your sin. Now it is your fault' (46).

And here the feminist critic finds herself unbounded, trembling at her keyboard, and uncertain – how will she attend to her own words?

Critical Implications

1. The feminist critic can follow Kristeva towards an analysis of abjection that is marked by suffering and a crisis in the subject: 'Where [abjection] ... emerges, where it is differentiated from chaos. An incandescent, unbearable limit between inside and outside, ego and other. The initial fleeting grasp: "suffering," "fear," ultimate words sighting the crest where sense topples over into the senses, the "intimate" into "nerves." Being as ill-being' (40). We recognize in this 'ill-being' a variation on Kristeva's 'semiotic,' though voided of *jouissance*. Jacqueline Rose has described Kristeva's analysis of abjection as 'a response to an idealization latent in her own formulations, ... [a reply] that the semiotic is no *fun* (27).

2. The feminist critic can follow Kristeva down another path towards psychoanalysis itself as that 'site of maximum abjection, the only place where the "savagery" of the speaking can be heard.' Thus *Don't* provides a safe place for verbal re-enactment and repetition within an analytic scene that refuses the traditional therapeutic authorization of the analyst over the analysand. 'Without ... biologizing language, and while breaking away from identification by means of interpretation, analytic speech is one that becomes 'incarnate' in the full sense of the term. On that condition only, it is 'cathartic' – meaning thereby that it is the equivalent, for the analyst as well as for the analysand, not of purification but of rebirth with and against abjection' (31).

3. The feminist critic can trace the shadow of another narrative embedded in the text – one that leads to the mother, and not simply as the object of blame. The mother's disappearance is elaborated in Tanya Modleski's analysis of the gothic (58–84). Several contemporary Canadian feminist writers identify the feminist daugh-

ter's enabling and disabling ambivalence to the mother. In Gail Scott's *Spaces Like Stairs*, the mother becomes the 'semi-Gothic character, a figure of *excess*, of *hope*, but also of terrible *absence* (128), a source of both oppression and rebellion.[8]

4. The feminist critic can accompany Danica through a labyrinthine descent in the mythological traces of Inanna, a journey that restores and heals the traveller. Individual sections of *Don't* are organized as a series of gates recalling the Sumerian Queen of Heaven and Earth, Inanna, 'who gave up, at seven successive gates, all she had accomplished in life until she was stripped naked, with nothing remaining but her will to be reborn' (Wolkstein xvi).[9]

5. The feminist critic can analyse how this incest narrative puts the lie to Freud's law of seduction. Danica's text provides a critique parallel to Luce Irigaray, who writes: 'If, under cover of the law [Freud's Oedipus complex in women], seduction can now be practiced at leisure, it seems equally urgent to question the *seduction function of law itself*. And its role in producing fantasies. When it suspends the realization of a seduced desire, law organizes and arranges the world of fantasy at least as much as it forbids, interprets, and symbolizes it' (Irigaray 38). *Don't* tells the other side of Freud's Oedipal seduction fantasy, interrupting the pleasures of prohibited desire.

6. The feminist critic can trace the movement of Danica's narrative into the public sphere by analysing how the early dissemination of a small feminist-press book to a community of feminist readers was superseded by the creation of a larger public sphere of listeners, owing in part to the award-winning interview conducted by Peter Gzowski on his CBC radio program. The book's popularity carried with it the shocking recognition that too many readings were informed by first-hand experience.

7. The feminist critic can explore what it means to narrate the scene of one's own violation. Remembering is so much a part of storymaking; language moves her from disembodied third-person fly on the wall to the first-person experience on the table or the bed. Did her disengagement and splitting in response to physical invasion lead not only to a survivor's amnesia, but to her life-long desire to write?

8. The feminist critic who writes about incest narratives, that is, *this* academic feminist, dissolves the boundaries between the subject of her study and her experience. Is this the writer in her? Or is this any reader's response to the political imperative of Dan-

ica's text? This particular feminist reader/critic is a white woman who has had a fortunate education, a middle-class economy, and a painful memory of child sexual abuse. Is it appropriate to speak of this?

ad-proprius

At lunch with a group of feminist scholars in a prairie city, I am told that sexual abuse and incest are inappropriate topics of conversation. I continue to speak. Is my stubborn talk vulgar self-interest or a reactive memory of my Wasp childhood dinner table where the monitoring of topics turned conversation from dialogue to competitive taboos? I am unsure of anything but a story my body has recently remembered. At that moment, I had no absolute memory of the abuser's identity, though I know he was male. I continue to tell my story of child sexual abuse just for a moment longer. I become aware that the others' resistance may derive from their own secreted memories. I ask myself once again whether my storytelling comes out of mere self-interest. Or am I responding to the interest of another woman at the table who reaches out to say, 'Sometimes it is important to tell the inappropriate story.'

Appropriate. AppropriAte. 'ad-proprius,' to render one's own. By speaking out of this secret space, my improper talk forces some of my listeners to vacillate between apathetic and inappropriate readings of my story. Marked by proximity, the inappropriate reading renders the story the reader's; the apathetic reading maintains the 'proper' distance.

This feminist critic can't maintain a critical distance. I call Elly Danica on the phone, ostensibly for an interview, but actually I want to talk back to her book. There are long silences in the interview. My questions are too elaborate to be effective. I worry about Danica's interpretation of my questions, then worry about worrying – what are the limits of intentionality? Spurred on by my apparent critical correctness, I tell Danica how, in numbering her paragraphs, she revises Wittgenstein's cautionary words: 'Where man cannot speak, there must he be silent.' 'Isn't this silence the place where women's words begin?' I ask Danica hopefully. Quietly she considers my question for a moment, then remarks, 'You have very definite ideas of what you want, ... and I'm not sure I'm answering your questions.' I feel myself resurface from my theoretical bunker and decide to spill the beans, the seed, the story. Out with it. I admit to 'framing my questions in this complex way in order to protect myself.' Danica replies with compassion: 'For too long we've been trying to fit into a male academic paradigm of what it is we should be saying and how we should be saying it. But [personal] engagement is very, very difficult and very painful and very risky in an academic environment' (Williamson 'an enormous risk'). I wonder what the line is between analysis and self-dramatization. How do I keep the lid on? Or as Armin Wiebe would say, 'Who is keeping the tarp tied down?'

Later I reread *Don't* in a restaurant. The inside story, a sordid affair; the outside story, business as usual. Between the two – *nothing more than two dots dark eyes stare out of a baby head ... two tiny memories of somewhere else someone under the same tender skin pulled inside out. A slit opens up in the middle of her mind slide of a man framed in the white cardboard of a window. Now that she's read the story of incest with the numbered paragraphs she wonders for a moment whether this memory is a lively re-creation of fictive imaginings or a crossover from a temporal elsewhere. On the page, the story of child sexual abuse oozes from her flesh. Memory returns like snatches of conversation in the writing it surfaces as a compulsion witout motive. Memory returns when the woman smells a smell not located in the room, twists and turns her sense closing in towards her own body shifts ground her vagina aches all day without reason and all day long the imagined smell of excrement fills her with revulsion. Her body, register of the unrecorded, knows what she doesn't. Her body, lost bearer of unfelt touch, of probing fingers, remembers in stages: there is no story. She, the third-person narrator, watches the history of her body peel away a texture of mental debris and lived surfaces – a voice (she/I) cries – 'don't.'*

The Sense of an Epilogue

Don't ends with this epiphanic 'Epilogue' of recovery and a visual image: 'Beginning. Always. From the secret place. Soul dwelling: found. Self: found. Heart: found. Life: found. Wisdom: found. Hope, once lost: found. Process: never lost' (93). This 'subject in process' is virtually represented in a reproduction of a drawing by Danica that follows this 'Epilogue,' doubling the ending as though recovery and healing exceed the ability of verbal language to describe it. Danica's 'Ikon' is a round airbrushed drawing reproducing in black and white a series of layered petals or lips. The round drawing reframes the female body in a sexual economy that refuses to figure the woman's body as lack, absence, hole, or wound. The boundaries of the palimpsestic surface (skin) are both fixed and unfixed in the shifting edges of superimposed repetition.

Elaine Scarry writes that creation and torture share a voculabury – ' "produce," "body," "project," "artifact." However, they share the same pieces of language only because the one is a deconstruction of the other, a reversal of the path of creation to decreation ... In the one, pain is deconstructed and displaced by an artifact; in the other, the artifact is deconstructed to produce pain' (*Body in Pain* 145).

Danica's vision of a female body's fluidity resists and reverses the un-imagining/imaginable tortured body. Danica's book begins with a single word interrupting defiant silence: 'Don't. I can not write with only this word' (7). The writing that follows negates the nightmarish inscription on her body of a father-torturer's humiliations. Writing is precisely her recuperation of an imagining creative subjectivity – a 'dreaming with a pen in hand.' Writing makes it possible for the subject to read her own words. 'Each scar holds a book' (93). The textualization of her body is less objectification than an 'objectifiction' which restores agency to her being. Writing reconstitutes the writer's body and world, making survival possible in a sensorium of particulars: 'Fingernails. Teeth. Determination' (93). These particulars are not simply body parts organized by a consciouness informed by the body/mind inner/ outer split and hierarchy of Cartesian dualism. The physical body is inhabited by 'determination' and will. The utopian body of Danica's 'Ikon' provides a visual correlative to Danica's recuperation in language of a body capable of subjective pleasure. *Don't*'s revisionary subject privileges relatedness and associative imagining: 'I dream. I love. I am' (93). The spare syntax of these three sentences announces a new subject whose recuperation depends upon a shared collective rereading of her body in pain.

Afterword

A 1990 McClelland and Stewart paperback edition that sells for less than half of the original price packages Danica's story with telling differences. A comparison of the covers of each edition suggests the effects of diverse design and marketing strategies. The

cover of the McClelland and Stewart edition reinforces an opposition between opaque forgetting silence and transparent bold telling with a chalk-white handwritten block-letter 'Don't' scratched
out of the surface. The female voice is represented in the typescript
letters below spelling out 'a woman's word.' The visual representation of the command *Don't* in the original Gynergy edition fore-
grounds the process of sounding a woman's voice in the insistent
and ascending intensity of repetitive visual echoes 'Don't. Don't.
Don't. Don't.' While the mass-market paperback suggests that
something hidden will be revealed in the book, the feminist edition
implies that the women's voice or the chorus of voices has become
progressively louder and more effective. What is obliterated in the
mass-market paperback is represented as increasingly powerful in
the feminist edition.

The original 'Introduction' by Nicole Brossard is now preceded
by Peter Gzowski's 'Foreword.' While Gzowski is 'hit hard' by
Danica's book, he maintains a journalist's reassuring distance from
the text itself; his words focus on the revelation of the 'ordinar-
iness' of child sexual abuse, contextualizing his original interview
with Danica in terms of recent discoveries by several friends that
they were survivors of child sexual abuse. Gzowski's identification
with the story is based on his professional history, which included
time 'as a young newspaperman' in Danica's home town, Moose
Jaw: 'unspeakable acts, I realized, could have occurred while I was
working down the street, and they had been perpetuated by men
I might have met – or, for that matter, written about in other
contexts' (x–xi). Gzowski's empathic but none the less detached
response to the text contrasts with Brossard's embodied response
as reader/writer where grief and pain are re-enacted and born 'in
ourselves': 'When I first read the manuscript, I experienced a range
of feelings – from outrage to utter dejection, from anger to the
deepest of sadness. It took me several days to finish reading it,
because this is a book that is read with a lump in the throat, a
tightness in the heart, tears. Reading this book, we bear the child
and the woman in ourselves. Reading this book, we share inti-
mately what seems beyond words' (xv).

Omitted in the new mass-market edition is Danica's visual image of petal-like vaginal imagery that affirms women's bodies
through a symbolic representation of female genitalia 'beyond
words.' In place of the visual image, Danica's own 'Afterword'
reinforces Gzowski's assertion of a happy ending to the story in

the writer's new-found joyful health. This revision not only eliminates any reference to the body, but psychologizes Danica's recovery. No longer 'victim,' she is 'a woman with her eyes and her heart open, strong, hopeful and more determined than ever before' (99–100).

Danica's transformation into a self-determined autonomous writer and speaker is celebrated in her new 'Afterword.' However, there is an intriguing comparison to be made of the publicity quotations on each publication's cover. In the earlier Gynergy edition, an extended excerpt of Brossard's introduction on the back cover alerts the reader to the socio-political context of the book, which 'reminds us how much sexual violence, whatever its form (incest, rape, pornography, flashing, verbal harassment), is not only a repeated assassination of our vitality, our dignity and our creativity, but also a way for men to occupy our lives, in the same way one "occupies" a country.' This political context dissolves in the M&S edition, where Brossard is replaced on the cover by Peter Gzowski, whose comment individualizes Danica's story, stressing the heroism of her text: '[An] unforgettably powerful book ... The pain, the reality, and the courage are now all of ours to share.' Ironically, Danica herself denies this heroization in her 'Afterword,' where she writes about the significance of feminist collectivity in the development of her writing. She also notes: 'There are now reviews which speak of my courage. I prefer to call it determination. Determination not to let men control or define who I am my whole life' (99).

Danica's 'Afterword' doesn't finally have the last word in this new edition of Don't. The last two pages of the book are devoted to publicity advertisements that announce 'More Great Titles from M&S Paperbacks ...'; two of the ten titles are by Joan Clark and L.M. Montgomery, the famous deceased Canadian children's author. The other books listed celebrate Canadian businessmen, male explorers, male private eyes, male humorists, and male aviators. Secrets, power, discovery, daring, and laughter are carefully ordered in masculine terms.

Who has the last word? In the world of mass-market publishing, will the new female subjects have a short shelf-life? In this transition from feminist to mass market, do we find ourselves at a moment of social transformation or political co-optation? Will this new community of readers embody a cultural hegemony that potentially invalidates the concerns of incest survivors and feminists?

These questions potentially lead us to take up a cultural pessimist position and negate the potential for transgression and resistance in 'the popular.' Is it more likely that the proliferation of stories by incest survivors may help to create an atmosphere whereby, increasingly, child care givers are conscious of the symptoms of abuse and are held accountable for their actions. The epigraph to this paper links 'Survival.' with writing, period. This reader/writer can attest to the potentially liberating effects of the telling story, the act of writing out a narrative of child sexual abuse.[10] Literary criticism may be something other than testimonial, but for some, psychic healing is in the telling.

NOTES

This paper is expanded and revised from a presentation at 'Women Writing and the Literary Institution,' organized by the Research Institute for Comparative Literature, University of Alberta, 11 November 1989, and is included in the published proceedings. I am grateful to the gathering for their insightful comments and warm support, and, in particular, to conference organizer Claudine Potvin, and to Caroline Bayard and Carole Gerson. Elly Danica's generous conversations clarified some of my responses to her work. Gary Watson provided a helpful editorial reading of this paper. Part of this paper was presented at the Association of Canadian University Teachers of English annual meetings (Kingston, 26 May 1991), where Jeanne Perrault's research and writing on 'body/pain' made productive dialogue possible.

1 A survivor of mother-daughter incest describes the trauma of disclosure. Anne Sexton, herself probably a father-daughter incest survivor, is accused by her daughter Linda of incest in *Anne Sexton: A Biography*.
2 Russell's definition of incestuous abuse is 'any kind of exploitative sexual contact or attempted contact that occurred between relatives, no matter how distant the relationship, before the victim turned eighteen years old. Experiences involving sexual contact with a relative that were wanted and with a peer were regarded as nonexploitative and hence nonabusive' (*The Secret Trauma* 41). Ian Hacking describes the philosophical framework of Russell's research and results as 'consciousness-raising,' a framework of empowerment through knowing that informs my study. Hacking explores the philosophical implications of the contemporary discourse on child sexual abuse, raising important questions that need to be developed in

further readings of incest narratives. He asks: 'What happens to the person who now comes to see herself as having been sexually abused? I am not now referring to the person who has merely kept an awful private secret, who now may feel liberated by being able to talk about it, or oppressed by having it brought to surface consciousness again. I am referring to placing oneself in a new world, a world in which one was formed in ways one had not known. Consciousness is not raised but changed' ('World-Making' 26). I am grateful to Ian Hacking for permission to quote from this unpublished paper. See also his 'The Making and Molding of Child Abuse.'

3 Russell suggests that 'father-daughter incest [is] the most traumatic form of incestuous abuse' because her research shows:
1. Fathers were more likely to have imposed vaginal intercourse on their daughters than the other incest perpetrators ...
2. Fathers sexually abused their daughters more frequently than other incestuous relatives and for a longer duration ...
3. Fathers were more likely than other relatives to use physical force (even though the use of force by incest perpetrators is extremely low) ...
4. The vast majority of fathers were also the victim's provider ...
5. Most of the fathers were at least twenty years older than their victims' (*The Secret Trauma* 231–2).

4 Risks in speaking out include negotiating the media. In a personal interview with me, Hryniuck described an interview with Winnipeg CBC Radio that was never aired. The three female producers wanted the interview broadcast as it had been taped. However, the male executive producer insisted that Hryniuk respond to an additional set of questions that would have forced her to represent the actual act of violation, a disclosure that Hryniuck's own written account critiques: 'They – only the men – ask point blank – only the men – was it sexual intercourse? That being the ultimate in sexual abuse. What's the difference between a finger, a broomhandle, and a penis? Why, in their minds, is intercourse the only legitimate form of sexual abuse? Finger. Broomhandle. Penis' (42).

5 Oughton also published Hryniuk's *walking inside circles* as another of the four chapbooks by West Word alumni.

6 Critic Mark Czarnecki also regrets the tone of the work, which 'tends to moralize the hard-won success of her present life' ('Ghosts of Evening Rendezvous' 61).

7 Feminist psychologist Rosa Spricer outlined these symptoms during a panel on 'Child Sexual Abuse' at the Women's Research Centre's Second Annual Feminist Forum, sponsored by Athabasca University and the University of Alberta, Edmonton, October 1989.

8 The 'gothic mother' is a central character in Daphne Marlatt's novel
  Ana Historic.
9 For critical readings of *Don't* in relation to this mythology, see Shirley Hartwell, 'Words Speaking Body Memory.'
10 See my 'Lucrece' in *Tell Tale Signs.* Winnipeg: Turnstone P 1991.

WORKS CITED

Allen, Charlotte Vale. *Daddy's Girl: A Very Personal Memoir.* Toronto:
  McClelland and Stewart 1980
Armstrong, Louise. *Kiss Daddy Goodnight: Ten Years Later.* New York:
  Penguin 1987
Czarnecki, Mark. 'Ghosts of Evening Rendezvous with Dad.' *Maclean's*
  3 Nov. 1980, 60–1
Danica, Elly. *Don't: A Woman's Word.* Charlottetown: Gynergy Books
  1988
Felski, Rita. *Beyond Feminist Aesthetics: Feminist Literature and Social
  Change.* Cambridge: Harvard UP 1989
Fraser, Sylvia. *My Father's House: A Memoir of Incest and Healing.*
  Toronto: Collins 1988
Froula, Christine. 'The Daughter's Seduction: Sexual Violence and Lit-
  erary History.' *Signs* 11.4 (1986): 621–43
Gzowski, Peter. 'Elly.' Interview with Elly Danica. *The Latest Morning-
  side Papers,* 116–30. Toronto: McClelland and Stewart 1989
Hacking, Ian. 'The Making and Molding of Child Abuse.' *Critical In-
  quiry* (1990–1): 253–88
– 'World-Making by Kind-Making: Child Abuse for Example.' Forth-
  coming in *How Classification Works.* Edinburgh: Edinburgh UP 1992
Haskell, Lori. 'Research on the Effects of Child Sexual Abuse: A Femin-
  ist Critique.' Critical Perspective Paper 4. Toronto: OISE Centre for
  Women's Studies in Education, n.d.
Hartwell, Shirley. 'Words Speaking Body Memory: After Reading:
  Don't: A Woman's Word. *Trivia* 13 (1988): 48–56
Herman, Judith. *Father/Daughter Incest.* Cambridge: Harvard UP 1981
Hryniuk, Angela. Personal interview. Winnipeg, November 1990
– *walking inside circles.* Charlottetown: Gynergy Books 1989
Irigaray, Luce. *Speculum of the Other Woman.* Trans. Gillian C. Gill.
  Ithaca: Cornell UP 1985
Johnston, Jill. 'Divided against Her Father.' *New York Times Book Re-
  view* 94 (21 May 1989): 50
MacKay, Barbara. 'Daddy's Girl.' *Books in Canada* 16.10: 3
Marlatt, Daphne. *Ana Historic.* Toronto: Coach House P 1988
Meigs, Mary. 'Memories of Age.' *Trivia* 13 (Fall 1988): 57–65

Middlebrook, Diane Wood. *Anne Sexton: A Biography.* Boston: Houghton Mifflin 1991
Modleski, Tanya. *Loving with a Vengeance: Mass-produced Fantasies for Women.* New York: Methuen 1982
Morris, Meaghan. *The Pirate's Fiancée: Feminism Reading Postmodernism.* London: Verso 1988
Rose, Jacqueline. 'Julia Kristeva: Take Two.' *Coming to Terms: Feminism, Theory, Politics.* Ed. Elizabeth Weed. London: Routledge 1989
Russell, Diane E.H. 'The Incidence and Prevalence of Intrafamilial and Extrafamilial Sexual Abuse of Female Children.' *Child Abuse and Neglect: The International Journal* 7 (1983): 133–46
– *The Secret Trauma: Incest in the Lives of Girls and Women.* New York: Basic Books 1986
Scarry, Elaine. *The Body in Pain: The Making and Unmaking of Language.* New York: Oxford UP 1985
– 'Introduction.' *Literature and the Body: Essays on Populations and Persons.* Baltimore: Johns Hopkins UP 1988
Underwood, Nora. 'The Abuse of Children.' *Maclean's* 27 Nov. 1989, 56–9
Wachtel, Eleanor. 'The Secret Is Out.' *Books in Canada* 10.1 (1981): 14
Wiebe, Armin. Public reading. Winnipeg, 2 Nov. 1989
Williamson, Janice. 'an enormous risk. but it's got to be done.' A conversation with Elly Danica, November 1989. In *Sounding Differences: Conversations with Seventeen Canadian Women Writers.* Toronto: U of Toronto P, forthcoming
– 'once I remembered, ... all the rest of it was there.' A conversation with Elly Danica, January 1990. In *Sounding Differences*
Wolkstein, Diane. 'Introduction.' In *Inanna: Queen of Heaven and Earth: Her Stories and Hymns from Sumer,* xv–xix. Ed. D. Wolkstein and S.N. Kramer. New York: Harper & Row 1983
Young, Katherine. 'Disembodiment: The Phenomenology of the Body in Medical Examinations.' *Semiotica* 73.1/2 (1989): 43–66

Whose Life Is It Anyway?
Out of the Bathtub
and into the Narrative

MARLENE KADAR

Life writing is the broad term used by Evelyn Hinz and Donald Winslow to refer to a genre of documents or fragments of documents written out of a life, or unabashedly out of a personal experience of the writer. In my view, life writing includes many kinds of texts, both fictional and non-fictional, though we tend to focus on the latter because they appear more 'true to life.' The texts that comprise life writing, and that are obviously life stories, are better named life-narratives, and as such fulfil Aristotle's minimum criteria for a whole story with a certain unity – a beginning, a middle, and an end (634–5). Put another way, a narrative is something that survives paraphrase or translation (Rimmon-Kenan 8), and in spite of Cleanth Brooks's 1947 notion that it is 'heresy' to paraphrase, life-narratives are paraphraseable.

But life writing includes more than just life stories, and it has the potential to cross genre boundaries and disciplines. The narratives within life writing are linked by their common thematic concern with a life, or the self, but in recent years they have come to share a more complex feature: a philosophical and linguistic imperative that comes first (and about which we will say more as we go), and then a sincere, probing disregard for genre and its rules, which has the effect of blending genres, creating new genres, and derailing the once-respected 'objective' speaker or narrator. The result has been that life writing is the playground for new relationships both within and without the text, and most important, it is the site of new language and new grammars, sometimes blended non-white languages, including Native-Canadian and African-American styles and dialects. It is the site of the other, and this other is 'autobiographical' in one sense, and not at all in another. Autobiography proper requires too much unity of the narrative, and too much 'objective' or reasoned thinking, too much author/ity of the author to be as irreverent as life writing can be.

Although we do not have a poetics of life writing, Jacques Derrida, Jane Gallop, and Shoshana Felman make their contribution to a theorizing of life writing when they celebrate the similarities between all types of narrative – official and unofficial, literary, historical, philosophical, and psychoanalytic. Virginia Woolf had a sense that autobiographical truth was in flux when she wrote in *A Room of One's Own* in 1929 that 'the impulse towards autobiography may be spent' (76). But a few pages later, as she walks through the streets of London, she becomes overwhelmed by what must be 'the accumulation of unrecorded life, whether from the women at the street corners with their arms akimbo ... talking with a gesticulation like the swing of Shakespeare's words' or from 'drifting girls whose faces, like waves in sun and cloud, signal the coming of men and women' (85). I say this realizing that Domna Stanton wants to create a case for what she calls autogynography and thereby insist that Woolf was wrong about autobiography (Stanton 3). But it may be that Woolf anticipated a new genre into which autobiography as she knew it was subsumed. There are merits to holding on to the old word and creating a case for 'women's autobiography' (as Sidonie Smith does), but is also incumbent upon us to try and theorize a new genre that goes beyond and yet includes the old word, the old gender, and the old style. We must name what is now.

However, this isn't so easy with genres. Like water, genres assume the shape of the vessel that contains them. Also like water, genres tend to exhibit certain properties. But if you empty the containing vessels, the better to see what's inside, you are bound to be tricked. Like water, the shape of genres does not really exist, and their essence can never really be captured. The central metaphors in metafictional novels exhibit this feature in the very nature of the narrative that, while being written, is also called into question. I am persuaded that Gail Scott's heroine in the novel of the same name must create the story from her vantage point in the bathtub because she has no confidence in the narrator's assigned place within the narrative (as if it were something apart from the bathtub point of view). Scott also tells us in *Spaces Like Stairs* that women's consciousness is quite likely *incontournable*, or *unskirtable* (quite gloriously unladylike) (117).

When it comes to the genre that claims to unite the life and the writing – and is not exclusively postmodernist (although the term life writing would not exist were postmodernism not the lens through which we look) – the New Critical wolf is always at the door, wondering, quite naturally, about all the exceptions. But, what about this or that story, or this or that convention? For which reason, I would suggest, the bilingual heroine of *Heroine* (1987) stays in the bathtub for 167 pages of the 183-page novel. When the narrative radically changes key and becomes a fever dream in italics (on page 167), the heroine, sometimes now called 'Gail,' decides to end her ablutions. Until now she has been able to put together the story because the door to the bathroom has been slightly ajar, she can see things in other rooms, and her memory has been stimulated by the water. But she cannot reasonably be contained by the womb of the tub if the story is going to come to an end. And, anyway, it is not she who needs cleansing now. It is Jon, the protagonist of the fever dream and her trendy Marxist lover.

Jon has numerous other lovers (he believes in – as Gail thinks she should for a time – non-monogamous relationships). In the dream he and another lover have turned into shiny fish standing upright on their fins in a fish tank. Scott, the author, then writes: 'Shhh, if the heroine keeps up like this she'll be sorry. I'll work better out of the tub. I'll have more distance' (167). It is distance that, ironically and metafictionally, she does not have and cannot have if she is truly interested in writing in her life. The question the narrator(s) has (have) in *Heroine* is: For what reason would I feign distance anyway? As Sylvia Plath's narrator says in *The Bell Jar* twenty-four years earlier, 'I never feel so much myself as when I'm in a hot bath' (21). There it is: the narrators feel their selves when they are in the tub. Put another way, they don't do as they think they are supposed to do. 'Gail' then gets dressed to go out to a cafe, but ruminates: 'Still, I don't know if a real heroine would do what she feels like doing next [i.e., get out of the tub and go out into the narrative]' (168). In the metafictional key, life writing elevates and complicates the once-presumed simple autobiographical impulse.

Under the influence of hermeneutics, reader-response theory, feminism, and psychoanalysis, the values of readers and critics have changed, and the ethos of the postmodern writer, and reader, has required a dense kind of autorepresentation. Even the theorist finds this expansiveness irresistible. Linda Hutcheon's preface to the paperback edition of *Narcissistic Narrative* writes her life into a rigorous (and 'ever developing') poetics 'of what we seem determined to call postmodernism' (x–xi). Although Hutcheon's preface is not autobiographical in the narrow sense, it does not mask her presence in a text that is otherwise 'theoretical,' otherwise 'objective.' I realize this is partly the mandate of the preface. But I would like to suggest for the moment that the *autos* (the I, the self) has been removed, theoretically speaking, from the conventional autobiography and spread more evenly and in greater variety in life writing of all sorts, including intricate, percipient contemporary poetics.

This gradual reworking of the idea of the self in writing signifies a rejection of an earlier imperative to mask the self, or pretend one has lost it in a third-person narrative. The distinction between objective and subjective truth, or between 'real' fiction and its assumed opposite, non-fiction, creates philosophical assumptions that decide what kind of literature is valid, and according to these assumptions autobiographical narratives, conventional or otherwise, are often omitted. It is possible, as Nicole Brossard says, that 'in reality, there is no fiction' (*Lovhers* 15; Blanchot 94). And, as the zen teachings would have it, in spite of unhelpful assumptions about a worthy self or soul, 'one never loses one's true Self even amidst the errors and delusions, or rather illusions, and also ... one does not gain it at the time of enlightenment, since it was always there' (Wood 93). So, the life and the writing are constants, no matter what we say about them or try to do to them. And if the *autos* is spread out, the style is irrevocably changed.

Let's go back to Gail again. In the two remaining chapters of the novel, the heroine is not in the bathtub. The first of these, 'Jealousy, A Fish Story,' is one of those tall tales that has been reduced to a series of italicized diary entries, and the heroine is absent from the narrative. We see that the middle entry, March 8 – which we know is International Women's Day – finds Gail flirting with an anglophone student 'doing a doctorate in a branch of semiotics.' The two are comparing French and English modernism when the metafictional crisis – which is also linguistic and philosophical – hits. Gail 'suddenly ... can't remember how to get to the end of a sentence ... "Each time I start, it's as if the memory

of the past (the noun, the sentence's beginning) wipes out the
present (verb). So I can no longer move forward in the words"'
(175). Her psychiatrist interprets the dream for her, again in italics:
'Gail, the problem is you've lost your boundaries [bathtub?] ...
caught as you are between wanting [writing?] to be your own self
AND the object [heroine] of his affection.' The irony is that 'being
caught' is Gail's present state; it is the verb that allows the story
to be told, to advance the narrative into the final chapter (which
is not a fish story), 'Play it Again, S,' where there are no italics
and no diary entries. Gail meditates on the nature of fiction, while
eating. 'She thinks that in the 80s a story must be all smooth and
shiny. For this pretends to be the decade of appearances ... Yet I
feel this terrible violence in me. In any story, it will break the
smoothness of the surface' (182).

It is no surprise that the novel ends with an unfinished sentence,
the feminine pronoun – 'She–.' You will remember that Gail names
the linguistic fissure above by declaring that the noun is the sign
that a memory of the past wipes out 'the present (verb).' This, too,
is how the life of a generation of feminist writers in Quebec is
remembered. This is writing in the feminine, *l'écriture au féminin*,
the culmination of the autobiographical impulse in a new feminist,
psychoanalytic, and even Platonic key. It may be necessary to distinguish two phases of life writing, the one akin in spirit to autobiographical impulse in a new feminist, psychoanalytic, and even
Platonic key. It may be necessary to distinguish two phases of life
writing, the one akin in spirit to autobiography and written by
men and some women, both white and black, roughly before Virginia Woolf; and the one written after Woolf wrote: 'As a woman,
I have no country. As a woman I want no country. As a woman
my country is the whole world' (*Three Guineas* 125). Thus, life
writing is propelled by a recent theoretical questioning of two
assumptions: (1) the idea of literary appropriateness (i.e., all texts
are not really texts?; or some texts [can be read in the family room]
but should not be taken out of the house), and (2) the philosophical
merits of what I will call, for lack of a better term, subjective
thinking (i.e., the more distance between the author and her subject or reader, the higher the quality of the text or its truth).

So you may ask, well, why bother with yet another new genre,
especially when feminists are challenging the notion of genre itself? To which the answer is another question: Well, whose life is
it anyway? And do I have access to it through any other genre, any

other writing? The answer is no, because first of all a tradition of writing already exits that is not just autobiography or confession or journal writing, and in which all life-naratives share something. And secondly, a needy readership, some would say a contemporary readership, has willed life writing into being because of its own generic and generic desires.

Women have found it easier to write in their lives because they have not always written, or spoken, in a language or style that suited the judges of good taste. Think, for example, how legitimate would be St Augustine's *Confessions*, and yet how absent from our reading experience the medieval female confessional *The Book of Margery Kempe* of 1432. When metaphors in the feminine have not been understood – take Margery Kempe's relationship to the body of Christ as an example – they have been dismissed as part of a narrative that is obviously hysterical, or just 'fiction,' or they have appeared to be just too 'personal,' perhaps 'emotional.' These misreadings reflect then a great loss for us, an unwanted and unwarranted ignorance of our fullest culture, and an unnecessary censoring of our reading experience and, hence, our ability to fantasize and understand our misapprehensions, our errors, what we envision as the unacceptable (Heilbrun 44). How else can we explain the rebirth and refashioning of the epistolary or diarized novel, especially among women of colour (Joy Kogawa's *Obasan*, Alice Walker's *The Color Purple*) and by francophone women in Quebec (Nicole Brossard's *La lettre aérienne* or Lise Gauvin's *Lettres d'une autre*)? In the western European tradition the epistolary novel is truly rooted in the New Testament epistles, letters delivered to the people, the disciples, the poor, and others on the margins who are eager to belong to the group mirrored by the letter writer and his or her vernacular, his or her resistance to purifying genre.

It is revealing to consider that life-narratives may emerge more directly out of the tradition established in the Socratic dialogues where the concept of the self is not one-dimensional. In this context it is also interesting to consider Parmenides' metaphoric *Fragments* (c. 504 BC) as life writing, in which the narrator speaks in the first person, and then listens to 'the Goddess,' who addresses him in direct quotations. Not unlike Nicole Brossard or Hélène Cixous, or Mieke Bal in theme, he too articulates the bodily nature of the mind: 'thinking consists in composition of bodily parts. For it is an excess in the body that constitutes thought' (Wheelwright

100). In *Technologies of the Self*, Michel Foucault documents the three Stoic techniques of self-knowing using Plato's unfinished dialogue, *Alcibiades I*. At its pinnacle the Platonist's self-knowing slips into self-care (Foucault 26–6; *Alcibiades* 480–92). Foucault names the following: the disclosure of self through constant writing activity, including letters to friends (27, 30); the examination of self and conscience in a 'notebook,' what we might call journals, which would reactivate 'the truths one needed' (27); and, on a different level, *askesis*, a remembering of the secret self. Foucault explains that the 'move to attain the renunciation of the self distinguishes Christian asceticism,' but *askesis* 'means not renunciation but the progressive consideration of self' (35). It intends to prepare the self so that it can access the reality of this world, not of another (35). The goal of the Stoic, it would appear, even though he is not female, is to engage in the process of becoming more subjective in order to subjectivize truth (35). Surely, then, contemporary life writing may well celebrate such a thing, a kind of new-age peripety, a reversal of fortune for the subject in which the 'I' (self-unity) has been unsettled (Benstock 21). Shari Benstock attributes this not to Stoicism, but to the feminist challenge of the 'modernist aesthetic of "impersonality"' (21).

Life writing culminates for me in its combination of feminism and narrative, fictional or non-fictional, in what has come to be known as *l'écriture au féminin*. *L'écriture au féminin* is represented by two traditions of feminists: the French and the Québécoise, following Hélène Cixous and Nicole Brossard and others, and the more empirical Anglo-American, following in the footsteps of Virginia Woolf. There is a will in both traditions to stay away from the pure term 'autobiographical,' because it does not tell the whole truth about either life writing or *l'écriture au féminin*, but also because the adjective has been used to dismiss women's text from the valued canon. Shari Benstock unknowingly makes another case for life writing when she authorizes 'the fissures in female discontinuity' as separating female autobiographies from male. One of the major features of *l'écriture au féminin* is 'fissure' – Gail Scott's climbing 'spaces' in her book of literary essays, *Spaces like Stairs*.

This writing in the feminine IS life writing (that is, Moll Flanders herself really did write it; she is not just a narrative device), and Catherine Clément and Hélène Cixous characterize it in *The Newly Born Woman* by its *jouissance*, a word that has simultaneously sexual, political, and economic overtones: total access, total participation, and total ecstacy, all at the same time. *Jouissance* is produced by writing that ultimately 'undermines notions of representation and truth which hold that there is some original presence, some source of truth that can be restored to the text' (Cixous and Clément 165–6).

So, in trying to answer whose life is it anyway, let me enumerate the features of life writing as I see it now, a genre that one would wish were mere not a private club, and that may have evolved in two distinct phases. *deep* —

1 Life writing comprises texts that present a simple or complex narrative, a narrative exhibiting some features of narrativity, some of which may indeed be deferred, fragmentary, or disunifying (Bal 20–1).

2 These life-writing narratives may be otherwise viewed as having Aristotle's beginning, middle, and end, even though we realize that 'the convention of unity ... is seductive because of its potential to keep the disturbing uncertainty of the subject buried' (Bal 21), or *incontournable* (117).

3 The *incontournable* allows us to read life writing as a process of becoming more self-conscious.

4 Sometimes the most self-conscious of life-writing narratives use and fragment the conventions of a text into what Patricia Meyer Spacks has called 'intimate dyadic exchanges' (65–91) – epistolary novels, personal letters, and even gossip.

5 It is probable that the highest goal of intimate dyadic exchanges in particular is a philosophical notion of self-knowing that, as Foucault explains, is linked to a related notion of self-care (Plato's Alcibiades, explains Foucault [22–39], cares for his self in order to know his soul).

6 Thus, in all the life-writing genres the life and the writing identify to their mutual benefit.

7 This identification is enhanced by a distance between the author and the reader that has been minimized either intentionally, as in metafiction, or by virtue of the nature of a particular narrative voice such as what we have named facetiously here the 'bathtub-point-of-view,' or the ('ordinary') point of view of the letter-writer.

oh? where, here? Marlene Kadar

8 Life writing is, none the less, sometimes appointed as high literature, sometimes not.

9 Most often in this century life writing is exploited by women writers (who are caring for women's *bios* ['life, way of living'], women's *aute* [authority and originality], women's *graphia* [signs] or hermeneutics) (Sidonie Smith 7).

10 Although life writing is not exclusively the property of women writers, it is always accessible to them, and then, to all readers, and their *jouissance*. please!

WORKS CITED

Aristotle. *Poetics* in *Introduction to Aristotle*, 624–67. Ed. and Trans. Richard McKeon. New York: Modern Library 1947

Bal, Mieke. *Lethal Love: Feminist Literary Readings of Biblical Love Stories*. Bloomington: Indiana UP 1987

Benstock, Shari. 'Authorizing the Autobiographical.' In *The Private Self: Theory and Practice of Women's Autobiographical Writings*. Ed. Shari Benstock. Chapel Hill: U of North Carolina P 1988

Blanchot, Maurice. 'Michel Foucault as I Imagine Him.' In *Foucault/ Blanchot*. Trans. Jeffrey Mehlman and Brian Massumi. New York: Zone 1987

Brooks, Cleanth. *The Well Wrought Urn*. New York: Harcourt, Brace and World 1947

Brossard, Nicole. *La lettre aérienne*. Montreal: Remue-ménage 1985
– *Lovhers.* 1980. Trans. Barbara Godard. Montreal: Guernica 1986

Cixous, Hélène. 'The Laugh of the Medusa.' Trans. Keith Cohen and Paula Cohen. *Signs* (Summer 1976): 875–93

Cixous, Hélène, and Catherine Clément. *The Newly Born Woman*. Trans. Betsy Wing. Theory and History of Literature 24. Minneapolis: U of Minnesota P 1986

Derrida, Jacques. *Positions*. Trans. and annotated by Alan Bass. Chicago: U of Chicago P 1981

Felman, Shoshana. *Le scandale du corps parlant*. Paris: Editions du Seuil 1980

Foucault, Michel. *Technologies of the Self: A Seminar with Michel Foucault*. Ed. Luther H. Martin et al. Amherst: U of Massachusetts P 1988

Gallop, Jane. *Reading Lacan*. Cornell UP 1985

Gauvin, Lise. *Lettres d'une autre*. Montreal: Hexagone 1984

Heilbrun, Carolyn. *Writing a Woman's Life*. New York: W.W. Norton 1988

Hoffmann, Leonore, and Margo Culley. *Women's Personal Narratives: Essays in Criticism and Pedagogy*. New York: MLA 1985

Hutcheon, Linda. *Narcissistic Narratives: The Metafictional Paradox*. 1980. New York and London: Methuen 1984

Kogawa, Joy. *Obasan*. Toronto: Lester and Orpen Dennys 1981

Mukherjee, Arun. *Towards an Aesthetic of Opposition*. Stratford, Ont.: Williams-Wallace 1988

Plath, Sylvia. *The Bell Jar*. 1963. London and Boston: Faber and Faber 1966

Plato. *First Alcibiades*. In *The Dialogues of Plato*, vol. 2. Trans. B. Jowett. Oxford: Clarendon 1935

Rimmon-Kenan, Shlomith. *Narrative Fiction: Contemporary Poetics*. New Accents. London and New York: Methuen 1983

Scott, Gail. *Heroine*. Toronto: Coach House 1987

– *Spaces like Stairs*. Toronto: Women's Press 1989

Simon, Paul. *Discerning the Subject*. Theory and History of Literature 55. Minneapolis: U of Minnesota P 1988

Smith, Sidonie. *A Poetics of Women's Autobiography: Marginality and the Fictions of Self-Representation*. Bloomington: Indiana UP 1987

Spacks, Patricia Meyer. *Gossip*. Chicago: U of Chicago P 1985

Stanton, Domna, ed. *The Female Autograph: Theory and Practice of Autobiography from the Tenth to the Twentieth Century*. Chicago: U of Chicago P 1987

Walker, Alice. *The Color Purple*. New York: Harcourt Brace Jovanovitch 1976; London: Women's Press 1982

Wheelwright, Philip. *The Presocratics*. New York: Odyssey 1966

Winslow, Donald J. *Life-Writing: A Glossary of Terms in Biography, Autobiography, and Related Forms*. A Biography Monograph. Honolulu: U of Hawaii P 1980

Wood, Ernest. *Zen Dictionary*. 1957. Harmondsworth: Penguin 1977

Woolf, Virginia. *A Room of One's Own*. 1929. London: Grafton 1977

– *Three Guineas*. 1938. Harmondsworth: Penguin 1977

◄҂ 10 ҂►
Reading Reflections:
The Autobiographical Illusion
in *Cat's Eye*

NATHALIE COOKE

I have been told by friends, relatives, colleagues, and teachers – in fact, by everyone I know who has read it – that Margaret Atwood's *Cat's Eye* is 'more autobiographical than her other books.' And, of course, they are right. It *is* more autobiographical – or, anyway, it is more obviously about self-representation[1] – than her other books. But it is autobiographical in the same way that *Lady Oracle* is gothic: it speaks to the form as much as it speaks from or within it.

The fascinating part about all this is that those experienced readers who would be embarrassed to classify *Lady Oracle* as just another costume gothic, or *Surfacing* as a simple unironic quest narrative, are the very same readers who seem to dismiss this novel by describing it as 'autobiographical.' They have been fooled by Atwood – yes – but also by the literary conventions she is exploring in this novel, those of autobiography itself. Most important, they have been fooled into looking at the autobiographical illusion that Atwood creates, and into overlooking the deft sleight of hand involved in its creation.

My argument is that autobiography is not so much a generic caterogy as it is a literary strategy. Atwood's readers must do more than classify *Cat's Eye* in terms of autobiography; they must focus their attention on the way autobiography is used in the novel. Accordingly, the emphasis of my discussion of the autobiographical elements in *Cat's Eye* lies more on Atwood's artistry than on the links between Atwood's life and her art.

I am choosing my terms carefully because as critics have come to question their confidence in the 'referentiality of language' and the 'authenticity of the self' [2] they have become increasingly uncomfortable about classifying autobiography at all, particularly about differentiating between autobiography, on the one hand, and fictional autobiography, on the other. After all, the project of categorizing various kinds of autobiographical writing places limits on a form that seeks to challenge limits – those between expression and experience, in particular. Northrop Frye, for example, traces autobiography back to 'a creative, and therefore fictional' impulse (307). And Paul Jay argues that 'the attempt to differentiate between autobiography and fictional autobiography is finally pointless. For if by "fictional" we mean "made up," "created," or "imagined" – something, that is, which is literary and not "real" – then we have merely defined the ontological status of any text, autobiographical or not' (16). However, by conflating forms of autobiography and fiction, Jay ignores the invitation that autobiographical fiction sends to its readers, to be read as *both* fiction and nonfiction – at the same time.[3] Readers of autobiographical fiction, that is, are asked to read with a kind of double vision. I am by no means suggesting that such writing is any less fictional than fiction itself, just that we are invited to believe it might be. Herein, to my mind, lies all the difference.

What reason do we have to identify autobiographical elements as distinguised from fictional ones? I think we suspect that autobiography *reads* differently from fiction. Before we open the cover, for example, we find ourselves wanting to know whether a book is fiction or non-fiction. To be sure, when we say that a work is autobiographical we suggest that it has a claim to truth.[4] This is why, as Alice Munro attests, those who classify a work as autobiographical go on to comment on its validity, and its author's 'good faith' or 'honesty' (223). In spite of ourselves, then, we readers check to see what shelf a book is on in the library; we read the dust jacket; we watch for markers within the text.

When we do these things with *Cat's Eye* we find quite a bit of evidence to suggest that it *is* autobiographical. Briefly, it is a first-person narratives about an artist who sanctions autobiographical readings of her own work. Then there is Margaret Atwood's dust-jacket biography that bears striking resemblances to the events of Elaine's narrative: the entomologist father, the brother, the summers in the countryside, the Toronto childhood, to name only a few things. Further, some of the episodes in Elaine's life cannot help but remind us of episodes in the lives of her fictional sisters. Take that Toronto ravine, for instance. It haunts Joan of *Lady Oracle* just as it haunts Elaine. And, by now, it has made a deep and lasting impression on all of Atwood's readers.

Ironically, too, Atwood's disclaimer only makes us focus our attention on the autobiographical elements within the novel. 'This is a work of fiction,' she tells us. 'Although its form is that of an autobiography, it is not one.' But we all know enough not to take Atwood's comments at face value, so we pursue the issue. In what way does *Cat's Eye* have the form of an autobiography? In what way is it fiction? Can we not assume that the incidents in *Cat's Eye*, as well as the first-person narrator, are grounded in Atwood's own life? I think we can; but how does that help us?

One answer is that *Cat's Eye* is both fiction *and* autobiography: a 'fictive autobiography,' to coin my own term, an autobiography composed by a fictional protagonist, which draws attention to its own problematical status as a fictive construct. As a result, we expect more from this book, and from Atwood herself: entertainment *and* honesty, craft *and* good faith. But that does not solve the problem. It is not enought for me to classify this *as* a fictive autobiography (as I have), as autobiography, as fiction, or, as Douglas Glover writes in his review (for *Books in Canada*), Atwood playing 'hide-and-seek at the place where autobiography and fiction meet, always ensuring there is a back door open for quick escapes' (11). More important than our trying to define *Cat's Eye* in relation to those two terms, fiction and autobiography, is our exploring the implications of Atwood's challenging us to try.

That is, Atwood is deliberately using the autobiographical form in her fiction. But why? I can think of at least three reasons for this: there are probably many more.

1 To Challenge the Reader

First, Atwood has always forced us to explore our assumptions as readers. When she writes, 'You fit into me / like a hook into an eye,' we are certain we understand the kind of relationship she is talking about: the solid, comfortable, close male-female kind. But then she makes us take another look. 'A fish hook,' she writes. 'An open eye' ('Epigraph,' *Power Politics*). What she is doing in *Cat's Eye* is an expanded version of this kind of pulling-the-rug-out-from-under-us. By now, in this post-Saussurean, post-postmodern literary era, we probably think that we can no longer be taken in by anything that has the ontological status of a literary text. However sophisticated we are as readers, though, we can all still be caught on the autobiographical hook. We think of ourselves as 'sophisticated readers,' after all, precisely because we enjoy reading; it satisfies an insatiable curiosity, a desire to solve questions, to find things out. And autobiographical fiction offers the lure of a particular individual's answers (in good faith) to the questions that concern him or her.

Further, when the writer is a woman, the temptation to ignore the distance between the text and the events represented in it seems to be even greater. Women have long been credited with the dubious honour of best being able to understand and communicate their emotions and personal experience (Domna Stanton 8–9). Mary Jacobus calls this the 'autobiographical "phallacy,"' – with a "ph" – 'whereby male critics hold that women's writing is somehow closer to experience than men's, that the female text *is* the author, or at any rate a dramatic extension of her unconsciousness' (520). But it is not only male critics who give credence to the 'autobiographical "phallacy"'; so too do feminists. Sylvia Plath proudly proclaims that women have long been associated with the 'blood-hot and personal' (Gilbert and Gubar 24). And as Molly Hite quite rightly notes, 'many of the Anglo-American feminist critics who began with the intent of doing justice to women's fiction as a chronicle of female experience seem to have found themselves in the process purveying an exaggerated theory of mimesis in which authors are simply mirrored in their own texts' (11–12).

In fine, when we read *Cat's Eye* we are drawn by the prospect of the author within the text, of finding out about Atwood, or perhaps by having those stories we have heard about her confirmed, by her. It is not that this book is any less fictional than her others, but rather that the autobiographical elements in it suggest that it might be.

Atwood knows this. She has recognized that autobiographical fiction, by its very definition, forces its readers to do a kind of double-take – the same kind of double-take she has always demanded for her readers. At first glance, that is, generic classification seems to be a central issue. On closer inspection, however, it becomes apparent that this is no more than a red herring. When we read *Cat's Eye*, we are forced to redirect our attention from

Atwood's presence or absence in this seemingly autobiographical text to ourselves and, in particular, to our assumptions about autobiographical fiction itself. This is indeed a book about self-reflection; and the reader's role is to reflect upon the various reflections of the self contained within it.

2 To Challenge Narrative Closure

Another reason why Atwood uses the autobiographical in her fiction is that it provides one alternative to the narrative closure that seems to make her so uncomfortable. Cause of much critical anxiety, you will remember, was the absence of closure in Atwood's novel *Surfacing*. Hiding silently at the end of the novel, the still-unnamed protagonist is unable to move, let alone set about reintegrating herself into society. The conclusion of Atwood's next novel, *Lady Oracle*, is still more unstable. Not only do we find out that a stranger has probably recorded what we have so far taken to be Joan's first-hand account of her life, but we find that Joan is unable to impose closure on the book she herself is writing. If closure is anywhere to be found in this novel, it is in the opening lines, where Joan describes the death she has orchestrated for herself. As soon as we read further, though, we find that this ending, like all closure within the novel, has been exploded. Other endings are problematic as well: think of *The Handmaid's Tale* or *The Edible Woman*. Certainly, Atwood resists the two endings frequently reserved for a novel's heroine: marriage or death. This limited option, as Rachel Blau du Plessis has pointed out, is inadequate for any female writer. Instead, du Plessis argues, some women writers choose to 'write beyond'[5] the traditional endings they inherit as a way of illustrating their problematic nature. And Atwood, in particular, has consistently shown her discomfort with narrative conventions by 'unwriting' the novelistic forms she takes up – the quest in *Surfacing*, the gothic in *Lady Oracle*, to name just two examples.

Of course, that *Cat's Eye* is a fictive autobiography would seem to eliminate the problem of closure: since the future is unclear to the autobiographer as well as to his or her audience, the ending of any autobiographical work is often ambiguous. And *Cat's Eye* is no exception in that the ending points to the limited nature of human perception:

Now it's full night, clear, moonless and filled with stars,
which are not eternal as was once thought, which are not
where we think they are. If they were sounds, they would
be echoes, of something that happened millions of years
ago: a word made of numbers. Echoes of light, shining
out of the midst of nothing.
  It's old light, and there's not much of it. But it's
enough to see by. (421)

But the autobiographical elements in *Cat's Eye* serve to challenge
closure in a different way. As we recognize material from both
Surfacing and *Lady Oracle*, we realize that Atwood draws upon
and uses the autobiographical in these novels too. And surely, this
is a way of forcing us to look beyond the text – to the unwritten
world of Atwood's own experiences, perhaps, but certainly to other
texts.

3 To Challenge Classification

Finally, Atwood used the autobiographical as a tool in her ongoing
challenge of classification, literary and otherwise. In her earlier
novels, discomfort with rigid schemes of classification was voiced
by the novels' heroines. Joan Foster, for instance, fights against
the gothic as it begins to encroach upon her life and her art, seeing
herself as a kind of 'escape artist.' Offred, too, attempts to escape
from the prison-house that her society has created around biblical
words and phrases. And even such an early protagonist as the
Surfacer is uncomfortable with the restrictions society imposes
upon women. To be sure, by alterting us to the fact that women
in the Quebec countryside have no names, she emphasizes her –
and yes, Atwood's – discomfort with naming. Neither the Surfacer
nor the protagonist of *The Handmaid's Tale* have names (although
Connie Rooke argues very convincingly that she has discovered
Offred's 'real' name). Generally, though, Offred is called 'The
Handmaid' by the academics of the text and within it who piece
together her story. And, as they suggest, the name 'Offred' is itself
only a 'patronymic, composed of the possessive preposition and
the first name of the gentleman in question' (318).
  For an Atwood heroine, though, Elaine Risley seems curiously
resigned to the ways in which she and her art are classified. When

Charna, one of the capital 'f' feminists in the book, describes *The Three Muses* as 'her disconcerting deconstruction of perceived gender and its relationship to perceived power, especially in respect to numinous imagery,' Risley agrees – up to a point. 'If I hold my breath and squint,' she says, 'I can see where she gets that' (406). As readers, though, we cannot help seeing that Charna's description of the painting is inadequate. It is not wrong, exactly; it is just limited. Because we see the paintings through Elaine's eyes, we are able to see more in them than feminist concerns.

What is happening, then, is that the heroine no longer has to battle against the hegemony of rigid classification precisely because the reader does it for her. Whereas, we readers are now very comfortable suggesting that the parodic elements in novels such as *Surfacing, Lady Oracle*, and *The Handmaid's Tale* are motivated by Atwood's 'feminist' concerns, we are suddenly uncomfortable with the term. Somehow that vexed tag 'feminist' – which means something different to Charna, Jody, Carolyn, Zillah, and Elaine, to name just a few examples – is more problematic than descriptive. And yet it is still necessary: for *Cat's Eye* is a book about the thoughts and images that make up Elaine's reflections – feminist, humanist, and personal.

To be sure, reviewers have already shown that they are uncomfortable putting any labels to *Cat's Eye*.[6] Just as in the past they have been quick to categorize – and recategorize – Atwood's work, they are now hesitating. Even more surprising than this resistance to classification, however, are the grounds upon which that resistance is based: the sense that this is *more* than a feminist tract, *more* than a postmodern exploration of literary self-reflection, precisely, because it speaks from and about the autobiographical form.

In other words, Atwood is forcing us to rethink our position – again. Just as we had become comfortable with the idea that a biographical reading is a reductive one, Atwood shows us that it is quite the opposite. It is precisely the autobiographical aspect in and of *Cat's Eye* that makes us resist our temptation to master the text. We want to say that *Cat's Eye* is all of fiction and autobiography, feminist tract and personal meditation, contemporary metafiction and classical narrative precisely because it is *more* than these. But to say that would be to admit that Atwood has restored our faith in story and in the magic of literary illusion; and we are surely much too experienced as readers to say that.

NOTES

A version of this paper was presented at the section on 'Margaret Atwood's Evolving Dialectics' at the 1989 MLA meetings in Washington, DC.

1 It should be noted that the question of self-representation in *Cat's Eye* demands two discrete responses: one that concentrates on verbal self-representation and another that concentrates on visual self-representation. This paper falls into the former category.

2 Sidonie Smith argues that these two assumptions underlie the commentary about autobiography by such critics as William Spengemann and James Olney (*A Poetics of Women's Autobiography* 5).

3 Autobiography, in my mind, is distinguished from fiction by the presence of the autobiographer in the text, and the claims of referentiality that he or she makes. In this, I agree both with Paul John Eakin (*Fictions in Autobiography* 4), and with Bella Brodzki and Celeste Schenck (*Life/Lines* 12–13).

4 See George Gusdorf ('Conditions and Limits' 44) and Barrett Mandel ('Full of Life Now' 62).

5 I am grateful to Rachel Blau du Plessis for her illuminating discussion of women writers' revisionist projects.

6 See, in particular, the commentaries by Douglas Glover, Alice McDermott, and Camille Peri.

WORKS CITED

Atwood, Margaret. *Cat's Eye*. Toronto: McClelland and Stewart 1989
– *The Handmaid's Tale*. Toronto: McClelland and Stewart 1985
– *Power Politics*. Toronto: House of Anansi Press 1971
Brodzki, Bella, and Celeste Schenck, eds. *Life/Lines: Theorizing Women's Autobiography*. Ithaca: Cornell UP 1980
Du Plessis, Rachel. *Writing beyond the Ending*. Bloomington: Indiana UP 1985
Eakin, Paul John. *Fictions in Autobiography*. Princeton: Princeton UP 1985
Frye, Northrop. *Anatomy of Criticism*. New York: Atheneum 1969
Gilbert, Sandra, and Susan Gubar. *The Madwoman in the Attic*. New Haven: Yale UP 1979
Glover, Douglas. 'Her Life Entire.' *Books in Canada* 17.7 (October 1988): 11–14
Gusdorf, Georges. 'Conditions and Limits of Autobiography.' In *Autobiography: Essays Theoretical and Critical*, 28–48. Ed. James Olney, Princeton: Princeton UP 1980

Hite, Molly. 'The Other Side of the Story' (manuscript). Another version of this paper appears in *The Other Side of the Story: Structures and Strategies of Contemporary Feminist Narrative*. Ithaca: Cornell UP 1989

Jacobus, Mary. 'Review of *The Madwoman in the Attic*.' *Signs* 6.3 (1981)

Jay, Paul. *Being in the Text: Self-Representation from Wordsworth to Barthes*. Ithaca: Cornell UP 1984

McDermott, Alice. 'Book Review: What Little Girls Are Really Made Of.' *New York Times*, 5 Feb. 1989, 7–8

Mandel, Barrett. 'Full of Life Now.' In *Autobiography*, 49–72 (*see* Gusdorf)

Munro, Alice. 'What Is Real?' In *Making It New: Contemporary Canadian Stories*. Toronto: Methuen 1982

Peri, Camille. 'Witch Craft.' *Mother Jones* 14.3 (April 1989): 28–45

Rooke, Constance. *Fear of the Open Heart*. Toronto: Coach House Press 1989

Smith, Sidonie. *A Poetics of Women's Autobiography: Marginality and the Fictions of Self-Representation*. Bloomington: Indiana UP 1987

Stanton, Domna C. 'Autobiography: Is the Subject Different?' In *The Female Autograph: Theory and Practice of Autobiography from the Tenth to the Twentieth Century*, 3–20. Ed. Domna Stanton. New York: New York Literary Forum 1984

Dreaming a True Story:
The Disenchantment of the Hero
in *Don Quixote*, Part 2

ELLEN M. ANDERSON

In the last chapter of the novel bearing his name, the imaginative gentleman Don Quixote of La Mancha falls ill from a fever whose cause is identified by the village doctor as extreme melancholy. After hearing this diagnosis, the protagonist falls into a profound sleep, which both his niece and his housekeeper fear may presage his death. From it he awakens to announce his return to sanity by means of the grace of God:

> My judgment is now clear and free from the misty shadows of ignorance with which my ill-starred and continuous reading of those detestable books of chivalry had obscured it. Now I know their absurdities and their deceits, and the only thing that grieves me is that this discovery has come too late, and leaves me no time to make amends by reading other books, which might enlighten my soul ...

> I am Don Quixote de la Mancha no longer, but Alonso Quixano, called for my way of life the Good. Now I am the enemy of Amadis of Gaul and of all the infinite brood of his progeny. Now all profane histories of knight errantry are odious to me. I know my folly now, and the peril I have incurred from the reading of them. Now, by God's mercy, I have learnt from my own bitter experience and I abominate them. (2:74, 935, 936)[1]

It is notable that Don Quixote here repents less of his deeds while mad than of his readings while sane. For what determines both the manner of his derangement and the manner of his recovery is that he is first, foremost, and always a reader who in part 1 searches ceaselessly for signs in his adventures that will show him that he is indeed a chivalric hero (Foucault 118; Robert 60, 159–60). It is also significant that on his recovery he contrasts his readings of chivalric fiction with his experiences of chivalric life. This separation of reading and living at the end of part 2 reverses their relationship in part 1, for in the latter it is difficult to imagine a more complete identification of fictional text and 'real life.' If part 1 can be seen as the story of how Don Quixote's illusion of heroism is created by himself and sustained by others, part 2 can be seen as the story of how this illusion is gradually destroyed.[2] For in the book, experiences that seem to denote the truth of history are set inside frames that apparently suggest the deceit of fiction. This complex form of the novel's key episodes (dreamlike life-stories, characters bewitched to appear what they are rather than what they should be according to the paradigms of the chivalric romance) mirrors faithfully the process they depict: a fact seen through the lens of a fiction indirectly reveals the original fact transformed by its union with fiction. The union of objective and subjective reality partakes of an almost feminine thinking, 'different from the conventional modes of rhetoric based on inductive or deductive thinking and organization ... eidetic (presented through detailed and accurate visual images which reproduce a past impression), open-ended and generative' (Van Wart 52). It is important for the history and poetics of life writing that the flexibility Van Wart attributes to the writing of women's diaries, especially modern journals, is also to be found in the fictional writing of a male novelist of the seventeenth century, and it is in the hope of extending the boundaries of the genre that this article is offered.

Within the novel the episodes through which Don Quixote's release from illusion is accomplished are called by four names: history, story, dream, and enchantment. How these words are used to describe the progress of the hero's disillusionment and self-recovery through the meeting of objective and subjective reality is the subject of this article. I shall first demonstrate how they overlapped semantically in Cervantes's time by describing what each term then meant and how it was used in the Spanish romance of chivalry, the object of Don Quixote's adoration and Cervantes's literary satire. I shall then demonstrate their use as ambiguous designations of four scenes crucial to Don Quixote's changing sense of himself: first, his descent into the Cave of Montesinos (2:22); second, his defeat in Barcelona by the Knight of the White Moon (2:64); third, his decision to take up the pastoral life (2:67); and fourth, his discovery of a changed self on his deathbed. All of these episodes provide Don Quixote, the arch-reader, with role-models that he can 'read,' imitate, or reject as models for his subsequent actions, if he will. The rest of this study will demonstrate how these alternatives stories and histories, experienced by Don Quixote as also enchantment and dreams, invite him to enter them as a character – exactly as all narratives invite all readers to do. And this invitation to the readers to participate in the protagonist's work of recognizing and remembering the secret self by interpreting the author's deliberately ambiguous presentation of these episodes as both text and experience allows *Don Quixote* to be seen as one of the earliest and most complex examples of fictional life writing.

History and Story

The Spanish word *historia* meant in the sixteenth century, as now, both 'history' and 'story' (Wardropper 82; Riley 164; Eisenberg, 'Pseudo-Historicity' 119). The ambiguity makes it possible for the fictional narrator Cide Hamete Benengeli to refer to what he writes as a true story. In some contexts this means, in Aristotelian terms, 'history' (what did happen) and in others, 'fiction' (what might have happened, or what should have happened [Riley 164–5]).[3] Garci Rodríguez de Montalvo, in his introduction to Don Quixote's favourite chivalric romance, *Amadís de Gaula*, distinguished three kinds of *historia*, two of which are important for my purposes. The first is the true history, or chronicle, whose author must record the heroic exploits of princes and their vassals exactly as they happened (*Amadis of Gaul* 17–18). Cervantes ironically allows Cide Hamete to affirm this definition of history in his account of the appearance of the 'enchanted' Dulcinea: ''but finally he noted the deeds down, although with fear and misgivings, just as our knight performed them, without adding or subtracting one atom of truth from the history, or taking into account any accusations of lying that might be laid against him' (2:10, 524).

Montalvo's second category is the fictional story, whose author weaves a tapestry of heroic deeds accomplished by noblemen who never existed (*Amadis of Gaul* 19). With respect to the world of its readers, Cide Hamete's book is a fiction because its hero never existed. However, the term 'false history' is never applied within *Don Quixote* to Cide Hamete's book: it is reserved for the work of Alonso Fernández de Avellaneda, the author of the apocryphal continuation of Cervantes's book, published in 1614 (2:61, 867). For, although Avellaneda really existed in Cervantes's world, he wrote a story about a hero who, with respect to Cide Hamete's Don Quixote, is an impostor.

Confusion between the chivalric fictions and the chronicles of historic deeds could occur not only because the same word was used for both kinds of writing, but also because both genres were purportedly written for the same purposes: to provide an example for the princes and noblemen who read them to imitate (Fogelquist 17–18). They were, then, not only keys to the past in the indicative and subjunctive moods but maps for the future, mirrors in which these readers might behold their own images. Thus, Don Quixote's self-transformation in imitation of his hero, Amadís, is only a more extreme version of the zeal Montalvo hoped to inspire in the audience of aristocrats he was writing for – presumably the only readers who would ever believe that they could, or should, literally do so. And if for inspiration and imitation great deeds are desired, those larger-than-life and more exciting exploits depicted in the romances of chivalry would do as well as – nay, better than – the merely historical deeds, because they appeal to the imagination so much more strongly (*Amadis of Gaul* 19). For it is imagination that moves the will to action. Men (and only men) inspired by great deeds of story or history might themselves do great deeds whose story would become history and the models of imitation for future generations.[4]

Dreams

While history and story, then, were similar in name, in form, in content, and in purpose, story was also equated by analogy with dreams. When the village curate tells Don Quixote that he doubts that knights errant really existed, he uses these words: 'I cannot by any means persuade myself, Don Quixote, that all the crowd of knights errant you have referred to have really and truly been people of flesh and blood living in the world. On the contrary, I think that it is all fiction, fable and lies – dreams told by men awake, or rather half asleep' (2:1, 478).

In other words, dreams are like fiction on which no form has been imposed by the imaginative genius of the author's mind. Now the priest's metaphor is not only his own. Originally penned by Petrarch, it became a commonplace repeated by the critics of Ariosto in Italy and by the opponents of the chivalric romances in Spain (Forcione 14). According to this point of view, fictions and dreams are false because they do not tell precisely and exclusively what objectively happened. But not being exactly like objective reality is not necessarily the same as being untrue, as other thinkers in Cervantes's own time acknowledged and as the novelist himself put into practice in the building of his novel's universe.

It was recognized by the poet Fernando de Herrera, in a well-known work published in Cervantes's lifetime, that dreams were often based on the memory of events or thoughts of the dreamer's waking consciousness, that is, the circumstances of his or her immediate past (Herrera 545, 548). They are thus made of the same raw materials as those of chronicles and histories: remembered experience. Now in certain texts, including Scripture and the romances of chivalry, dreams predict what may or what will happen.[5] Dreams, then, can accomplish (but need not accomplish) for characters inside a narrative what historians should do for readers outside it: they project forward in time from the past to suggest the one objectively correct course of action for the future.

But if, as Montalvo and his contemporaries thought, chronicles are faithful transcriptions of what *did* happen, then mistakes cannot be made in applying the lessons they so clearly teach. For there will be a unanimous understanding by all right-thinking readers of the correct lesson to be learned from the univocal meaning of the events described on the page. Dreams, by contrast, mix the remembered images of the dreamer's experience with archetypal symbols in order to depict what *may* happen, or what may have happened. Like Aristotle's universal truth of poetry (which in Cervantes's time also meant prose fiction [Riley 35], the dream must be interpreted to be understood. Truth in these forms lies not in itself alone but in the kind of match it makes with the mind that scrutinizes it. In the words of Saint Augustine's *Confessions* (a passage Cervantes probably knew[6]): 'The world will not supply an answer to those who question it unless they also have the faculty to judge it ... It would be nearer the truth to say it gives an answer to all, but it is only understood by those who compare the message it gives them through their senses with the truth that is in themselves' (bk. 10, ch. 6, 213).

The dream-interpreters of the Bible and of *Amadís de Gaula* are wise-men who infallibly hit on *the* right answer for the dream's riddle by matching its contents with their superior intelligence. The dreamer is consequently enabled to make correct choices. But in Cervantes's novel the interpreters of Don Quixote's experience in the Cave of Montesinos are a madman and two mere mortals, one of whom is illiterate. What the experience means, and even if it really happened, are questions that can never be definitively answered within the book. Indeed, Don Quixote spends much of part 2 wondering whether his vision is a true one and trying to find in it a clue to the 'disenchantment' of Dulcinea. This uncertainty is clearly a parody of the prophetic and infallible character of dreams in literature, as opposed to their equivocal nature in the real life of the average person.

Enchantment

Dreams, then, are as false and as true as story, and their interpretation can affect the future like the exemplary reading of history. Dreams, fiction, and history also partake of some of the qualities of enchantment, the last word I shall analyse. Unlike the other words discussed so far, enchantment is not analysed in the novel, but its effects on its victims are graphically, and comically, described by Don Quixote. The first is that it makes people and things appear to be what they are not (Predmore 39). In this it, like story, resembles deceit, and many of the so-called enchanters in the book are indeed people who are deceiving Don Quixote and Sancho for reasons of their own. Its spells also resemble fiction, which creates a plausible image of people and episodes that never happened in real life. One could say that Don Quixote has been bewitched by fiction's quasi-magical power to make the nonexistent vividly present to the senses, as occurs when he hacks at Maese Pedro's puppets, while believing them to be actual characters of the romances of chivalry.

The essence of the ironic sorcery peculiar to part 2, then, is this: from the mad knight's point of view, things have been enchanted to appear uglier than the archetypes of perfection they should be, so that they look to him as they look to everyone else (Predmore

40). Because knights errant should see only marvellous things, and (he believes) he is a knight errant, all things he sees should be marvellous. If they are not so, they must have been changed by malevolent enchanters, as the sorceress Alcina changes men into beasts in *Orlando furioso* (6.51), one of the books in Don Quixote's library. But Ariosto's beast-men started out, not as swine, but as valourous – albeit somewhat lecherous – knights. The Princess Dulcinea, on the other hand, was originally the peasant girl Aldonza Lorenzo, as readers of part 1 know. Therefore, Sancho's pretence to his master that the ugly peasant woman both see before them is the peerless Dulcinea, appearing ugly and common only to her hapless knight (2:10), in fact changes her from her universal, poetic 'self' to her historical, prosaic identity. But to Don Quixote, who in part 2 believes that his renaming of her constitutes a revelation of her true, archetypal self (Parker 114), she has been changed in appearance by malevolent, not to say comic, enchanters. This double inversion, in which others' deceit restores the objective and prosaic truth that Don Quixote's imagination originally transformed into the subjective stuff of poetry, provides the pattern of his eventual disillusionment – or, as one might say, his disenchantment.

For Don Quixote is also his own enchanter. In his madness he has re-created himself as an archetype of perfection, one who does not grow old, is never defeated, and is virtuous, prudent, strong, and humble. Such characters, unlike mere mortals, never change because they are already everything they are ever going to be. Any change can only be a descent from the moral and social summit they occupy from birth. They are, therefore, immobilized in their own fame. Both kinds of *historia*, history and story, also fix their heroes in a past that cannot be changed (Avalle-Arce 218). Magic, or enchantment, can render its victims immobile, too, either through unconsciousness or paralysis as Don Quixote states from his cage on an oxcart, a prison he believes to have been constructed for him by malevolent enchanters: 'anyone enchanted, as I am, is not at liberty to dispose of his will' (1:49, 435). Metaphorically speaking, this is also Don Quixote's spiritual and psychological position: he does not believe that he can or should change, and in part 2 he defends himself from recognizing that his present role is a change from the man he had been for most of his life. For if he were to believe such a thing, he would not know himself as a knight errant knows himself in the books he has read, and he would therefore be, not a real chevalier, but an imaginary one. He would cease to be what he 'is' now, which is glorious story, 7 and return to what he used to be, which is uninteresting history. And that would be a descent from the higher universal truth of poetry to the lower particular truth of his original life-history.[8]

The fact that history, story, dream, and enchantment are not semantic opposites but neighbours in a spectrum of experience that is refracted from the light of truth makes it possible for Cervantes to use all four words to show how Don Quixote can discover his true self by means of the very mental structures that caused him to lose it. Now that I have clarified these terms, I shall spend the rest of this article telling a story of how Don Quixote's dreams lead him to disenchant the contents of his memory so that he can take his place in his own history.

The Cave of Montesinos

What Don Quixote says happened in the Cave of Montesinos is a vision fantastic by the standards of both fiction and history because in it what the left hand of fiction giveth, the right hand of history taketh away. He meets an old man who claims to be the great Montesinos, the hero of a cycle of Spanish Carolingian ballads that Don Quixote believes to be historically accurate. By his own testimony, Montesinos is at least five hundred years old. Within the conventions of romance, this is improbable because there the hero never grows old. He disappears, and one of his decendants takes his place in a new cycle of adventures, as Esplandián and his sons and grandsons follow Amadís (Fogelquist 133–5). Nevertheless, the aged Montesinos greets the fifty-year-old Don Quixote as the valorous knight for whom the adventure of disenchanting the cave's inhabitants has been reserved.

At long last, Don Quixote has been recognized as an equal by the heroes whose life-stories he has tried to emulate, and he has been given a mission that will justify his chivalric vocation. However, contrary to those of most enchantments, whose literary purpose is to create a wrong for the hero to right, the victims of this spell do not know how or why they were bewitched or how they can be rescued. If no one knows how to be saved, how is the hero to know what he is supposed to do? Might he not make a mistake or commit a sin, thereby spoiling his life-story?

The effects of the spell in the cave conform to the pattern set by the comic enchantments of Don Quixote himself in part 1 and of Dulcinea in part 2. The victims are immobilized or their appearance does not live up to what history or story proclaim to be true. The hero Durandarte lies stretched out on his tomb, apparently dead, as his story proclaims; nevertheless, he speaks from time to time, contradicting Montesinos's experience of their shared history. Perplexed, the latter asks, 'And yet, despite my knowing that this knight really died, how is it that ever and anon now he complains and sighs as if he were alive?' (2:23, 617) This incongruous juxtaposition of the 'facts' of the 'historical' past and the impossible appearances of an enchanted present is followed by the arrival of the motionless knight's beautiful lady, Belerma, who, true to the events of the ballads, carries Durandarte's mummified heart. However, she is ugly, contrary to those same ballads. Among the other figures who inhabit the cave, Don Quixote sees 'three peasant girls ... and no sooner did I see them than I realized that one of them was the peerless Dulcinea del Toboso' (621). The comic pairing of the epithet 'peerless Dulcinea' and 'three peasant girls' shows that the Manchegan knight now believes that for the present his mortal eyes can see her only in her prosaic guise – that is, the only way those eyes have ever been able to see her. (This bit of historical evidence does not convince the listening Sancho of the reality of his master's experience because he knows that he himself invented that enchantment which to his master is now Dulcinea's actual plight.) But she also behaves like the commoner she now resembles. She asks of her knight a small loan of money; unfortunately, this is the one thing the impoverished chevalier cannot promise her because he does not have it. Money is, moreover, something the knights of romance never condescended either to use or to discuss, as Don Quixote has repeatedly reminded Sancho when the latter requested a vulgar, fixed salary (Eisenberg, 'A Typical Romance of Chivalry' 6). So Don Quixote offers her, instead of the useful thing he cannot give, the impractical, but proper, thing she does not ask for: a vow to release her from her enchantment. With these words, his account of his adventure ends and his quest for his lady's deliverance begins. Nevertheless, as Hughes (111) has argued, the intrusion of money signifies the corruption of Don Quixote's ideal from without that meets the decay of his ideal from within.

The story of Don Quixote's adventure in the Cave of Montesinos is one of only two episodes in the entire novel that are left unexplained for its readers: the other is the immediate cause of the protagonist's death, as we shall see. Cide Hamete, the narrator, seconds Sancho Panza's scepticism about its factuality (2:24, 624). Like a good historian, he transcribes only what he knows: the story Don Quixote tells. But he cannot decide what to call it. Is it a dream that Don Quixote believes is real? Did he in fact see the heroes of the Spanish Carolingian ballads, as he claims (history)? Or did he make it up, as an alleged apocryphal tradition claims, to fit in with the adventures he had read of in his histories (or stories)? No answer is offered, so that the readers are expressly invited to match the details of the story with the patterns that seem most plausible to their own judgment.

I shall take up Cide Hamete's challenge by placing myself four-square behind the textual authority of Maese Pedro's monkey (2:25, 637) and Don Antonio Moreno's 'enchanted' head, a sculpture of bronze (2:62, 874). Both these omniscient oracles reply to Don Quixote's queries as to whether the adventure of the Cave of Montesinos is truth or a dream by equivocating with scholarly probity and prudence. They reply that it is a bit of both, false and plausible. And yet, the hybrid form of their answers reveals indirectly to the questioning hero what the reader of part 1 already knows: because a fallible and human Don Quixote himself, not an omniscient fate, created his and Dulcinea's identities in a fit of dementia, he cannot truly be considered a knight errant nor can she be called a princess. These identities are plausible only to a mind that no longer can distinguish between history and story. Thus, the mad hero's life as Don Quixote is like the curate's definition of the romances themselves, the dream of a man half-asleep. But it is through the fiction of his vision that he can begin to dream the truth of his identity as the creator of the life-story he wishes to read through his living.

The form and content of the adventure itself reveal this in miniature. When Don Quixote is dragged from the cave his appearance is described as follows: 'his eyes were shut, *as if* [my italics] in sleep ... after some time he came to himself, stretching his limbs *as if* [my italics] waking from a deep sleep' (2:22, 614) This is an exact physical equivalent of the curate's definition of the imperfect conscious control exercised by their authors over the composition of romances of chivalry. Thus, Don Quixote's tale may be fiction or dream and is metaphorically both. The apparently random sequence of events and the absurd parade of personages grotesquely deformed from the nobility and beauty appropriate to aristocrats in fiction and in history betray to the readers of Don Quixote's time the lack of an ordering imagination. Don Quixote, its narrator, is creating exactly what he will later accuse Avellaneda of having written: whatever turns out (2:71, 925). But if there is little apparent form in the telling of this story, there is a shape in its narrator's interpretation of it; 'the sweetest existence and most delightful vision any human ever enjoyed or beheld' (2:22, 614). There is no reason to doubt that Don Quixote did indeed find it so. After all, the narrator finally got to meet the personages he believes really existed and he discovered that they were not dead, but sleeping, so that there was something for him to resurrect in his imitation of their famous exploits. However, they are also decaying very slowly – perhaps like himself. This is, I think, why he can say in the very next sentence: 'Now, indeed, I positively know that the pleasures of this life pass like a shadow and a dream, and wither like the flowers of the field.' There are too many resemblances between the speaker and the figure of Durandarte for the reader not to see, even if Don Quixote himself does not, that the latter's dream of himself may also decay. Durandarte's muscular hand looks like Don Quixote's hand as he describes it to Maritornes in part 1 (43, 393) – and he was comically enchanted by her words into hanging by that hand from her window in a position of grotesque immobility, just as Durandarte has been rendered paralysed on his own tomb. If the dead paladin so greatly resembles Don Quixote then the doubts the former expresses as to whether the latter can free her from this spell can be seen as metaphorical statements that (1) Don Quixote has embalmed his heart – his true self – in his dreams of glory, even as Montesinos has embalmed Durandarte's, and (2) there is no one but he for whom this disenchantment is reserved and, even so, he may not be able to do it unaided. Consequently, as this vision is either a conscious or unconscious creation of the mad knight's own making in solitude, then even his dreams are unfaithful to the splendour of the chivalric *historias*, whether stories or histories.

Don Quixote's Defeat in Barcelona

The Cave of Montesinos prepares the reader to accept the likelihood that the course of Don Quixote's remaining adventures will not follow the triumphant pattern of the heroes of the chivalric

romance and that he will be defeated by forces that he understands
no better than Montesinos understands the means and purposes
of the spell that imprisons him. Don Quixote is knocked off his
horse by the Knight of the White Moon, who extracts from him,
on his honour as a knight errant, a promise to stop being one by
returning to his village and refraining from feats of arms for one
year. Significantly, Sancho's response to this event is described as
follows: 'all this episode seemed to him to be happening in a dream,
and the whole business to be a matter of enchantment' (2:64, 891).
Why? Because Don Quixote is the hero of a book. By the laws of
romance he cannot be defeated within the reality of a text except
by enchantment or in a dream, which by definition have subjective,
but not objective, reality. This is all either the knight or his squire
ever knows because neither man learns what the reader does: that
the Knight of the White Moon is one of Don Quixote's neighbours,
who has devised the episode as the culmination of a plot to get
the madman home for a year to see if peace, quiet, and boredom
may not cure him of his delusions of grandeur. It is one more
example of the ironic mirroring of truth and fiction that, for Don
Quixote to forsake knight-errantry, it has become necessary for
someone to enter his world and fight him as an equal on his own
terms, thus lending this imagined universe 'historical' validity.

The treatment does indeed seem to work. For the first time in
the novel, Don Quixote does not attribute a disaster to enchanters
or to fate or to any agent other than his own imprudence. This is
not to say that he does not still believe that he is a knight errant.
However, he now accepts that he must live out what he believes
to be his true vocation in a different manner: 'When I was a knight
errant, valiant and daring, my arms brought credit to my exploits,
and now that I am a common squire I will bring credit on my
words by fulfilling the promise I made' (2:66, 896). Ironically, the
defeat he recognizes as an objective fact accomplishes the same
results as those of enchantment: he can no longer make manifest
by his actions what he thinks is his real self, but must present a
prosaic false front to the world. However, story and fiction are
reversed once again. What he presents as a mask is in fact his true,
prehistoric, self: the nameless gentleman, or squire, of La Mancha.
And there is one other danger to his chivalric self in accepting
retirement: he realizes that he can change. Heroes, as we have seen,
do not change except in a kind of slow decay. If Don Quixote can

change, is he still a hero? If the answer is no, who, and what, is he?

Don Quixote Takes Up the Pastoral Life

As yet, he asserts that it is possible to be a knight errant in retreat. But as that identity cannot be acted out, there is an emptiness in his soul where his self should be. And because nature and art abhor a vacuum, he rushes to fill it with a new identity: that of the shepherd Quijotiz. He decides to live like a literary shepherd with such friends as he can persuade to join him. Because there is a literary precedent for this decision, one he has read, there would seem to be no danger of dishonour or unfaithfulness to his chivalric self in following its example. For the hero of the chivalric romance *Amadís de Grecia* adopts the life of a shepherd to be near the shepherdess with whom he has fallen in love. The crucial difference between Don Quixote and his model is that our hero has no such excuse. He will be no nearer to Dulcinea by pretending to be Quijotiz than he is by believing he is. It is therefore a gratuitous act, rather like his feigned penance in the Sierra Morena (1:25). This gratuitous quality is, I think, important for understanding the significance of his decision to take up the pastoral life. For the first time in part 2 he knows himself as someone he has always been: a man capable of playing a part. He does not believe that he has been bewitched, or that he is dreaming, or that he *is* a shepherd. The very nature of his chivalric identity prevents him from reaching this last conclusion for the reason I have mentioned before: knightly heroes do not change the quality of their self-knowledge.

However this stratagem may seem to safeguard his chivalric identity, it in fact leads to its dissolution, because the mechanism of creating the shepherd Quijotiz is exactly the same as the one his nameless former self employed to create the knight Don Quixote. He gives himself and other important characters names in the pastoral style, exactly as before he had named in the chivalric fashion. He even gives his lady the same name he had baptized her with once before because, he says, it will do as well for a shepherdess as for a princess (2:68, 903). But this time he knows that he is assigning roles rather than discovering archetypal identities, and this time, unlike the first, he has before him eyewitnesses who can remind him, should he forget, that the pastoral world is one not reserved for him, but created by him.

However, there were in fact witnesses he did not see when he created his first fictional world. Lurking in the back of his mind is the memory of a certain conversation with the Duchess, which took place when, as he thought, he was at the height of his glory. She, like nearly everybody else in part 2, has read part 1. Because Don Quixote has not read it, he cannot refute her claim that in his life-history it says that Dulcinea 'does not exist on earth, but is a fantastic mistress, whom your worship engendered and bore in your mind, and painted with every grace and perfection you desired' (2:32, 680). He may no longer remember, and therefore may not believe, that he did this,[9] but he has heard from a lady of rank whom he trusts that, in Cide Hamete's allegedly true story, which he himself has defended against Avellaneda's fictitious continuation, it says that he did. Furthermore, the Knight of the White Moon was able to defeat him although he had commended himself to Dulcinea's protection. Now he sees himself, as do the others who agree to play his game with him, repeating the action that the book of his life declares him to have performed once before. The accumulation of evidence from his own life-story that he was not always Don Quixote and that Dulcinea was not always Dulcinea reaches in his mind the proportions of an avalanche, burying his certainty of his own chivalric infallibility. This is, I think, why he takes to his bed immediately after laying his plans with his friends to live out a pastoral fantasy. He knows that this role is a fiction, to him a lie, and the means of its creation casts doubt on the integrity of the life on which he has staked his enduring fame. If this is not the reason for his illness, then his decline and fall appears to be an awkward deus ex machina dragged in arbitrarily because Cervantes wanted to finish off his hero to get the authentic part 2 to press as soon as possible after the publication of Avellaneda's version.

The Death of Don Quixote as the Recovery of Alonso Quixano, the Good

The hero's recovery of his true self is the logical conclusion of the double inversion of fiction and fact, dream and enchantment that the story of his life has been throughout part 2. It is also constructed as a reversal of his experience in the Cave of Montesinos.

Here he falls asleep and remains asleep so deeply that those around him believe that he will remain so, perhaps in death, forever. Now the Spanish word for 'sleep,' *sueño*, is also the word for 'dream.' There are then two possible translations for the Spanish original: 'he slept so deeply that his niece and housekeeper thought he would remain in his sleep' or, 'in his dream.' It is part of the genius of Cervantes that he never reveals what, or if, Don Quixote dreamed during those six hours. As with the vision of the Cave, readers must judge for themselves, projecting their own images on to a blank screen. My projection is the final story I shall tell here.

When Don Quixote emerged from the Cave of Montesinos, he did so with the dream that he was under a spell of immobility, even as he was perhaps beginning to fall under the spell of his own unacknowledged self-doubt. In sleep, as we have seen, consciousness and the will it directs are relaxed, so that images from the memory may rise to the mind's eye. St Augustine compares the memory to a great field or a spacious palace, a metaphor that resembles Don Quixote's description of the pleasant fields and crystal palace he finds in the Cave of Montesinos (Hughes 113 n.8). In the memory, says the saint, 'I meet myself ... I remember myself and what I have done, when and where I did it, and the state of my mind at the time' (bk. 10, ch. 8, 215) I suggest that in that deep sleep Don Quixote goes to the bottom of the cave of his memory, walks through its spacious palaces and great fields and meets there not only Don Quixote and Dulcinea, but the gentleman of La Mancha and Aldonza Lorenzo, who can now live again because they were not dead, but sleeping. He dreams his own true story, and thereby disenchants the images of his past in his memory. He then returns to consciousness with a new name, now his real name, and to a recognition of himself as a man who can change, a privilege beyond the prerogatives of the perfect, or finished, knight errant. He now knows himself to be, not a hero of chivalry, but a man capable of dreaming such a protagonist out of texts, and thereby becoming the hero of another book. Here are his words: 'I was mad but now I am sane. I was Don Quixote de la Mancha, but today, as I have said, I am Alonso Quixano the Good. May my sincere repentance restore your former esteem for me' (2:74, 938).

Now repentance requires, apart from sorrow for the past and a desire to amend the future, the turning of the soul to the truth of its own past to acknowledge the good and the evil it has done and to reject nothing that really happened. In this, the soul's duty to itself and the historian's duty to the reader are the same: to add nothing to, and to subtract nothing from, the truth – even the apparent mistakes by which it has been discovered. There is only one thing the dying man rejects: Avellaneda's continuation, which is bad fiction rather than a good story, for it is not even, as a dream is, the shadow of the truth. What he does not reject is Cide Hamete's book, contained in Cervantes's book, a true story of what he was but is no longer. As a true story of an imagined reality, it can serve as an example for readers, noble and common, *not* to imitate in their future actions, a kind of anti-history. This is the final and most subtle showing of truth by means of fiction: the novel itself. It is exemplary in the negative and that is why Don Quixote's life-story is the story of the last knight errant. It is also why it is the subject of this article, which appears in a volume devoted to life writing, a genre-in-the-making. It is a book that refuses to name once and for all experiences of reading and living, thereby inviting readers to find in the silences between its words their own names for the experiences that become their possessions through their acts of reading and interpreting the text. If, as Ruth El Saffar has argued (xii), Cervantes recovers truth through the acceptance of the feminine in his fiction, then the reader of Cervantes can choose to recover from *Don Quixote's* startling anticipation of the imaginative flexibility of postmodern writing by women, a new kind of text: not *l'écriture féminine*, but *l'écriture humaine*, writing in the human – and in the humane.[10]

NOTES

1 The English translation of *Don Quixote* is cited here and henceforth by part, chapter, and page.
2 The critical bibliography of Don Quixote is enormous; as a result, I have chosen to refer, where possible, to sources available in English to the readers of this volume. The meaning of Don Quixote's disillusionment is one of the most disputed in Cervantine scholarship, and the interpretation offered here is not the only one possible. Mancing's examination of this question is one of the most detailed analyses available in English, although our conclusions about the ultimate end of the process of disillusionment differ; his bibliography lists most previous authors. To his list should be added Williamson, who analyses the process in terms of Cervantes's experimentation

with, and satire of, the narrative techniques of the chivalric romances.

3 The fullest analyses of Renaissance theoretical discussions of the relative truth of story and history and their implications for Cervantes's work are to be found in Wardropper ('Don Quixote'), Riley (Cervantes's Theory of the Novel 163–8), and Forcione (Cervantes, Aristotle and the Persiles 58–9).

4 Fogelquist (El Amadis 17–18) points out that for Montalvo and his sixteenth-century contemporaries history was a mirror for the reader (speculum historiale), because 'the reading of history as a didactic genre assumes a cyclical concept of time. That is, man can learn from the reading of history because the same deeds are repeated and reflected during the whole of time [my translation].'

5 One example is Pharaoh's dream of the seven fat years followed by the seven lean years, which Joseph correctly interprets to devise a plan of action that gets Egypt safely through the years of famine (Genesis 41:25–57). Another is Amadís's dream of the arrival of the Damsel of Denmark bearing his lady Oriana's pardon, a dream that foretells the eventual reunion of the lovers at Miraflores (2:48, 464–5). The hermit with whom Amadís has taken refuge explains the enigmatic symbols of this dream for the benefit of the hero himself and for the readers of the book (2:51, 484–5). Fogelquist (219–25) presents a complete catalogue of the numerous prophetic dreams in the romance.

6 Cervantes's familiarity with Augustine's works, especially the Confessions and The City of God, has been studied by DiSalvo.

7 'I am a knight errant – not one of those whom Fame has never thought to record in her memory, but one who, in despite and defiance of envy itself, and of all the Magi ever born in Persia . . . shall write his name in the temple of immortality, to serve as a pattern and example to future ages, wherein knights errant may see what steps they should follow if they would climb to the honourable summit and pinnacle of arms,' declares Don Quixote – from his undignified position as an 'enchanted' prisoner in an oxcart (1:49, 422).

8 In the words of Aristotle: 'Hence poetry is more philosophical and more serious than history, for poetry deals more with things in a universal way, but history with each thing for itself' (Poetics 51a36, 81). The theorist Alonso López Pinciano, whom Cervantes almost certainly read, explains Aristotle's concept of the universality of poetry as 'an art superior to Metaphysics, for it contains much more and extends its reach to what is and is not' (Philosophía antigua poética 1:220 [my translation]).

9 I do not wish to imply that Don Quixote does not remember that Aldonza Lorenzo and Dulcinea are the same person. I suggest in-

stead that he does not in part 2 remember how he 'fell in love' with 'Dulcinea' in the same way that the narrator of part 1 explains it, that is, as the hero's creation of a nonexistent ideal lady from the image of a woman who does exist in a most un-ideal form. As Don Quixote explains to the Duchess (2:32, 680–1), he believes that he has stripped away the vulgar appearance of Aldonza Lorenzo that hides the ideal essence, and hence, the real being, of Dulcinea. He loves the universal in the particular, in accordance with the dictates of Neoplatonic love. In Parker's words, 'The Neoplatonic victory of reason over passion is here depicted as in fact the subjugation of reason to the imagination' (*Philosophy of Love* 114). Therefore, the process of his return to sanity might also be described as the recovery of the particular from the universal.

10 Much of the research for this article was originally conducted under the erudite and humane guidance of Professor Geoffrey L. Stagg, to whom it is dedicated. It has been revised from a talk presented at the annual meeting of the American Association of Teachers of Spanish and Portuguese (Ontario Chapter) in Toronto, Ontario, in November 1986.

WORKS CITED

Amadís of Gaul. Books I and II. Trans. Edwin B. Place and Herbert C. Behm. 1508. Lexington: UP of Kentucky 1974

Aristotle. *Poetics* (selections). In *Literary Criticism: From Plato to Dryden*, 69–124. Ed. and trans. Allan H. Gilbert. 1940. Detroit: Wayne State UP 1970

Augustine of Hippo, Saint. *Confessions.* Trans. R.S. Pine-Coffin. 1961. Harmondsworth: Penguin 1975

Avalle-Arce, Juan Bautista. 'Tres comienzos de novela.' In *Nuevos deslindes cervantinos*, 215–43. Barcelona: Ariel 1975

Cervantes Saavedra, Miguel de. *The Adventures of Don Quixote.* Trans. J.M. Cohen. 1950. Harmondsworth: Penguin 1983

DiSalvo, Angelo J. 'St. Augustine and the *Persiles* of Cervantes.' In *Studies on 'Don Quixote' and Other Cervantine Works*, 55–64. Ed. Donald W. Bleznick. York, sc: Spanish Literature Publications Co. 1984

Eisenberg, Daniel. 'The Pseudo-Historicity of the Romances of Chivalry.' In *Romances of Chivalry in the Spanish Golden Age*, 119–30. Newark, Del.: Juan de la Cuesta 1982

– 'A Typical Romance of Chivalry.' In *Romances of Chivalry in the Spanish Golden Age*, 55–74

El Saffar, Ruth. *Beyond Fiction: The Recovery of the Feminine in the Novels of Cervantes.* Berkeley: U of California P 1984
– ed. *Critical Essays on Cervantes.* Critical Essays on World Literature. Boston: G.K. Hall 1986
Folgelquist, James Donald. *El Amadís y el género de la historia fingida.* Madrid: Studia Humanitatis / José Porrúa Turanzas 1982
Forcione, Alban K. *Cervantes, Aristotle and the 'Persiles.'* Princeton: Princeton UP 1970
Foucault, Michel. '[Don Quixote in the Lettered World].' In *Don Quixote: Critical Essays on Cervantes,* 171–21 (*see* El Saffar). Repr. from *The Order of Things: An Archaeology of the Human Sciences,* 46–50. New York: Random House 1973
Herrera, Fernando de. *Obras de Garcilaso de la Vega con anotaciones de Fernando de Herrera.* 1580. Facsimile edition. Prologue and intro. by Antonio Gallego Morell. Madrid: Consejo Superior de Investigaciones Científicas 1973
Hughes, Gethin. 'The Cave of Montesinos: Don Quixote's Interpretation and Dulcinea's Disenchantment.' *Bulletin of Hispanic Studies* 54 (1977): 107–13
Kadar, Marlene. 'Whose Life Is It Anyway? Some Preliminary Remarks on Life-Writing.' In *Essays in Life-Writing,* 5–21. Ed. Marlene Kadar. Robarts Centre for Canadian Studies Working Paper 89-WO3. North York, Ont.: York U
López Pinciano, Alonso. *Philosophía antigua poética.* Ed. Alfredo Carballo Picazo. 3 vols. Biblioteca de Antiguos Libros Hispánicos, Serie A. Vols. 29–31. 1596. Madrid: Consejo Superior de Investigaciones Científicas 1953
Mancing, Howard. *The Chivalric World of Don Quixote: Style, Structure and Narrative Technique.* Columbia: U of Missouri P 1982
Parker, Alexander A. *The Philosophy of Love in Spanish Literature, 1460–1680.* Ed. Terence O'Reilly. Edinburgh: Edinburgh UP 1985
Predmore, Richard L. *The World of 'Don Quixote.'* Cambridge: Harvard UP 1967
Riley, E.C. *Cervantes's Theory of the Novel.* Oxford: Clarendon 1962
Robert, Marthe. *The Old and the New: From 'Don Quixote' to Kafka.* Trans. Carol Cosman. Berkeley: U of California P 1977
Van Wart, Alice. 'Life Out of Art': The Writing of Elizabeth Smart.' In *Essays in Life-Writing,* 49–59. Ed. Marlene Kadar. Robarts Centre for Canadian Studies Working Paper 89-WO3. North York, Ont.: York U
Wardropper, Bruce W. '*Don Quixote:* Story or History?' In *Critical Essays on Cervantes,* 80–94 (*see* El Saffar, ed.). Originally published in *Modern Philology* 63 (1965): 1–11
Williamson, Edwin. *The Half-way House of Fiction: 'Don Quixote' and Arthurian Romance.* Oxford: Clarendon 1984

PART FOUR

POETICS AND
LIFE WRITING

PART FOUR INCORPORATES two conventional scholarly essays in and about poetics. Post-structuralist vs. humanist notions of the self underpin the essays in this volume, but here they are theorized explicitly. The contributors do not focus on one primary text. They examine theoretical issues that, at this early stage in its 'new' history, nevertheless impinge on how we conceive the genre and the critical practice we here call life writing. This section relates the issues at stake in life writing: generic, historical, formal, social, theoretical, epistemological, and political. However, as Shirley Neuman suggests in her concluding remarks, there is no systematic poetics of life writing, for 'such a poetics cannot be systematized; it can only be accumulated from the ongoing writing and reading of many autobiographers, many readers, occupying many simultaneous *and* sequential subject positions.'

It is obvious that life writing refers to a body of written and oral literature that is not yet fixed, and that is by its very nature immersed in the political life of contemporary poetics and literary theory. Thus, several issues emerge in the forefront of the discussion to name and harness life writing: Does it have any structural, even classical, unity we can speak of? Is it more like drama and less like narrative? Is it particularly useful as a home for feminist discourse? Is it well suited to deliver anti-hegemonic discourses in general? Can it accommodate the discourses of feminism alongside those of antiracism? And is life writing in the end more about the 'self' than other kinds of writing are about the 'self'? Or does it open up a new territory for the complex subject to inhabit in its multitudinous forms, and especially in its more naked forms?

~ぎ 12 ぎ~
Mimesis:
The Dramatic Lineage
of Auto/Biography

EVELYN J. HINZ

'To speak is to act'

Sartre

Auto/biographical documents[1] come in a variety of forms, appeal
to a diverse audience, and provide valuable data for scholars from
numerous disciplines; in the past couple of decades, auto/biog-
raphy has also emerged as one of the most popular and prolific
forms of literature. Small wonder, then, that the need to formulate
a 'poetics' of this material has become so urgent, but that attempts
to do so have met with such little concrete or comprehensive success.

Yet perhaps the problem has less to do with the heterogeneity
of auto/biography and more to do with the way the hegemony of
the novel has misled critics into using a generic analogy that is
too purely literary. For despite their disparateness and variety,
auto/biographical documents do have three basic features in common: an element of conflict and dialogue, a sense of performance
and/or spectatorship, and a mimetic or referential quality. If one
notes that these are also the major characteristics of drama – and,
moreover, that drama shares with auto/biography an interdisciplinary dimension and a catholicity of appeal – then one begins to
sense that possibly what has impeded the formulation of a 'poetics'
of auto/biography may be the failure to recognize its dramatic
affinities and the tendency instead to liken it to prose fiction.[2]

In his 'Manifesto' for the inaugural issue of biography (1978), for example, Leon Edel's strategy for proclaiming biography as a literary art was to emphasize its 'narrative' qualities and to compare the biographer's craft to that of the novelist. Similarly, novelistic analogies are repeatedly used by theoreticians of autobiography, even when their concern is to distinguish autobiography and biography and even when their intention is to argue that autobiography cannot be reduced to 'fiction' (Mandel).

It is of course true that most auto/biographies do have a narrative quality, but if by narrative we mean a causal sequence of events, then so also is drama a type of 'story.' Nor will it do to argue that drama lacks a necessary written component, since many plays are scripted; conversely, to insist that auto/biography must have a written component is to evidence myopia concerning oral forms of such material.

Where drama would seem to be an inappropriate analog is in its visual immediacy or quality of actual presence. Yet that auto/biography does aspire to this condition may be seen in its frequent recourse to pictorial metaphors. 'Portrait,' for example, repeatedly occurs in the titles of auto/biographies, and 'vivid' is the adjective used by reviewers to express commendation. Similarly, some of the earliest forms of biography – that is, the pictographs in Egyptian tombs – are visual articulations; the autobiographical impulse of numerous modern artists – such as Van Gogh – takes the form of self-portraits, and photographs constitute a major component in many contemporary biographies.

A case for drama as the 'sister-art' of auto/biography can also be made on genetic or historical grounds. In classical tragedy, for example, one finds the earliest depiction of individual lives, and the titles of the earliest forms of biography highlighted their dramatic ancestry: for instance, Acts of the Apostles, Acts of the Martyrs. Nor when biography acquired its more secular and domestic character was its dramatic lineage forgotten. Indeed, in his attempt to define biography by distinguishing it from history, John Dryden specifically invoked Aristotle's notion of 'unity of action' as a way of defending the narrowed focus of this 'new' mode of writing. Even more important, the first real theoretician of life writing, Roger North, aligned narrative art with history and argued that the true relative of biography was dramatic comedy. Finally, the first great biographer, Boswell, employed distinctly dramatic metaphors to describe his objectives in his life of Johnson: to enable the reader 'to see him live,' and to ' "live o'er each scene" ' with him, as he actually advanced through the several stages of his life' (22).

If the coming of age of auto/biography coincided with the emergence of the novel in the eighteenth century, in short, this situation is scarcely grounds for seeing prose fiction as the model being emulated by auto/biographers. To the contrary, the format of the first great novels – Fielding's fictional biography of *Tom Jones*, Defoe's fictional autobiography of *Moll Flanders*, or Richardson's fictional letters/diary of *Pamela* – suggests that auto/biography is their 'parent' form, just as the epic or melodramatic nature of these novels suggests that drama is their 'grandparent.'

With regard to the nineteenth century, if the major contribution of the romantic period was the notion of 'self,' in the case of Wordsworth's *Prelude* this articulation took the form of poetry (or high mimesis) and 'rehearsal.' Equally, John Henry Newman's *Apologia pro Vita Sua* is a profoundly conflictual piece, and its 'spiritual' dimension is in keeping with the origins of drama in religious ritual.

At the beginning of the twentieth century, one finds no less eminent a biographer than Lytton Strachey experimenting with a dramatic format in his *Elizabeth and Essex*, a work that had its genesis in an early play he wrote entitled *Essex: A Tragedy*. Later in the century, Gertrude Stein quite literally 'staged' her 'disguised' autobiography in *The Mother of Us All*, an opera based on the life of Susan B. Anthony (see Winston). In *Memories of a Catholic Girlhood*, Mary McCarthy textually sets up a struggle between past experience and present commentary, and in the crucial 'Tin Butterfly' section she ponders the question of whether her early rendition of the experience might not have had its origins in a play she had started writing in college (82). In *Stop-Time*, Frank Conroy frames his autobiography with a 'Prologue' and an 'Epilogue,' and in *The Woman Warrior*, Maxine Hong Kingston not only gives her autobiography a dramatic title, but also echoes the ancients' metaphor for the nature of plot in drama in her presentation of herself as a 'knot-maker' (190). As for examples of the contemporary connection between biography and drama, one might note that one of the most applauded plays of our time – *Amadeus* – is a 'life' of Mozart; that Swiss-German playwright Max Frisch used a dramatic format in his significantly titled *Biography, A Game*; and that playwright Romulus Lenney has written a play on the life of Byron.

Yet perhaps the most persuasive way of suggesting that drama is at the heart of auto/biography is to observe how this idea keeps surfacing in modern criticism. At the outburst of interest in this area, for example, James Olney published his pioneering *Metaphors of Self* (1972), and despite the fact that his title signals his linguistic orientation or that his Greeks are Plato and Socrates, he specifically mentions the affinities of autobiography and drama (xi) and throughout his study he is concerned with the *agon* of self-dramatization. Around the same time, William L. Howarth drew attention to the histrionic stance adopted by Benvenuto Cellini, Franklin, and O'Casey in their autobiographies; accordingly he went on to identify the 'dramatic' as one of three autobiographical strategies. More recently, a discontent with narrative analogies and an implicit shift in the direction of drama may be seen in such speech-act studies as Elizabeth Bruss's *Autobiographical Acts: The Changing Situation of a Literary Genre* or Albert E. Stone's *Autobiographical Occasions and Original Acts*. Finally, although he titles his work *Fictions in Autobiography*, Paul John Eakin's way of emphasizing the fictional component is via a dramatic analogy: 'When we settle down into the theater of autobiography, what we are ready to believe – and what most autobiographers encourage us to expect – is that the play we witness is a historical one, a largely faithful and unmediated reconstruction of events that took place long ago, whereas in reality the play is that of the autobiographical act itself, in which the materials of the past are shaped by memory and imagination to serve the needs of the present' (56). As much as Eakin is arguing for an ultimate difference between autobiography and drama, in short, so much does his emphasis upon the presentness of the experience highlight the affinities of the two art forms.

In keeping with the archaeological nature of auto/biography itself, and following the practice of its earliest critics and theoreticians, the best way to initiate a 'dramatic' poetics of life-writing may be to turn to the oldest attempt to define the generic features of drama: namely, Aristotle's *Poetics*. Writing as a biologist, Aristotle prefaced his taxonomy by first observing that mimesis is a universal and instinctual impulse, just as is our 'pleasure' in viewing such 'copies.' Such an observation, it seems to me, perfectly explains the ubiquity of auto/biography and its ability to attract readers of the most diverse kinds.

More specifically, Aristotle's emphasis on the concept of mimesis directs us to the most basic similarity between drama and auto/biography and their distinctiveness from more imaginative art forms – their factual referential quality, or premise that something empirically real is being imitated, something that has an existence outside of or prior to the text. Thus, while theoretically all art has experience in the 'real' world as its point of departure, in drama and auto/biography the imitation of 'real' life or the notion that something 'real' is being imitated is a sine qua non.

However 'realistic' a novel might be, a sense of referential actuality is not a major concern; what is imitated is other modes of discourse. Indeed, to Henry James the novel came of age when authors began to assert their own *données*, and the formulation of a 'poetics' of the novel became possible only when its non-referential nature was recognized.

Novels are intertextual, in short, but drama and auto/biography are inherently contextual; in the novel we delight in the pretence of imitation and the absence of constraints, whereas in drama and auto/biography freedom is the illusion and the pleasure (and pain) principle arises from contending with the reality principle. In both cases, art is less a matter of imaginative creation and more a matter of imaginative re-creation, less a matter of inventing and more a matter of reshaping. In both, what we take pleasure in is allied less with the product than the process, the mimetic impulse itself. Aesthetic pleasure in fiction depends upon a sense of the autonomy of the art object, whereas in drama and life writing what we delight in is a sense that the subject can never be pinned down, that what we are witnessing is a performance, and that what is being imitated can never be fully expropriated or superseded by the copy.

More important than the fact that auto/biography and prose fiction have narrative in common, therefore, is the fact that they differ radically in the area of mimesis. And the importance of a dramatic analogy is that it enables one to recognize the historical/ referential component of auto/biography while still arguing for its artistry, whereas the use of a novelistic model leads to the nihilistic cul-de-sac of denying the reality and the humanity of the individual and of arguing that existence itself is 'ultimately fiction' (as Petrie titles his study of biography).

To illustrate more concretely the referential nature of auto/bi-ography, one might consider why life-writing documents by or

about the 'famous' attract more public attention or have greater
market value than do the lives of the 'unknown': does it not have
something to do with the extent to which the reader is in a position
to compare the 'original' and the 'copy,' and is not this also the
informing (albeit in reverse) attraction of the exposé – itself a central ingredient of drama. Similarly, with regard to lives of the
unknown, one might note how such documents tend initially to
be treated either as history or as fiction until their subjects lose
their anonymity, and that it is only when comparison between the
original and the copy (or various copies) is possible that any meaningful criticism can begin. Paradoxically too, as much as 'mock'
life-writing documents sport with this notion of referentiality, so
much does our pleasure depend upon our recognition of the rule
that is being invoked and broken. Hence, one might also consider
why referential materials (pictures, reproductions of letters, clip-
pings, and so on) seem appropriate in auto/biography but are dis-
tracting in even a historical novel. Why also do we accept the
notion of unreliability in life writing but object to deliberate fal-
sification, and conversely, why, despite their appetite for biographical details, do traditionalist readers object to fiction that is
too autobiographical?

   Auto/biography as well can be too 'subjective,' and here is another area in which dramatic analogies are helpful. In the same
way that an actor/actress assumes the role of another, so autobiography involves coming to terms with another self (either earlier or hitherto unrecognized). In both cases, a sacrifice of ego is
involved, and the degree of pleasure is in proportion to the amount
of conflict. Hence the dislike of autobiographies that are too self-
glorifying – a failing, significantly, that usually takes the form of
too much narrative and too little dramatization. Hence also the
reason that the intensely autobiographical preoccupation of dram-
atists like Eugene O'Neill and Tennessee Williams does not jeop-
ardize their aesthetic success. Hence too the special tension of
watching a performance by famous actors or reading autobiographies of those we know, in contrast to what might be called a
narrative response when we do not know those in question. That
acting and autobiography go hand in hand might also be seen from
the fact that our most famous twentieth-century diarist, Anaïs
Nin, was an aspiring stage performer. Perhaps, too, it's their fas-
cination with role-playing that explains the proclivity for autobiography on the part of many actors (such as Errol Flynn or Dirk

Bogarde, Anne Baxter or Shirley MacLaine). The concept of the persona, in short, is central to autobiography, and its dynamics are best understood by way of its functioning in drama.

In biography, too, an ability to sacrifice ego and to assume the identify of another is required. Here an observation by Ronald Hayman, the biographer of Bertolt Brecht, is extremely relevant: 'Working at a biography, I always feel a bit like an actor who needs to steep himself so deeply in his character's habits of thinking that he can say the words as if they were spoken for the first time' (187–8). A former actor, Hayman was also once a director, and equally profitable are the analogies that can be drawn in this respect. Both director and biographer are in a position of relative authority, on the one hand, but at the mercy of their materials, on the other. Both make their presence known through their interpretation, and in both instances their artistry frequently results in their getting equal billing with their subjects. Just as we speak of Laurence Olivier's *Hamlet*, for example, so we speak of Richard Ellmann's *James Joyce*. As much as we recognize the biographer's signature, however, we never lose sight of his or her referential subject or think of these biographies as totally autonomous artworks. Without Theodore Dreiser there would be no *Sister Carrie* and without Doris Lessing there would be no *Martha Quest*; but without Edel's biography we would still have a Henry James. It may be their imitation of current self-reflexive novelistic practice that accounts for the mistaken attempts of certain modern biographers to write themselves into their texts, whereas it could be said that great biographers succeed in keeping themselves unobtrusive because of their adherence to dramatic principles of composition.

The first of these dramatic ground rules, according to Aristotle, is the priority of plot over character delineation, a principle that would at first seem to be at total odds with auto/biography. What Aristotle was decrying, however, was the notion that a compendium of details will yield a sense of character, and this same principle explains why 'composite' or 'chronicle' biographies (like Carlos Baker's *Ernest Hemingway* or Bernard Crick's *George Orwell*) are less appealing than single-authored or interpretative ones. Moreover, Aristotle's notion of the priority of plot lies behind the current view that preliminary to the actual writing of a biography one must first have determined what is the 'life-myth' of the sub-

ject. If we do not use the term 'myth' loosely, and if we recall that
to Aristotle plot was the illustration of a law of life, then we are
now also in a position to account for the 'universal' appeal of auto/
biography: just as a drama can be repeatedly performed by various
sets of actors, so auto/biography has a paradigmatic or archetypal
component that goes beyond the individual example. Hence the
paradox noted by Susanna Egan: that despite the uniqueness of the
individual life, autobiographies collectively reveal recurrent 'patterns of experience.'

By virtue of its teleological nature, auto/biography also accords
with Aristotle's definition of a good plot as one wherein the end
arises inevitably out of the beginning. In contrast to the serial
nature of plot and sense of possibility that characterizes the traditional novel, in auto/biography we watch the plot 'unfold' and
emotional tension takes the place of intellectual curiosity. Diaries
might seem to constitute an exception here, until one considers
that the impetus for keeping a journal typically derives from the
diarist's sense that he or she is predestined. Significantly, this same
sense of destiny distinguishes the correspondence of autobiographers from the letters of others. As in drama, therefore, auto/
biography typically works toward or culminates in a 'recognition'
scene – frequently the recognition that in the process of articulating the would-be self one discovers the real but hitherto latent
self.

A scientist and logician, Aristotle was mainly concerned with
the way dramatic plot adhered to laws of physics; as he saw it,
plot could best be described as the trajectory of an action, in which
the beginning equalled the starting-point of the motion and the
ending its completion. Utilizing such an interdisciplinary perspective, one sees that it is really a narrow literary notion of plot
that lies behind the current argument that autobiography, in particular, is not an attempt to recall the past. That is, even if we
want to describe autobiography as a 'happening' rather than a recollection of what 'happened,' the term itself points us in the direction of drama (rather than narrative). In turn, as much as one
might want to argue that the self that emerges in the course of
articulation is different from the self that began the project, still
the fact remains that there was a starting-point and that the ending
arose out of the beginning. If the impression generated by autobiography is that the self is never finished, we nevertheless have
a sense that an arc of experience or activity has been completed.

To illustrate the closed-circuit quality of life writing one might consider why we are hesitant to accord authority to biographies of the living. Consider, too, why ongoing diaries seem less commanding than autobiographies, or why original diaries published during an author's lifetime have less impact than posthumous or (self)edited ones. Indeed, the public appeal of an autobiographical document would seem to depend greatly on whether it has a self-contained quality. A specific case in point here is the serially published diaries of Anaïs Nin, which, according to statistics, decreased in popularity in proportion to their movement into the present and to the degree that Nin did less and less retrospective editing. Significantly, too, the difference between the earlier and later volumes could be described as a shift from a dramatic to a narrative mode.

What the Nin diaries at their best also illustrate is the way in which life writing approximates drama in its spatialization of time. Thus, just as drama takes the form of acts and scenes, and just as Aristotle denigrates the episodic plot, so successful life writing eschews temporal sequence and presents development in terms of clearly demarcated phases – frequently, indeed, using places of residence as a structuring principle. It is this view of life in terms of distinct phases, moreover, that explains why an autobiography can deal with only a segment of a life and yet provide a sense of completeness. So also, this synecdochal principle explains how a biographer can write the 'life' of a living person.

Another way that time is spatialized in auto/biography is through the presentation of genealogy as 'setting' or expository material. Time is always the eternal present in drama, and in auto/biography historical issues are typically of importance only insofar as they highlight the subject's problems. Hence the great difficulties of the 'life and times' approach. Such an approach tends to be successful only to the extent that the author ascribes to a 'great man' theory of history; when this is not the case, a work loses its popular appeal and also tends to be used as a reference text – as biographical data rather than as a primary document in its own right. Significantly, the same situation pertains in drama, wherein the more that social setting is emphasized the more a play begins to read like a novel.

It is also by virtue of its focus on the individual that auto/biography approximates the unity of time and place in drama; and hence in both forms the matter of length becomes a real issue.

According to Aristotle, to be impressive a drama must have 'magnitude' but not be of such a scope that the whole is lost sight of. When auto/biography fails, I would argue, the cause frequently has to do with lack of adherence to this principle: from adopting a narrative rather than a compositional approach or from making the beginning and end of the life-story conform to the beginning and end of the subject's historical life-span. Forgotten here is that it is not action per se that moves a plot but a rising action, so that the matter of length must also be gauged in terms of how much inexorability a reader can stand without becoming impatient or frustrated. It is, perhaps, not the sheer welter of details that turns many readers away from behemoth life-writing documents, but rather that the reader's emotional stamina is too severely taxed. Because they are fictional, novels can go on and on; in auto/biography as in life, the climax (death) cannot be indefinitely postponed.

If we turn now from plot to characterization, Aristotle's major contention that character must be revealed in action would again initially seem to be at odds with the practice in auto/biography, which so frequently deals with 'uneventful' or 'secret' lives. Significantly, it was precisely in this connection that E.M. Forster – who first articulated a 'poetics' of the novel – took issue with Aristotle and championed the superiority of prose fiction. To Forster, the great virtue of the novel – in contrast to the limitations of drama – is the artist's concern with what goes on behind the scenes and is never acted out, and Forster especially applauded the fact that the novelist can 'talk about his characters as well as through them' (92). Much as this sounds in theory like the art of the biographer, however, in biographical practice such a procedure is disastrous. In the novel we can accept authorial intrusions and descriptive stage directions because the world is one of the author's making; in biography, the world is real – our world; thus authorial commentary makes us feel that we and the subjects are being manipulated, and what we want to see instead is the way the self manifests itself in action and out of struggle. Nor should one object that in the case of autobiography the conflict is of an internal and 'linguistic' variety, for actually it was in the context of criticizing speeches which do not reveal choices that Aristotle argued his 'character in action' principle.

Moreover, to the extent that Aristotle was arguing for physical interaction with others or the environment, he also draws our attention to a hitherto ignored feature of auto/biography: namely, the emphasis upon activity. What makes Edel's biography of Henry James so convincing is not merely his evocation of setting but the way he presents James as 'moving' in these settings – we see him climbing stairs, riding horseback, entering apartments. Similarly, in *Stop-Time* Frank Conroy is continually 'driving'; peripatetic self-articulation is central to Alfred Kazin's *A Walker in the City*; in the *Excursion* Wordsworth is always walking (toward encounters); and to Robert M. Pirsig, Zen and motorcycling go hand in hand. Conversely, but to the same effect, a feeling of immobility or a sense of having failed to act frequently constitute the impetus for autobiography. In the 'lives' of women, for example, the major subtext is often the desire to translate verbal aggression into real combat.

As for Aristotle's contention that the protagonist of drama (specifically tragedy) should be above the common level, here too auto/ biography has definite affinities. Although many subjects of biography or writers of autobiography are not 'eminent' in any historical sense, both are treated or treat themselves as special cases, with the effect of the project – the immortalization through publication – being to make them so. In turn, Aristotle's theory that the protagonists in drama should be true to life and yet truer than life provides ancient precedent for postmodernist theories concerning the fictionality of autobiography. Similarly, it is in terms of Aristotle's emphasis upon the evolutionary consequences of such idealized mimesis that one best addresses the current argument that in rewriting the past the autobiographer changes the self of the present and projects its future.

Understanding these dynamics one begins to see less difference between the 'exemplary' lives of the past and the 'realistic' lives of today. It is not really the hagiographic impulse that makes some early auto/biographical documents unsatisfactory, but rather the tendency to narrate rather than to 'dramatize.' For if actions speak louder than words, drama in itself also militates against moralizing. Partly this is a result of the immediacy of the experience: when one is caught up in an action one is not in a position to judge. Partly it is a result of the closed nature of the form: moralizing is possible only when the premise is that things might have been different. In auto/biography, this premise is ruled out by the retrospective vantage point of the telling. Accordingly, when moralizing does occur in successful auto/biography – Plutarch's *Lives*, for example, or McCarthy's *Memoirs* – it typically occurs outside the framework of the plot (in a prologue or epilogue) or is somehow distinct from the main action (like the chorus).

What also militates against moralizing in drama and auto/biography is the process of identification that takes place, and herein Aristotle's affective theory concerning audience response also provides helpful analogues. However much auto/biography might appeal to a sense of curiosity, and howsoever much such work might be well crafted, the measure of success is the degree of emotional response that is evoked. To Aristotle, the twin poles of such response were 'pity and fear,' and here one might notice the resonance of this concept in the repertoire of adjectives used to praise auto/biographies: 'profoundly moving' ... 'shocking' ... 'understanding' ... 'sympathetic' ... 'passionate' ... 'tormented.' Significantly, when the research itself is praised, the standard adjective is 'painstaking.' In this light, one also begins to sense that it is not critical immaturity but something inherent in auto/biographical documents that explains why reviews of this material tend to be subjectively toned, or why reading biographies and autobiographies seems to be a personal matter and not something one can delight in if pressured to do so.[3]

In emphasizing emotional response, Aristotle was speaking primarily of the 'tragic' effect caused by scenes of wounding or death, and these ultimate scenes are also the spectres that haunt auto/biographies and provide an undercurrent of vulnerability, even when the life purports to be a story of invincibility. As such, regardless of whether its subject is a regal or a menial figure, auto/biography also adheres to Aristotle's contention that the action of drama must be 'serious.' Aristotle felt that the language of tragedy should accord with this seriousness, and solemnity of tone and dignified diction are similarly the hallmarks of auto/biography.

A last key similarity between drama and auto/biography has to do with the essential situation at the heart of each: in tragedy we typically have a protagonist who is prompted by inner demons to pit him- or herself against the status quo; in autobiography we have an individual who wants to be sui generis or self-authorized (writing the 'definitive' version in the case of the biographer). In both cases, such hubris leads to a defeat that is also paradoxically a victory. Although life goes on in both instances, something has been added that the future needs to consider.

Despite the new insights into auto/biography that result from recognizing its affinities to drama, to construct a 'poetics' of this material also requires addressing an issue that in its extant form Aristotle's *Poetics* leaves relatively untouched: namely, the way that drama evolved out of ritual and reflects an archaic mind-set. Significantly, however, it was this aspect of drama that first sparked the interest of cultural historians/anthropologists and early psychologists, and it is through a consideration of various features of ritual that one is able not merely to place into proper perspective certain would-be 'new' theories about auto/biography but also to question the related notion that such literature is a uniquely modern phenomenon (Gusdorf).

According to Mircea Eliade, nothing so characterizes the archaic mind-set as a concern with origins, and surely this is the distinguishing feature of auto/biography. What both also have in common is that the impetus for ritual act derives from a crisis situation or a sense of vulnerability (a feeling of diminished status/power), and both reflect a belief that a return to origins is a means of recuperating lost vitality and stability. Thus, the more we want to argue that auto/biography is not a nostalgic project, the more we should recall that in archaic ritual, too, the return to the past is a way of cancelling historical contingencies and of enabling a fresh start.

Even more akin to auto/biography is the type of mimesis that characterizes ritual and the related belief in the efficacy of imitation that distinguishes such mimesis from a purely aesthetic exercise or 'realistic' reproduction. As Jane Ellen Harrison explained in her pioneering study, ritual is not statically but dynamically representational; anticipating the current penchant for wordplay in discussions of mimesis, she observed that ritual is a combination of the re-presentational and pre-presentational. As such, in ritual we have the basis for the current theory that autobiography is an active re-living of the past and for the notion that in the course of articulating the self one creates the self. In the same way, in the magic attached to naming in primitive cultures one finds precedent for the current emphasis upon the role of verbalization in autobiography.

Insofar as autobiography has a therapeutic dimension and involves a confession of guilt, there is echoed here the primitive notion of exposure as a cure and of psychic healing as a process that entails practical measures. Equally, the confessional aspect of autobiography tends to have less to do with Judaeo-Christian concepts of wrongdoing and more to do with primitive concepts of transgression, breaking taboos, or having lost face; thus, the language of initiation ceremonies seems more appropriate to describe the valorization of the self than does a vocabulary of conversion and redemption. To the extent that autobiography frequently features persons who confess their failings as a way of flaunting their success, much can also be learned from a knowledge of the antics of the 'trickster' in primitive culture.

In the light of these observations, we are now in a position to address the prevailing argument that writing about the self is a uniquely civilized phenomenon and that the sense of personality that empowers it is totally alien to the communal sense of identity that prevails in a primitive world-view. Such an argument, however, is based upon the mistaken belief that primitive societies are totally without forms of auto/biographical expression and thus reveals a very superficial and technology-oriented approach to such literature. Moreover, if primitive societies are highly ritualistic, and if the purpose of ritual is to restore communal values, then the need for such rituals would seem to suggest a tendency toward individualism on the part of members. Conversely, if modern auto/biography is characterized by a celebration of the self, such self-justification frequently constitutes a request for re-admission to the group or a desire to be understood. Perhaps, therefore, the reason auto/biographical documents are rare in primitive societies has to do with the fact that ritual performs a self-exorcising role for their members; and perhaps the reason auto/biographical documents are so abundant in the Western tradition has to do with the extent to which they provide a sense of the communal that we lack.

To summarize briefly, then, if a 'poetics' of auto/biography must be based on the premise that we can approach life only in terms of metaphors, it becomes all the more important that we choose our analogues carefully. Although modern forms of auto/biography technically share a narrative element with prose fiction, the internal dynamics of life writing are much closer to dramatic art, and the language of the stage affords us a much better vocabulary for describing the impact of this kind of literature than does the critical terminology of prose fiction. Indeed, what especially recommends seeing drama as the most appropriate 'sister-art' for auto/

biography is that this analogue enables one not only to encompass all the essential features of life writing noted by theoreticians, but also to avoid the incestuous and reductive binds into which a novel-oriented approach inevitably leads. To rescue auto/biography from history by claiming its affinities with fiction, for example, leaves us with the problem of explaining how it is different or deserves to be regarded as a distinct genre; the dramatic model, in contrast, enables one to emphasize the referential dimension of auto/biography without surrendering claims about its artistry, just as there is sufficient difference between drama and auto/biography to prevent the latter from being stripped of its own distinctive signature.

When we appreciate the genealogical ancestry of auto/biography, and when we recognize that drama is the oldest literary art form, then we can also make a better case for the larger claims by theoreticians that an autobiographical and ludic element informs all types of discourse. Insofar as auto/biography is associated with identity formation, we might point to the fact that prior to the speech phase the child is engaged in play. In the same way, if we want to argue that storytelling is a universal tendency, we might note that its most basic form is the 'tall tale' or dramatic exaggeration rather than an autonomous exercise of imagination.

Recognizing the dramatic affinities of auto/biography also throws new light on the question of the popularity of this literature. Novel-oriented critics tend to see the current appetite for auto/biography as an inverse effect of the way postmodernist fiction fragments any notions of a unified self (see Nadel). Valid as this may be for academics, such explanations overlook the fact that most of the consumers of auto/biography know nothing about the 'literature of exhaustion.' To account for the current appeal of auto/biography what we need to focus on is the way this popularity is paralleled by the current interest in native cultures and alternative lifestyles.[4]

The appeal of auto/biography today, I would argue, is best understood through an awareness of its ritual nature and in terms of how it answers to spiritual needs: the need for role models who inspire feelings of 'pity and fear' by reason of the limited stage upon which they perform, the need to face mortality, and the need to establish a living connection with the past. Instead of serving to reinforce a sense of the unique individual, auto/biography appeals because it counters such 'loneliness.' Viewed in this light, the coming of age of auto/biography in the eighteenth century might be interpreted less as the natural outgrowth of the 'age of enlightenment' and more as a counterbalance to the secularization of values and the deification of the self-made 'man.'

NOTES

This essay is a revised and expanded version of the introduction to *DATA and ACTA*, a special issue of *Mosaic* on Life Writing (see Winston on p. 212, below).

1 When I am referring to both autobiography and biography, I conjoin the two – i.e. auto/biography; when I am referring only to autobiography I omit the slash.

2 I should emphasize at the outset that by 'novel' I am referring to the canonical model and that in treating prose fiction and narrative as synonymous with the novel, I am for the purposes of this essay merely following the conventional view.

   Accordingly, I should also emphasize that I have elsewhere objected to this tendency to view all prose fiction as 'novelistic.' Specifically, just as Northrop Frye called for a distinction between the novel and confession or autobiography, so I have argued for a difference between the novel and the romance, arguing that the distinguishing feature of the latter is its dramatic nature. In this light, one way of salvaging the narrative model might be to argue for the similarities between life writing and romance – focusing for example on the way in which both feature heroes or heroines, both present society as an antagonistic force, and both proceed in a relatively straightforward fashion from crisis to crisis toward a climax. Moreover, the more a novel has an autobiographical nature – e.g., the *Künstlerroman* or *Bildungsroman* – the more it resembles romance. To this effect, C.S. Lewis structures his romance *Till We Have Faces* in the form of an apologia, and James Branch Cabell collectively titles his romances *The Biography of Manuel*; similarly, Doris Lessing uses an autobiographical mode in her science-fiction mythic narrative *Memoirs of a Survivor* and Ursula K. Le Guin uses a diary form in *The Left Hand of Darkness*.

3 An interesting example here is the response of one life-writing specialist to the 1986 survey conducted by George Simson regarding the best and worst biographies for 1985: 'I never read biographies right away. I am usually three or four years late ... A biography is something one gets around to' (*biography* 9.4 [1986]: 289).

4 For a stimulating discussion of the connection between the primitive *communitas* and the modern commune syndrome see Turner,

who also prefaces his study by noting the kind of sacrifice of Western biases required of the modern anthropologist.

WORKS CITED

Boswell, James. *Life of Johnson*. Ed. R.W. Chapman. 3rd ed. London: Oxford UP 1970

Bruss, Elizabeth W. *Autobiographical Acts: The Changing Situation of a Literary Genre*. Baltimore: Johns Hopkins UP 1976

Dryden, John. 'The Life of Plutarch.' In *Biography as an Art: Selected Criticism 1560–1960*, 17–19. Ed. James L. Clifford. New York: Oxford UP 1962

Eakin, Paul John. *Fictions in Autobiography: Studies in the Art of Self-Invention*. Princeton: Princeton UP 1985

Edel, Leon. 'BIOGRAPHY: A Manifesto.' *biography* 1.1 (1978): 1–3

Egan, Susanna. *Patterns of Experience in Autobiography*. Chapel Hill: U of North Carolina P 1984

Eliade, Mircea. *Cosmos and History: The Myth of the Eternal Return*. Trans. Willard R. Trask. New York: Harper 1959

Forster, E.M. *Aspects of the Novel*. 1927. Harmondsworth: Penguin 1964

Frye, Northrop. *Anatomy of Criticism*. Princeton: Princeton UP 1957

Gusdorf, Georges. 'Conditions and Limits of Autobiography.' In *Autobiography*, 28–48 (*see* Olney)

Harrison, Jane Ellen. *Ancient Art and Ritual*. New York: 1913

Hayman, Ronald. 'Bertolt Brecht.' In *The Craft of Literary Biography*, 186–98. Ed. Jeffrey Meyers. New York: Schocken 1985

Hinz, Evelyn J. 'Hierogamy vs. Wedlock: Types of Marriage Plots and Their Relationship to Genres of Prose Fiction.' *PMLA* 91.5 (1976): 900–13

Hong Kingston, Maxine. *The Woman Warrior: Memoirs of a Girlhood among Ghosts*. New York: Random House 1977

Howarth, William L. 'Some Principles of Autobiography.' *New Literary History* 5 (1974): 363–81. Repr. in *Autobiography*, 84–114 (*see* Olney)

Mandel, Barrett J. 'Full of Life Now.' In *Autobiography*, 49–72 (*see* Olney)

McCarthy, Mary. *Memories of a Catholic Girlhood*. 1957. New York: Harcourt 1974

Nadel, Ira Bruce. *Biography: Fiction, Fact and Form*. London: Macmillan 1984

North, Roger. *General Preface and Life of Dr. John North*. Ed. Peter Millard. Toronto: U of Toronto P 1984

Olney, James, ed. *Autobiography: Essays Theoretical and Critical*.

Princeton: Princeton UP 1980
- *Metaphors of Self: The Meaning of Autobiography.* Princeton: Princeton UP 1972
Petrie, Dennis. *Ultimately Fiction: Design in Modern American Literary Biography.* West Lafayette, Ind.: Purdue UP 1981
Stone, Albert E. *Autobiographical Occasions and Original Acts.* Philadelphia: U of Pennsylvania P 1982
Turner, Victor. *The Ritual Process.* Chicago: Aldine 1969
Winston, Elizabeth. 'Making History in *The Mother of Us All.*' In *DATA and ACTA: Aspects of Life-Writing,* 117–29. Ed. Evelyn J. Hinz. Winnipeg: U of Manitoba *Mosaic* 1987

❦ 13 ❧
Autobiography:
From Different Poetics to
a Poetics of Differences

SHIRLEY NEUMAN

I

For most readers and writers of autobiography, the genre contracts that its authorial and narrating 'I' is verifiably an actual person to whom that 'I' refers.[1] That is, autobiography's definitive feature is that it seeks to represent, or at least is figured upon, a (perhaps impossible) correspondence between its narrating 'I' and a subject actually-in-the-world. This remains true whether we grant the 'self' ontological status or whether we theorize a 'subject' as the product of discursive and ideological structures – whether we see the reference of autobiography as to a self already existent in the world or as to a subject brought into being through the act of writing the autobiography. It remains true of even the 'new autobiography' such as Derrida's *The Post Card* or *Roland Barthes by Roland Barthes*: its dislocations and displacements of the narrating 'I' or of the authorial signature, which question the notion of a unified self and assert the impossibility of its representation in literature, create a 'negative space' that calls attention to the kind of subject and the kind of referentiality we know as autobiographical by noting their absence (Ulmer 47). As Paul Smith has astutely observed in *Discerning the Subject*, what is at stake in this debate about the subject in autobiography is epistemology: 'Wherever the "I" speaks, a knowledge is spoken; wherever a knowledge speaks, an "I" is spoken. This is the dialectical mechanism of a certain *presumption* of the "subject": that is, a "subject" is presumed to exist, indexed as an "I" and loaded with the burden of epistemologies, wittingly or not' (100).

Theorists of autobiography, however, have not approached this subject/their subject through the burden of epistemologies. Rather, they have outlined various poetics that attempt to explain how the narrator of autobiography, indexed as an 'I,' creates a 'self' in the text and establishes, or cannot establish, a referential relation between that 'self' and a 'self'-in-the world that may, or may not, exist apart from its discursive production. They have, variously, posited the self as individual and unified, as split, as textually produced, and as impossible of production. Doing so, they have made contradictory claims for autobiography that have echoed, with scarcely a hesitation, the claims made for different literary theories.

The concept of the self as an indivisible entity, ontologically and textually self-identical while at the same time individual and distinct from others, underpinned the earliest work on autobiography and still forms the basis of the 'contract' through which all but theoretically sophisticated readers approach the genre. The *historical* importance of this concept cannot be overestimated: the humanist foundations of the notion of a textually and experientially unified self made it possible to take autobiography seriously within the literary institution. In 1956, Georges Gusdorf made room for the genre within the category 'literature' on the grounds that autobiography has a canon and a history consistent with and dependent upon the traditions of Western humanist thought and its conception of the self as individuated and unified; in 1972, James Olney reinforced the humanist case on the grounds that autobiography is 'more universal than it is local, more timeless than historic, and more poetic in its significance than merely personal' (viii). In a humanist *poetics* of autobiography, the autobiographer is seen as discovering meaningful pattern in the flux of past experience in order to arrive at an understanding of himself as unique and unified. His text is the product of an imperative to make the act of writing and the memories of the past that he writes about consubstantial within the autobiographical 'I' and to make that 'I' simultaneously unique *and* representative of other 'I's' – his 'semblables' as Rousseau would have it (5). Memory is the catalyst of such autobiographical 'truth,' but it is also the agent of its impossibility (an impossibility acknowledged and explored within humanist poetics of the genre), for what is forgotten or misremembered may be at least as important to the 'truth' of the sought-for 'self' as what is remembered.

From this recognition it is not far to various poetics of the genre which suggest that the autobiographical subject, split between narrated past and writing present, can never be identical with him/ herself for, as Paul Jay notes, autobiography, like psychoanalysis, 'turns on the subject's formulation of his past into a narrative, not on the past itself' (26). From this conviction of the impossibility of becoming autobiographically fully present to oneself it is a logical step to those poetics that describe the self of autobiography in terms of textual production rather than of social, familial, or personal production. All these descriptions ultimately rest, as Paul Jay notes, on Nietzsche's demystification in *The Will to Power* of the self as 'a natural, privileged, and potentially unified psychological condition' and on his recognition of the self as 'a historically constituted set of ideas and assumptions whose referents are complexly dispersed within the very language we must use to think the self into being' (28). A poetics that posits the autobiographical subject as textually produced posits each autobiography as a 'performance' of the self (Bruss 172) or as an 'art of self-invention' or re-invention (Eakin 55, 276), although both the performance and the invention are still held to have referential significance even if they can scarcely be called mimetic. The concept of the unified self completely deconstructed, autobiography becomes, in Paul de Man's formulation, impossible, disfiguring that which it figures forth. An autobiographer, such as Derrida or Barthes, can only displace and dislocate the signature and the 'I' of the text, can only enact the impossibility of making the self present, so to speak, to oneself.

What emerges from this theoretical trajectory is the fact that the study of autobiography, first justified on the grounds that the genre has a canon and a history embodying the humanist ideal of the individuated and unified self, is now often justified on the grounds that the genre is marginal to those same ideals (now discredited as serving hegemonic interests), that it enacts the impossibility of the construction of a unified self, and that it constructs fictions of the self that function discursively rather than referentially. However, poststructuralist poetics of autobiography have, in *practice* if not in theory, produced a 'subject' almost as hegemonically powerful as the humanist 'self' they attempt to destabilize. That practice becomes evident when we look at the canon that supports 'mainstream' attempts at a poetics of the genre. Whether, in these attempts, the 'self' is theorized as ontological

or as discursively produced, the canon of autobiography from which
it is theorized runs – and I parody only slightly the bulk of critical
commentary on the genre – from Augustine, through Montaigne,
Rousseau, Franklin, Wordsworth, Adams, James, Sartre, Leiris,
Barthes, and – now that it is obligatory to offer token proof that
we are not sexist or racist – one or two of Gertrude Stein, Maya
Angelou, Malcolm X, and Maxine Hong Kingston. What binds
both humanist and poststructuralist theorists of autobiography to
this canon is their common focus on the *literary* text and its author. The first may see the author as creating a 'universal' self and
the second may see the author as dead and the textual subject as
destabilized; however, their common posture of self-effacement
before the text and the struggle on the part of each to control the
decrees promulgated in the name of 'literature' have led both to
restrict their observations to the recognizably 'literary' and to skirt
the subject of the reader.

Theorists who acknowledge their own presence as readers have
given rise to two kinds of poetics of autobiography that step outside 'literature' as it has been defined by the main trends of Euro-
American criticism. One, under the double impulse of deconstruction and European sociological criticism, maintains the need not
only 'to deconstruct the illusion of the unity of the subject which
supports the genre of autobiography,' but also 'to decenter the
study of the genre, which has a tendency to enclose itself in the
magic circle of literature' (Lejeune 1980, 316). This project has led
Philippe Lejeune to consider the autobiographical impetus of the
non-literary autobiographies ghostwritten for 'ceux qui n'écrivent
pas' (1980) or those published by France's largest vanity press (1986).
The second response from readers – and the one to which I will
address myself – has come from those who have asked irreverent
questions of the autobiographical canon: Who's there? Whose self
is this anyway? they have demanded of these theorists of the autobiographical 'subject,' and have often concluded that this 'subject' has nothing to do with themselves and their knowledge.
Opening the door on a poetics of autobiography grounded on the
concept of the individual, such a critic has most often found a
privileged white male subject that implicitly, and sometimes explicitly, denies fully realized selfhood to at least some, and often
all, women, people of colour, colonial subjects, and so on. Susan
Stanford Friedman has summed up what she calls the 'fundamental
inapplicability of individualistic models of the self to women and

minorities': they do not 'take into account the importance of a culturally imposed group identity for women and minorities' and they 'ignore ... the differences in socialization in the construction of male and female gender identity' (34–5). But, opening the door on any of the various poststructuralist poetics, another critic, Biddy Martin in this case, enters on a territory marked by the 'institutional privileges enjoyed by those who can afford to disavow "identity" and its "limits" over against those for whom such disavowals reproduce their invisibility' (78).

In thinking about autobiography, such readers/theorists have challenged and relinquished what disables them in both humanist and poststructuralist poetics, and have taken what enables them. Thus, they have appropriated the poststructuralist project of decentring the universal subject for precisely such decentring has made space for the experience of racial minorities, the working classes, colonial and postcolonial peoples, women, non-heterosexuals. At the same time they have refused to relinquish the possibility of a unified self: why give up a visibility and a position from which to act, a visibility and a position only just beginning to become available in either social praxis or literary theory to those who are not Euro-American, white, middle-class and male?[2] Moreover, for women, people of colour, colonial peoples, the poor, non-heterosexuals, various arguments run, the understanding of the *material* as well as the discursive circumstances of their oppression is a primary step towards freedom from that oppression through self-possession. To posit an understanding of the subject as only a product of discourse rather than as also a product of oppressive historical and material circumstances is to deny the experiential, even the corporeal, sources of some of these subjects' self-knowledge. It is to deny that, for some autobiographical subjects, 'It's not on paper that you create but in your innards, in the gut and out of living tissue – *organic writing* I call it' (Anzaldúa 172).

These simultaneous appropriations of and challenges to the dominant humanist and poststructuralist theories of autobiography have led to a plethora of different poetics of the genre. These different poetics most often seek to describe how particular group identities function in the discursive creation of the 'self' in autobiographies by women, Afro-Americans, aboriginals, lesbians, and so forth. In the considerable body of recent writing on women's autobiography, for example, a consensus has emerged that, as Mary Mason first put it, 'the self-discovery of female identity seems to acknowledge the real presence and recognition of another consciousness, and the disclosure of female self is linked to the identification of some "other" ' (22). Friedman argues that women autobiographers create an identity that is not individualistic, not collective, and not a poststructuralist alienated self 'disconnected from ... referentiality'; that 'women's autobiographical writing is often based in, but not limited to, a group consciousness – an awareness of the meaning of the cultural category WOMAN for the patterns of women's individual destiny' (40–1). Indeed the entire process of inventing a self in autobiographies by women or in poetics of women's autobiography is often defined as a double gesture by which the narrator presents herself or is read as culturally defined as a woman and as 'different from cultural prescription' (Friedman 39), as both the product of social discourse and as individual. Poetics of women's autobiographies such as Sidonie Smith's or Carolyn Heilbrun's *Writing a Woman's Life*, therefore, pay considerable attention to the ways in which their narrators negotiate cultural prescriptions for women, by appropriating or re-writing androcentric models for autobiography (Smith 50), or by demarcating decisive moments in the life that are different from those established by male models or that have to be read differently from what seem to be similar moments in men's lives (Heilburn, passim).

In poetics of Afro-American autobiography, such as William Andrews's *To Tell a Free Story*, the quest for individual autonomy without renouncing a collective identity with other Afro-Americans emerges as a structure that is modified, but not abandoned, in the history of this writing from slave narratives to contemporary autobiographies. At the same time, white Americans emerge as the specific audience to which the autobiographies are often addressed, giving them strong links with genres such as the exemplum and with the rhetorics of emancipation and conversion. However, in some recent autobiographical writing by Afro-American women such as Bernice Reagon, the group identity is no longer Afro-Americans but Afro-American *women*, the audience addressed no longer white but those same Afro-American women: 'Black women, as a group within the Black community ... have to take on the task of understanding what or who Black people are as a people and how we, Black women, must move so that there will be our people today and tomorrow ... We are people builders, carriers of cultural traditions, key to the formation and continuance of culture. We are the ones who touch the children first and most consistently' (81).

My point here is not to go on outlining in this sketchy way the major premises of each of these poetics that seek to describe a group-identified 'self' as different from a 'self' described by humanist and poststructuralist theorists. Nor is it my aim to minimize the worthwhile complexity and increasing specificity introduced into our understanding of autobiography by these different poetics. Instead I would like first to register some qualms about the problems of *categorization* inherent in these different poetics and then to suggest some of the issues a poetics of autobiographical difference more particular and more complex, and therefore less exclusionary, than what we have might take up.

II

Each of these different poetics is constructed around a category: 'woman,' 'native,' 'black,' 'lesbian,' and so on. But those categories contain *within* themselves both their own exclusions and their own erasures of difference. Feminists' struggles to overcome their own and others' racism have taught us how often the category 'woman' excludes rather than includes these other categories, how often 'woman' has been construed as white, heterosexual, middle-class. Major discussions of working-class autobiographies, such as David Vincent's, include few women subjects, a misrepresentation scholars such as Juliet Swindells and Regenia Gagnier are only beginning to redraw. The poetics of Afro-American autobiography, by contrast, has failed to address the self-representation of a growing, if hardly predominant, Afro-American middle class. The correctives to date to such exclusionary practices present their own set of problems. A growing awareness of racism and heterosexual bias within the feminist movement has, for example, led to some excellent essays on 'women of colour' and lesbians in recent critical collections. But such inclusions, based on often conflicting feminist orthodoxies, have not escaped other, if different, exclusionary and self-censuring practices. In a climate of increasing awareness about racism and heterosexual bias in our criticism, for example, Carolyn Heilburn writes with 'trepidation' about ' "a select group of college-educated, middle and upper class, married white women" ' (1988, 62) and only after arguing that their 'complaints ... [which] include sexual abuse and the miseries of a hunger that

is not physical ... can be felt by women of all races and classes'
(63), a universalizing justification she would not need to make at
this historical juncture for discussing the work of an aboriginal or
Afro-American woman. Similarly, while lesbians' autobiographies,
which most frequently take the form of 'coming out' narratives,
almost all acknowledge the feminist movement as empowering
their opposition of 'negative stereotypes' with more positive constructions, the extrapolation of a poetics of lesbian autobiography
or even of lesbianism from these stories has, as Biddy Martin points
out, 'mask[ed] the role of rhetoric' in constructing this new lesbian
and 'rendered invisible' or 'anachronistic' the lesbian who 'came
out' before this new narrative structure was in place (88).

The much larger difficulty with the categorization that underlies
all these problems is what Vietnamese writer, composer, and film-
maker Trinh Minh-ha calls 'planned authenticity.' 'Every notion
in vogue,' she reminds us, 'including the retrieval of "roots" values, is necessarily exploited and recuperated' and the invention of
the need to recover an 'authentic' 'ethnic' self goes hand-in-hand
with the hegemonic culture's role of 'saviour' of the ' "endangered
species." ' 'Today,' she further observes, 'planned authenticity is
rife; as a product of hegemony and a remarkable counterpart of
universal standardization, it constitutes an efficacious means of
silencing the cry of racial oppression. We no longer wish to erase
your difference. We demand, on the contrary, that you remember
and assert it' (1989, 89). Literary critics have not even begun to
examine the extent to which such self-definition in terms of non-
hegemonic group identity might in fact play into the hands of
dominant groups who, by encouraging the self-reinforcement of
the disabling identity, could disallow 'the cry of racial [or other]
oppression.' To mark one's difference in some circumstances may
be simply to reinscribe one's oppression in a more self-satisfied
manner. Such an examination seems particularly imperative in theory of autobiography where different poetics founded on racial,
gender, and sexual identities are being proposed as a corrective to
earlier theorists' efforts.

What is certain is that the demand for 'authenticity' in terms of
these group identities is producing theory of autobiography in
which differences within the group are blurred and sometimes
erased in poetics that can verge on the ahistorical. Discussions of
aboriginal autobiography by critics such as David Brumble III or
Gretchen Bataille and Kathleen Sands, for example, have formally

distinguished between pre-conquest oral narrative, 'autobiographies' solicited by anthropologists and mediated by their enquiries and their writing, and more recent autobiographies written at the intersection of aboriginal, post-colonial cultures with non-aboriginal literary forms. Indeed, both anthropologists' transcriptions of autobiographical narratives and theirs and literary critics' interpretations of those narratives have been subjected to a telling critique by Helen Carr of the ways in which they pursue 'an essence' of Indian-ness (134). What critics of aboriginal autobiography have only just begun to do, however, is to document precisely the radically different sociocultural contexts these narratives come out of – sociocultural contexts that include familial and gender roles, ways of being in the environment, particular historical junctures, modes of tribal and imperialist 'government,' and relationships beyond the tribal unit.[3] Discussions of women's autobiography do pay attention to the historical circumstances of the writings they address, but at the same time there creeps into some of them the judgment that women have only written fully 'successful' autobiography in the wake of the 1960s feminist movement. Such a judgment encodes the notion that the 'successful' autobiography is the one that re-presents the fully autonomous, individuated self thought typical of men's autobiographies, and, indeed, of 'literary' character from the Enlightenment on. While this is an equity to which the feminist movement legitimately aspires, to privilege it in a poetics of women's autobiography is in fact to reinscribe the values of the androcentric culture that denied validity to earlier women's expression and is, perhaps, to be blind to some of the ways in which such women did find expressions for the 'self.'

Moreover, such theories of group identity prove reductive of differences in at least two ways. They engage in an 'essentialism of otherhood' (Lazreg 97) for they are theories founded on difference *from* hegemonic identity – from whiteness or maleness or imperialism or socio-economic privilege – and they therefore usually fail to account for complicities, overlaps, commonalities between the non-hegemonic identity and the hegemonic identity from which it differs.[4] Furthermore, such categories fail to take into account differences *within* or *from* the non-hegemonic identity. It makes a difference whether the 'woman of colour' is black or Vietnamese or Chinese-American; whether the 'black' is Afro-American, Puerto Rican, Brazilian, or Kenyan, whether she lives in Harlem or Tennessee; whether the 'aboriginal' is a Quecha, a

Hopi, a Stoney; what bloods are mixed in a Métis, what different tribal and Euro-American inheritances are hers. It makes a difference whether the child gets up on a religious holiday to 'fried thick pink slabs of home-cured ham and ... the grease [poured] over sliced red tomatoes. Eggs over easy, fried potatoes and onions, yellow hominy ... crisp perch ... [and] cathead biscuits ... three inches in diameter and two inches thick' (Angelou 36), or whether she gets up to 'bread dripping clarified butter, and curried brains, and cumin eggs, and a peculiarly potent vermicelli, soaked overnight in sugar and fatted milk' (Suleri 30). Nationality, historical juncture, and governments make a difference to 'self'-realization, as do varying family structures, educational patterns, and psychic, social, and physical traumas suffered collectively or individually. Gender, sexuality, attitudes about our bodies, and socio-economic class all figure crucially in the autobiographer's representation of self, whether that self is conceived of as socially constructed or as forged in determined individualistic resistance to social forces. Not only will any given autobiographer necessarily represent his or her 'self' at the intersection of several such categories, but, as Trinh Minh-ha puts it, 'despite our desperate, eternal attempt to separate, contain and mend, categories always leak' (1989, 94). Alicia Dojovne Ortiz, an Argentinian living in Paris and writing *Buenos Aires* in French, describes such leakage: 'I have no roots. It's a fact. A tragic mixture of blood runs in my veins. Jews, Genovese, Castillians, Irish, Indians, maybe Blacks, find in me a bizarre and motley meeting place. I am a crowd, a one-woman march, procession, parade, masquerade' (81-2). Whether such a 'self' is an 'empty self' (81) and a 'masquerade' as Ortiz claims, a plenitude of selves, or a multilayered subject is a question with which the poetics of autobiography has not yet come to terms; what is certain is that the different poetics we have elaborated are vastly reductive before the experience of autobiographers such as Ortiz.

III

Let me be very clear: I fully grant the exceptional usefulness of these different poetics of group-identified subjects for challenging hegemonic notions of the self, for giving us detailed studies of some particular autobiographies, and for revising the canon of autobiography. But just as the binary opposition between the self conceived as individual and the subject conceived as discursively

produced can blind us to the dialectic between knowledge and the
subject it presumes, so these different poetics are bedevilled by a
binary opposition between the group consciousness they assert and
that from which it is different. I want very briefly to suggest some
ways in which these different poetics might be integrated into
what we might more properly call a *poetics of differences*, without
assimilating them or appropriating them to the hegemonic discourses they resist. I want to do so by suggesting that the theorist
and reader of autobiography enact a series of *simultaneous* and
multiple gestures.

The first of these gestures involves a return to the debate between humanists and poststructuralists as to whether the 'subject'
is individuated and universal or whether the subject is discursively
produced. At stake here is the question of whether the subject is
the product of social and ideological forces, of whether she is 'subjected to' a group identity over which she has no autonomous
control. Or does she have agency? Can she choose or will at least
some aspects of the self? An adequate poetics of autobiography, I
would suggest, would acknowledge that subjects are constructed
by discourse but it would *also* acknowledge that subjects construct
discourse. That is, it would acknowledge that, if the autobiographical self is to some extent passive before the ideological forces
constructing its group identity, it also has agency: that, as Paul
Smith puts it, 'by virtue of the contradictions and disturbances in
and among subject-positions, the possibility (indeed the actuality)
of resistance to ideological pressure is allowed for' (xxxv). The
autobiographies of so-called minorities and postcolonial peoples,
I would suggest, often particularize a dialectic between these two
generalized subject-positions, between the subject as acted upon
and produced by social discourse and the subject as acting to change
social discourse and, therefore, its own subject-position. Such a
simultaneous and *dialectic* recognition, by critics and theorists of
autobiography, of the subject as socially constructed and constructing[5] might enable a poetics of difference that would allow
for the particularities of discourse and experience producing and
changing any given subject in autobiography.

Such a poetics would conceive the self not as the product of its
different identity *from* others but as constituted by multiple differences *within* and *from* itself. Here Paul Smith's 'disenclosing'
of the subject is helpful once again. He understands the 'subject'
as 'a series of *positions*, subject positions, provisional and not nec-

essarily indefeasible, into which a person is called momentarily
by the discourses and the world that he/she inhabits' (xxxv). Such
a conception of the subject accounts for the experience of actual
autobiographers that they inhabit simultaneously or sequentially
more than one of the categories delineated in different poetics of
autobiography *and* corrects the essentialism of those categories.
For if we define women subjects, for example, not only in terms
of difference *from* the male subject, but in terms of difference
within, we have a poetics elastic enough and precise enough to
accommodate the experience of an Alicia Ortiz, or to accommodate the differences between the autobiographies of a Margery
Kempe, a Rosamond Lehmann, and a Maxine Hong Kingston.

Such a poetics of differences would allow us to heed the ways
in which any given autobiographical subject exists at particular
and changing intersections of race, nationality, religion, education,
profession, class, language, gender, sexuality, a specific historical
moment, and a host of material conditions. It would allow us to
begin to examine the ways in which the autobiographical self is
produced by and products 'systemic institutional relationships'
among these differences (Martin 78) and the ways in which it resists the stabilization of such systemic institutional relationships,
the ways in which it insists on what Trinh Minh-ha argues is a
'critical difference from myself' (1989, 90) '*which undermines the
very idea of identity*' (96) in the leakage between 'the natures of
I, i, you, s/he, We, we, they and wo/man,' which 'constantly over-
lap' (94). It would allow us to question our very categories, to begin
to hear Sara Suleri when she warns us in *Meatless Days* that 'the
third world is locatable only as a discourse of convenience' and to
begin to make sense of her assertion that 'there are no women in
the third world' (20): to begin to see that if the Third World is a
discursive and not a geographical location it can provide no ground
on which a flesh-and-blood woman can walk, that Woman too
may be 'locatable only in a discourse of convenience,' that the
category Woman is a construct of Euro-American culture and may
have no applicability in Lahore in the 1950s 'where the concept of
woman was not really part of an available vocabulary: we were
too busy for that, just living, and conducting precise negotiations
with what it meant to be a sister or a child or a wife or a mother
or a servant' (1). At the same time it pushes us to question Suleri's
'we,' to ask how far she can speak for all the women of Lahore in
the 1950s.

That is, without sacrificing a recognition of the effects of discursive structures and of group consciousness in the production of the autobiographical 'self,' a poetics of differences also accommodates the specificity and the possible agency of that self. A subject conceived of as the matrix of differences *within* and *from* itself as well as of differences from others is a subject conceived of with a specificity that resists appropriation to a hegemonic poetics and resists the demand for 'planned authenticity,' all the while that it allows for some kinds and degrees of intersubjectivity. Such a subject is neither the unified subject of traditional theory of autobiography nor the discursively produced and dispersed subject of poststructuralist theory. Nor is it a self 'silenced' by hegemony, an 'empty self,' or a self marked only by its 'difference,' its otherness in relation to a hegemonic subject. It is a complex, multiple, layered subject with agency in the discourses and the worlds that constitute the referential space of his or her autobiography, a self not only constructed by differences but capable of choosing, inscribing, and making a difference.

IV

My logical next step, the one seemingly demanded by such a hortatory positioning as I have taken here, would be to formulate the descriptive features of the poetics of differences I have just called for. Failing that I should at least have the grace to excuse myself by an allusion something along the line of 'Had we but world enough and time.' In fact, I do not think any one scholar can systematize a poetics of differences. For where to stop between the broadest outline of *issues* at stake in such a poetics, such as I have tried to suggest here, and a catalogue, as endless as the writing of autobiographies in this world, of all the different permutations and combinations of subject-positions their narrators have occupied at different textual moments? How to form the descriptive system we usually demand of a 'poetics' without falling back into the problems of categorization I have tried to point to here? However, it is *precisely* the value of an unwritable 'poetics' of differences, I would argue, that it cannot be contained within a descriptive system such as we usually understand by the term *poetics*. For however descriptive a poetics of differences might eventually prove to be, it should also allow for the leakages between the categories of such a system, the leakages out of the system itself. What I am arguing for, then, under the rubric 'poetics of differences,' is in fact a praxis that would emphasize the *textual particularities* of autobiographies and would foreground the knowledge borne by *their* narrators' saying 'I' rather than subsume those particularities, that knowledge, under categories that are often *indifferent* to them.[6] A poetics of differences can mark autobiographical subjects' differences from other identities and from and within their own identities. It can also mark the nodes of intersubjectivity that occur as the autobiographical 'I' is 'called momentarily' into this or that discourse, this or that subject-position. But such a poetics cannot be systematized; it can only be accumulated from the ongoing writing and reading of many autobiographers, many readers, occupying many simultaneous *and* sequential subject-positions.

NOTES

I delivered earlier versions of this paper as a plenary address at a session on autobiography organized by Linda Hutcheon at the meetings of the Canadian Comparative Literature Association at the Learned Societies, Quebec City, May 1989, and to the Department of English, University of Saskatchewan, October 1989. I am grateful to Linda Hutcheon and Carol Morell for providing these occasions, to members of both audiences for useful questions and comments, and to Asha Varadharajan and Len Findlay for their especially acute observations. The leisure necessary for the revision of the paper was provided by a most welcome McCalla Research Professorship from the University of Alberta. (*November 1989*)

1 This is the 'pact' outlined by Philippe Lejeune (1975). Although he would himself criticize it as overly formalist in 'The Autobiographical Pact (bis),' the formal terms of the pact do imply the terms of both 'identity' and 'truth' in almost all autobiography received by critics as 'literature.'

2 This project of both de-centring the 'universal' subject and reclaiming the humanist subject for those previously rendered invisible in its construction, is the fundamental strategy of feminism. For recent formulations of this, see Elizabeth Weed ('A Man's Place' 75), Paul Smith (*Discerning the Subject* 148–51), and, about autobiography, Celeste Schenck: 'The poetics of women's autobiography issues from its concern with constituting a female subject – a precarious operation, which, as I have described it elsewhere, requires working on two fronts at once, *both* occupying a kind of center, assuming a subjectivity long denied, *and* maintaining the vigilant, disruptive stance that speaking from the postmodern margin provides' ('All of a Piece' 286). The strategy is one answer to Nancy Miller's question,

'In the face of a prevailing institutional indifference to the question of women, conjoined with a prevailing critical ideology of the subject which celebrates or longs for a mode beyond difference, where and how to move? On what grounds can we remodel the relations of female subjects to the social text?' ('Changing the Subject' 116).

3 Hertha Wong's 1989 essay 'Pictographs as Autobiography' is a major step in re-thinking the question of the forms and sociocultural significance of 'autobiography' in such different contexts. Arnold Krupat has also made a major contribution in *For Those Who Came After*; there historical circumstances, modes of textual production, and the ways in which the notion of the 'author' must be reconceived to account for aboriginal autobiographers all figure in his discussion of their works.

4 The ways in which Western-trained feminist critics (among others) both 'homogenize' ('A Literary Representation' 246) Third World subjects and engage in a 'translation' of them into first-world feminist terms that 'violate' them ('Imperialism and Sexual Difference' passim) has been the burden of much of Gayatri Spivak's critique of feminism. Marnia Lazreg, writing of feminist social science, makes the point that the 'complicity' of Third World scholars in such 'translation' is often 'a conscious act involving social class position, psychological identification and material interests' ('Feminism and Difference' 89).

5 Paul Smith (*Discerning the Subject* 148–51) argues that such a recognition would enable literary theory generally.

6 The charge that contemporary theory 'often shows itself unable to approach the political dilemmas left open by its own consistent and elaborate privileging of a view of difference which can best be described as *indifference*' has been made by Paul Smith with regard to the 'subject' (159) and by Teresa de Lauretis with regard to the 'lesbian' subject.

WORKS CITED

Andrews, William L. *To Tell a Free Story: The First Century of Afro-American Autobiography, 1760–1865.* Urbana: U of Illinois P 1986

Angelou, Maya. *I Know Why the Caged Bird Sings.* London: Virago 1984. First published New York: Random House 1969

Anzaldúa, Gloria. 'Speaking in Tongues: A Letter to 3rd World Women Writers.' In *This Bridge Called My Back: Writings by Radical Women of Color.* Ed. Cherríe Moraga and Gloria Anzaldúa. 2nd ed.; New York: Kitchen Table Women of Color P 1983

Barthes, Roland. *Roland Barthes by Roland Barthes.* Trans. Richard Howard. New York: Hill and Wang 1977. First published as *Roland*

Barthes par Roland Barthes. Paris: Editions du Seuil 1975

Bataille, Gretchen M., and Kathleen Mullen Sands. *American Indian Women Telling Their Lives*. Lincoln: U of Nebraska P 1984

Brodzki, Bella, and Celeste Schenck, eds. *Life/Lines: Theorizing Women's Autobiography*. Ithaca: Cornell UP 1988

Brumble, H. David III. *American Indian Autobiography*. Berkeley: U of California P 1988

Bruss, Elizabeth. *Autobiographical Acts: The Changing Situation of a Literary Genre*. Baltimore: Johns Hopkins UP 1976

Carr, Helen. 'In Other Words: Native American Women's Autobiography.' In *Life/Lines*, 131–53 (*see* Brodzki and Schenck)

de Lauretis, Teresa. 'Sexual Indifference and Lesbian Representation.' *Theatre Journal* 40 (1988): 155–77

de Man, Paul. 'Autobiography as De-Facement.' *Modern Language Notes* 94 (1979): 919–30

Derrida, Jacques. *The Post Card: From Socrates to Freud and Beyond*. Trans. Alan Bass. Chicago: U of Chicago P 1987. First published as *La carte postale: De Socrate à Freud et au-delà*. Paris: Flammarion 1980

Eakin, Paul John. *Fictions in Autobiography: Studies in the Art of Self-Invention*. Princeton: Princeton UP 1985

Friedman, Susan Stanford. 'Women's Autobiographical Selves: Theory and Practice.' In *The Private Self: Theory and Practice of Women's Autobiographical Writings*, 34–62. Ed. Shari Benstock. Chapel Hill: U of North Carolina P 1988

Gagnier, Regenia. 'The Literary Standard, Working-Class Lifewriting, and Gender.' *Textual Practice* 3 (1989): 36–55

Gusdorf, Georges. 'Conditions and Limits of Autobiography.' Trans. James Olney. In *Autobiography: Essays Theoretical and Critical*, 28–48. Ed. James Olney. Princeton: Princeton UP 1980. First published as 'Conditions et limites de l'autobiographie.' In *Formen der Selbstdarstellung: Analekten zu einer Geschicte des literarischen Selbstportraits*, 105–23. Ed. Günther Reichenkron and Erich Haase. Berlin: Duncker and Humblot 1956

Heilbrun, Carolyn G. 'Non-Autobiographies of "Privileged" Women: England and America.' In *Life/Lines*, 62–76 (*see* Brodzki and Schenck)

– *Writing a Woman's Life*. New York and London: Norton 1988

Jay, Paul. *Being in the Text: Self-Representation from Wordsworth to Roland Barthes*. Ithaca: Cornell UP 1984

Krupat, Arnold. *For Those Who Came After: A Study of Native American Autobiography*. Foreword by Paul John Eakin. Berkeley: U of California P 1985

Lazreg, Marnia. 'Feminism and Difference: The Perils of Writing as a Woman on Women in Algeria.' *Feminist Studies* 14 (1988): 81–107

Lejeune, Philippe. 'The Autobiographical Pact.' In *On Autobiography*,

3–30. Trans. Katherine Leary. Ed. Paul John Eakin. Minneapolis: U of Minnesota P 1989. First published in *Le pacte autobiographique*, 11–46. Paris: Editions du Seuil 1975.

– 'The Autobiographical Pact (bis).' In *On Autobiography*, 119–37. First published as 'Le pacte autobiographique (bis).' In *Moi aussi*, 13–35. Paris: Editions du Seuil 1986.

– 'L'autobiographie à compte d'auteur.' In *Moi aussi*, 292–309. Paris: Editions du Seuil 1986.

– *Je est un autre: L'autobiographie, de la littérature aux médias*. Paris: Editions du Seuil 1980. My translations

Martin, Biddy. 'Lesbian Identity and Autobiographical Difference[s].' In *Life/Lines*, 77–103 (see Brodzki and Schenck)

Mason, Mary G. 'The Other Voice: Autobiographies of Women Writers.' In *Life/Lines*, 19–44 (see Brodzki and Schenck). First published in *Autobiography: Essays Theoretical and Critical*, 207–35. Ed. James Olney. Princeton: Princeton UP 1980

Miller, Nancy K. 'Changing the Subject: Authorship, Writing, and the Reader.' *Subject to Change: Reading Feminist Writing*, 102–21. New York: Columbia UP 1988

Olney, James. *Metaphors of Self: The Meaning of Autobiography*. Princeton: Princeton UP 1972

Ortiz, Alicia Dujovne. '*Buenos Aires* (an excerpt).' Trans. Caren Kaplan. In *She, The Inappropriate/d Other*, 73–82. Ed. Trinh T. Minh-ha. Special issue of *Discourse* 8 (1986–7)

Reagon, Bernice Johnson. 'My Black Mothers and Sisters or On Beginning a Cultural Autobiography.' *Feminist Studies* 8 (1982): 81–96

Rousseau, Jean-Jacques. *Les Confessions de J.J. Rousseau. Oeuvres complètes de Jean-Jacques Rousseau*. Vol. 1: 2–656. Ed. Bernard Gagnebin and Marcel Raymond. Paris: Gallimard 1959

Schenck, Celeste. 'All of a Piece: Women's Poetry and Autobiography.' In *Life/Lines*, 281–305 (see Brodzki and Schenck)

Smith, Paul. *Discerning the Subject*. Theory and History of Literature 55. Minneapolis: U of Minnesota P 1988

Smith, Sidonie. *A Poetics of Women's Autobiography: Marginality and the Fictions of Self-Representation*. Bloomington: Indiana UP 1987

Spivak, Gayatri Chakravorty. 'Imperialism and Sexual Difference.' In *Sexual Difference*, 225–40. Ed. Robert Young. Special issue of *Oxford Literary Review* 8 (1986)

– 'A Literary Representation of the Subaltern: A Woman's Text from the Third World.' In *In Other Worlds: Essays in Cultural Politics*, 241–68. New York and London: Routledge 1988

Suleri, Sara. *Meatless Days*. Chicago: U of Chicago P 1989

Swindells, Julia. 'Working Women Autobiographers.' In *Victorian Writing and Working Women: The Other Side of Silence*, 115–206.

Minneapolis: U of Minnesota P 1985
Trinh, T. Minh-ha. 'Difference: "A Special Third World Women
  Issue." ' In *Woman, Native, Other: Writing Postcoloniality and Fem-
  inism*, 79–116. Bloomington: Indiana UP 1989. Earlier version pub-
  lished in *She, The Inappropriate/d Other*, 11–37. Ed. Trinh T. Minh-
  ha. Special issue of *Discourse* 8 (1986–87)
– 'Introduction.' In *(Un)Naming Cultures*, 5–17. Ed. Trinh T. Minh-ha.
  Special issue of *Discourse* 11 (1989)
Ulmer, Gregory L. 'The Post-Age.' *Diacritics* 11 (1981): 39–56
Vincent, David. *Bread, Knowledge and Freedom: A Study of 19th-Cen-
  tury Working Class Autobiography*. London: Methuen 1982
Weed, Elizabeth. 'A Man's Place.' In *Men in Feminism*, 71–7. Ed. Alice
  Jardine and Paul Smith. New York and London: Methuen 1987
Wong, Hertha D. 'Pictographs as Autobiography: Plains Indian Sketch-
  books of the Late Nineteenth and Early Twentieth Centuries.' *Ameri-
  can Literary History* 1 (1989): 295–316

Biographical Notes

Ellen M. Anderson is an assistant professor of Spanish at York University. She is co-editor of the *Bibliography of Old Spanish Texts*, second edition, and has recently published 'Self Representation in the Work of Sor Juana Inés de la Cruz' in *Essays in Life-Writing*, edited by Marlene Kadar, Roberts Centre for Canadian Studies Working Paper (1989). Her most recent publication is 'The Lover into the Beloved Transformed: Neoplatonic Love as a Means for Self-Transformation in Cervantes' *El Rufián dichoso'* in the Proceedings of the Thirty-sixth Annual Meeting of the Renaissance Society of America.

Helen M. Buss is an assistant professor at the University of Calgary, working on women's autobiographical accounts in archival collections. She has published articles on Canadian literature and on women's life writing in Canada and the United States. She is the author of *Mother and Daughter Relationships in the Manawaka Works of Margaret Laurence* (Victoria UP 1985) and *Reading Canadian Women's Autobiography* (McGill-Queen's UP, forthcoming). Under the name Margaret Clarke she has published two novels, *The Cutting Season* (NeWest 1984) and *Healing Song* (NeWest 1988).

Elizabeth S. Cohen, a social historian by training, has published in *Histoire sociale/Social History* and *Quaderni storici* on gender and social relationships in early modern France and Italy. Her current writing explores the zone where history, anthropology, and literary studies mingle. In collaboration with Thomas V. Cohen, she is preparing two book-length studies that use criminal-court records to explore social behaviour in Renaissance Rome. She teaches History and Humanities at York University.

Thomas V. Cohen is associate professor of History and Humanities at York University. He is interested in spoken language, social gestures, patterns of exchange, and the structure of personal alliances in early modern Europe, especially in mid-Italy. He has written, for instance, on Purim pranks (*Sixteenth Century Journal* 1988), on the politics of adultery (with Elizabeth S. Cohen) (*Continuity and Change* 1989), and on the guile of a mad hermit (forthcoming); he is finishing an essay on the logical structure of a peasant insurrection.

Sally Cole received her Ph.D. from the University of Toronto in 1988. Her research and writing has involved recording the life stories of Inuit teenagers in the Canadian Arctic, of women in rural Portugal, and of Portuguese fishermen in Newfoundland and on Lake Erie. She is a Canada Research Fellow in Anthropology at McMaster University. Her book *Women of the Praia: Work and Lives in a Portuguese Coastal Community* records women's stories in the context of an exploration of women's work and economic development in rural Portugal (Princeton UP 1991). She is currently a Beatrice M. Bain Affiliated Scholar at the University of California at Berkeley.

Nathalie Cooke is an assistant professor of English at McGill University, where she teaches Canadian literature. She is also the co-editor of the revised Oxford *Anthology of Canadian Literature in English* (1990). Her recent publications include work on Mary di Michele for *Canadian Poetry*, Susan Musgrave, and Lorna Crozier.

Evelyn J. Hinz is Professor of English at the University of Manitoba, where she is also editor of *MOSAIC*. She has written numerous essays on literature and culture. Her books include the definitive edition of Roger Williams's *A Key to the Language of America* and an edition of Henry Miller's *World of D.H. Lawrence* (with J.J. Teunissen). She has also edited a collection of critical essays on life writing (*DATA and ACTA*). She has been awarded the William Riley Parker Prize for an outstanding essay in *PMLA* and has been a recipient of the Rh Institute Award for Interdisciplinary Scholarship. The official biographer of Anaïs Nin, she has edited *A Woman Speaks*, a collection of Nin's public addresses in American, British, French, and German editions.

Marlene Kadar is a Canada Research Fellow in the Humanities Division and the Robarts Centre for Canadian Studies at York University. She revised her dissertation on 'Partisan Culture in the Thirties ...' for publication in the *Canadian Review of Comparative Literature* (September 1986). Since then she has published numerous articles in the general area of life writing, including the Robarts Centre Working Paper *Essays in Life-Writing* (1989). She is preparing a collection of Earle Birney's unpublished correspondence, and a *Reader in Life Writing* (Oxford UP). Having won the Harcsár Memorial Prize for scholarship in Hungarian studies in 1983, Kadar is now exploring a feminist literary ethnicity. Kadar interviewed Mordecai Richler for *Other Solitudes* (Oxford UP 1990), edited by Linda Hutcheon and Marion Richmond, and reviews children's books for *Canadian Children's Literature*.

Shirley Neuman is Professor of English at the University of Alberta. Her work on autobiography includes several essays, the chapter on life writing in volume 4 of *Literary History of Canada* (1989), and the monographs *Gertrude Stein: Autobiography and the Problem of Narration* (1979) and *Some One Myth: Yeats's Autobiographical Prose* (1982). She is working on a book on the representation of bodies in autobiography.

Eleanor Ty is an assistant professor of English at Wilfrid Laurier University. She has done research on women novelists of the 1790s and is currently working on a scholarly edition of Mary Hays's *Victim of Prejudice* (originally published 1799) for Broadview Press.

Alice Van Wart has a Ph.D. in Canadian literature and currently teaches at the University of Toronto. Her publications include articles on Canadian writing and two collections of poetry. She is also the editor of *In the Meantime: A Collection of Unpublished Poetry and Prose by Elizabeth Smart*, *Necessary Secrets: The Early Journals of Elizabeth Smart*, *Elizabeth Smart's Juvenilia*, and *Elizabeth Smart's Garden Journals*.

Christl Verduyn is an associate professor at Trent University. Initially appointed to the French Department (1980), she became first chair of the Women's Study Program (1987), and is currently a member of the Canadian Studies Program. She has published on Quebec and English-Canadian feminist writing and literary theory, and is the editor of *Margaret Laurence: An Appreciation* (Broadview Press 1988). She is currently preparing a major study of Marian Engel's work.

Janice Williamson teaches English and Women's Studies at the University of Alberta and publishes on women's writing and feminist cultural studies. Her fictions have been collected in *Tell Tale Signs* (Turnstone Press 1991). She was the principal editor of *Up and Doing: Canadian Women and Peace* with Deborah Gorham (Women's Press 1989), and she co-curated and wrote with Bridget Elliott *Dangerous Goods: Feminist Visual Art Practices* (Edmonton Art Gallery 1990). Her latest work, *Sounding Differences: Conversations with Seventeen Canadian Women Writers* (U of Toronto P, forthcoming), focuses on women writers whose work explores issues of sexuality, race, ethnicity, and feminist politics.

THEORY/CULTURE SERIES